This Book Comes With Lots of
FREE Online Resources

Nolo's award-winning website has a page dedicated just to this book. Here you can:

KEEP UP TO DATE. When there are important changes to the information in this book, we'll post updates.

GET DISCOUNTS ON NOLO PRODUCTS. Get discounts on hundreds of books, forms, and software.

READ BLOGS. Get the latest info from Nolo authors' blogs.

LISTEN TO PODCASTS. Listen to authors discuss timely issues on topics that interest you.

WATCH VIDEOS. Get a quick introduction to a legal topic with our short videos.

And that's not all. Nolo.com contains thousands of articles on everyday legal and business issues, plus a plain-English law dictionary, all written by Nolo experts and available for free. You'll also find more useful **books, software, online apps, downloadable forms,** plus a **lawyer directory.**

Get updates and more at
www.nolo.com/back-of-book/DEPO.html

13th Edition

Tax Deductions for Professionals

Stephen Fishman, J.D.

THIRTEENTH EDITION	JANUARY 2018
Editor	DIANA FITZPATRICK
Cover Design	SUSAN PUTNEY
Book Production	SUSAN PUTNEY
Proofreading	ROBERT WELLS
Index	SONGBIRD INDEXING SERVICES
Printing	BANG PRINTING

ISSN 2163-5668 (print)
ISSN 2325-2952 (online)

ISBN 978-1-4133-2460-0 (pbk)
ISBN 978-1-4133-2461-7 (epub ebook)

This book covers only United States law, unless it specifically states otherwise.

Please note

We believe accurate, plain-English legal information should help you solve many of your own legal problems. But this text is not a substitute for personalized advice from a knowledgeable lawyer. If you want the help of a trained professional—and we'll always point out situations in which we think that's a good idea—consult an attorney licensed to practice in your state.

Acknowledgments

Many thanks to:

Lisa Guerin and Diana Fitzpatrick for their superb editing.

About the Author

Stephen Fishman is a San Francisco-based attorney and tax expert who has been writing about the law for over 20 years. He is the author of many do-it-yourself law books, including *Deduct It! Lower Your Small Business Taxes* and *Working for Yourself: Law & Taxes for Independent Contractors, Freelancers & Consultants*. All of his books are published by Nolo.

He is often quoted on tax-related issues by newspapers across the country, including the *Chicago Tribune, San Francisco Chronicle*, and *Cleveland Plain Dealer*.

His website and blog are at Fishmanlawandtaxfiles.com.

Table of Contents

Introduction

I f you're a professional, no one needs to tell you that taxes are one of your largest expenses. The best way to minimize your taxes and maximize your take-home income is to take advantage of every tax deduction available to you.

The IRS will never complain if you don't take all the deductions you're entitled to—and it certainly doesn't make a point of advertising ways to lower your taxes. In fact, many professionals miss out on all kinds of deductions every year simply because they aren't aware of them—or because they neglect to keep the records necessary to back them up.

That's where this book comes in. Specially tailored for the unique needs of professionals, it shows you how you can deduct all or most of your business expenses from your federal taxes—everything from advertising to vehicle depreciation.

This book, the first of its kind, is about tax deductions for all types of professionals, including:

- accountants
- architects
- chiropractors
- consultants
- dentists
- doctors
- engineers
- lawyers
- marriage and family therapists
- optometrists
- pharmacists
- psychologists, and
- veterinarians.

It can be used by professionals who work by themselves, or by those involved in group practices. You can use this book no matter how your practice is legally organized—whether you are a sole proprietor, or are involved in a professional corporation, a partnership, or an LLC.

This is not a tax preparation guide—we do not show you how to fill out your tax forms. (By the time you do your taxes, it may be too late to take deductions you could have taken if you had planned the prior year's business spending wisely and kept proper records.) Instead, this book gives you all the information you need to maximize your deductible expenses—and avoid common deduction mistakes. You can (and should) use this book all year long, to make April 15 as painless as possible.

Even if you work with an accountant or another tax professional, you need to learn about tax deductions. No tax professional will ever know as much about your business as you do; and you can't expect a hired professional to search high and low for every deduction you might be able to take, especially during the busy tax preparation season. The information in this book will help you provide your tax professional with better records, ask better questions, obtain better advice—and, just as importantly, evaluate the advice you get from tax professionals, websites, and other sources.

If you do your taxes yourself (as more and more small business owners are doing, especially with the help of tax preparation software), your need for knowledge is even greater. Not even the most sophisticated tax preparation program can decide which tax deductions you should take or tell you whether you've overlooked a valuable deduction. This book can be your legal companion, providing practical advice and information so that you can rest assured that you are not paying more to the IRS than you need to.

Get Updates to This Book on Nolo.com

When there are important changes to the information in this book, we'll post updates online, on a page dedicated to this book:

www.nolo.com/back-of-book/DEPO.html

CAUTION
There have been proposed changes to tax, health care, and other laws that could affect information covered in this book. If there are any significant changes due to laws enacted after the publication of this book, we will post updates online at the link included above. You can check the Nolo update webpage to make sure you have the most current information.

Tax Deduction Basics

The tax code is full of deductions for professionals—from automobile expenses to wages for employees. Before you can start taking advantage of these deductions, however, you need a basic understanding of how businesses pay taxes and how tax deductions work. This chapter gives you all the information you need to get started. It covers:

- how tax deductions work
- how to calculate the value of a tax deduction, and
- what professionals can deduct.

How Tax Deductions Work

A tax deduction (also called a tax write-off) is an amount of money you are entitled to subtract from your gross income (all the money you make) to determine your taxable income (the amount on which you must pay tax). The more deductions you have, the lower your taxable income will be and the less tax you will have to pay.

Types of Tax Deductions

There are three basic types of tax deductions: personal deductions, investment deductions, and business deductions. This book covers only business deductions—the large array of write-offs available to business owners, including professionals.

Personal Deductions

For the most part, your personal, living, and family expenses are not tax deductible. For example, you can't deduct the food that you buy for yourself and your family. There are, however, special categories of personal expenses that may be deducted, subject to strict limitations. These include items such as home mortgage interest, state and local taxes, charitable contributions, medical expenses above a threshold amount, interest on education loans, and alimony. This book does not cover these personal deductions.

Investment Deductions

Many professionals try to make money by investing money. For example, they might invest in real estate or play the stock market. They incur all kinds of expenses, such as fees paid to money managers or financial planners, legal and accounting fees, and interest on money borrowed to buy investment property. These and other investment expenses (also called expenses for the production of income) are tax deductible, subject to strict limitations. Investment deductions are not covered in this book.

Business Deductions

Because a professional practice is a profit-making enterprise, it is a business for tax purposes. People in business usually must spend money on their businesses—for example, for office space, supplies, and equipment. Most business expenses are deductible, sooner or later, one way or another. And that's what this book is about: How professionals may deduct their business expenses.

You Pay Taxes Only on Your Profits

The federal income tax law recognizes that you must spend money to make money. Virtually every professional, however small his or her practice, incurs some expenses. Even a professional with a low overhead practice (such as a psychologist) must pay for office space and insurance. Of course, many professionals incur substantial expenses, even exceeding their income.

If you are a sole proprietor (or owner of a one-person LLC taxed as a sole proprietorship), you are not legally required to pay tax on every dollar your practice takes in (your gross business income). Instead, you owe tax only on the amount left over after your practice's deductible expenses are subtracted from your gross income (this remaining amount is called your net profit). Although some tax deduction calculations can get a bit complicated, the basic math is simple: The more deductions you take, the lower your net profit will be, and the less tax you will have to pay.

EXAMPLE: Karen, a sole proprietor, earned $100,000 this year from her child psychology practice. Fortunately, she doesn't have to pay income tax on the entire $100,000—her gross business income. Instead, she can deduct from her gross income various business expenses, including a $10,000 office rental deduction (see Chapter 3) and a $5,000 deduction for insurance (see Chapter 13). These and her other expenses amount to $20,000. She can deduct the $20,000 from her $100,000 gross income to arrive at her net profit: $80,000. She pays income tax only on this net profit amount.

The principle is the same if your practice is a partnership, or an LLC, LLP, or S corporation: Business expenses are deducted from an entity's profits to determine the entity's net profit for the year, which is passed through the entity to the owners' individual tax returns.

EXAMPLE: Assume that Karen is a member of a three-owner LLC, and is entitled to one-third of the LLC's income. She doesn't pay tax on the gross income the LLC receives, only on her portion of its net income after expenses are deducted. This year, the LLC earned $400,000 and had $100,000 in expenses. She pays tax on one-third of the LLC's $300,000 net profit.

If your practice is organized as a C corporation, it too pays tax only on its net profits.

You Must Have a Legal Basis for Your Deductions

All tax deductions are a matter of legislative grace, which means that you can take a deduction only if it is specifically allowed by one or more provisions of the tax law. You usually do not have to indicate on your tax return which tax law provision gives you the right to take a particular deduction. If you are audited by the IRS, however, you'll have to provide a legal basis for every deduction the IRS questions. If the IRS concludes that your deduction wasn't justified, it will deny the deduction and charge you back taxes, interest, and, in some cases, penalties.

The Value of a Tax Deduction

Most taxpayers, even sophisticated professionals, don't fully appreciate just how much money they can save with tax deductions. A deduction represents income on which you don't have to pay tax. So the value of any deduction is the amount of tax you would have had to pay on that income had you not deducted it. A deduction of $1,000 won't save you $1,000—it will save you whatever you would otherwise have had to pay as tax on that $1,000 of income.

Federal and State Income Taxes

To determine how much income tax a deduction will save you, you must first figure out your marginal income tax bracket. The United States has a progressive income tax system for individual taxpayers, with six different tax rates (often called tax brackets) ranging from 10% of taxable income to 39.6% (see the chart below). The higher your income, the higher your tax rate.

You move from one bracket to the next only when your taxable income exceeds the bracket amount. For example, if you are a single taxpayer in 2017, you pay 10% income tax on all your taxable income up to $9,325. If your taxable income exceeds that amount, the next tax rate (15%) applies to all your income over $9,325—but the 10% rate still applies to the first $9,325. If your income exceeds the 15% bracket amount, the next tax rate (25%) applies to the excess amount, and so on until the top bracket of 39.6% is reached.

The tax bracket in which the last dollar you earn for the year falls is called your marginal tax bracket. For example, if you have $160,000 in taxable income, your marginal tax bracket is 28%. To determine how much federal income tax a deduction will save you, multiply the amount of the deduction by your marginal tax bracket. For example, if your marginal tax bracket is 28%, you will save 28¢ in federal income taxes for every dollar you are able to claim as a deductible business expense (28% × $1 = 28¢).

The following table lists the federal income tax brackets for single and married individual taxpayers.

2017 Federal Personal Income Tax Brackets		
Tax Bracket	Income If Single	Income If Married Filing Jointly
10%	Up to $9,325	Up to $18,650
15%	$9,326 to $37,950	$18,651 to $75,900
25%	$37,951 to $91,900	$75,901 to $153,100
28%	$91,901 to $191,650	$153,101 to $233,350
33%	$191,651 to $416,700	$233,351 to $416,700
35%	$416,701 to $418,400	$416,701 to $470,700
39.6%	All over $418,400	All over $470,700

Income tax brackets are adjusted each year for inflation. For current brackets, see IRS Publication 505, *Tax Withholding and Estimated Tax.*

You can also deduct your business expenses from any state income tax you must pay. The average state income tax rate is about 6%, although seven states (Alaska, Florida, Nevada, South Dakota, Texas, Washington, and Wyoming) don't have an income tax, and New Hampshire taxes only gambling winnings and dividends and interest. You can find a list of all state income tax rates at the Federation of Tax Administrators website at www.taxadmin.org.

Social Security and Medicare Taxes

Everyone who works—whether a business owner or an employee—is required to pay Social Security and Medicare taxes. The total tax paid is the same, but the tax is paid differently depending on whether you are an employee of an incorporated practice or a self-employed owner of a partnership, an LLC, or an LLP. Employees pay one-half of these taxes through payroll deductions; employers must pony up the other half and send the entire payment to the IRS. Self-employed professionals must pay all of these taxes themselves. These differences don't mean much when you're an employee of a business you own, since the money is coming out of your pocket whether it is paid by the employee or employer.

These taxes are levied on the employment income of employees, and on the self-employment income of business owners. Self-employment taxes consist of two separate taxes: the Social Security tax and the Medicare tax.

Social Security tax. The Social Security tax is a flat 12.4% tax on net self-employment income up to an annual ceiling, which is adjusted for inflation each year. In 2017, the ceiling was $127,200 in net self-employment income. Thus, a self-employed person who had at least that much in net self-employment income would pay $15,773 in Social Security taxes.

Medicare tax. There are two Medicare tax rates: a 2.9% tax up to an annual ceiling—$200,000 for single taxpayers and $250,000 for married couples filing jointly. All income above the ceiling is taxed at a 3.8% rate. Thus, for example, a single taxpayer with $300,000 in net self-employment income would pay a 2.9% Medicare tax on the first $200,000 of income and a 3.8% tax on the remaining $100,000. This 0.9% Medicare tax increase applies to high-income employees as well as to the self-employed. Employees have to pay a 2.35% Medicare tax on the portion of their wages over the $200,000/$250,000 thresholds (their one-half of 2.9% (1.45%) plus the 0.9%). In addition, Medicare taxes must be paid by high-income taxpayers on investment income. (See "The Medicare Net Investment Income Tax" in Chapter 2.)

For both the self-employed and employees, the combined Social Security and Medicare tax is 15.3%, up to the Social Security tax ceiling.

However, the effective self-employment tax rate is somewhat lower than 15.3% because (1) you are allowed to deduct half of your self-employment taxes from your net income for income tax purposes, and (2) you pay self-employment tax on only 92.35% of your net self-employment income. But taxpayers who earn more than the $200,000/$250,000 thresholds, can't deduct the 0.9% increase in Medicare tax from their income.

Like income taxes, self-employment taxes are paid on the net profit you earn from a business. Thus, deductible business expenses reduce the amount of self-employment tax you have to pay by lowering your net profit.

Total Tax Savings

When you add up your savings in federal, state, and self-employment taxes, you can see the true value of a business tax deduction. For example, if you're single and your taxable business income (whether as an employee of an incorporated real estate business or a self-employed owner of a partnership or an LLC) is $100,000, a business deduction would be worth 28% (in federal income tax) + 15.3% (in self-employment taxes) + approximately 6% (in state taxes)—depending on what state you live in. That adds up to a whopping 49.3% savings. (If you itemize your personal deductions, your actual tax savings from a business deduction is a bit less because it reduces your state income tax and therefore reduces the federal income tax savings from this itemized deduction.) If you buy a $1,000 computer for your business and you deduct the expense, you save about $493 in taxes. In effect, the government is paying for almost half of your business expenses.

This is why it's so important to know all the business deductions you are entitled to take and to take advantage of every one.

 CAUTION
Don't buy things just to get a tax deduction. Although tax deductions can be worth a lot, it doesn't make sense to buy something you don't need just to get a deduction. After all, you still have to pay for the item, and the tax deduction you get in return will only cover a portion of the cost. For example, if you buy a $3,000 computer you don't really need, you'll probably be able to deduct less than half the cost. That means you're still out over $1,500—money you've spent for something you don't need. On the other hand, if you really do need a computer, the deduction you're entitled to is like found money—and it may help you buy a better computer than you could otherwise afford.

What Professionals Can Deduct

Professionals are business owners, and as such they can deduct four broad categories of business expenses:

- start-up expenses
- operating expenses
- capital expenses, and
- inventory costs.

This section provides an introduction to each of these categories (that are covered in greater detail in later chapters).

> ⚠ CAUTION
>
> **You must keep track of your expenses.** You can deduct only those expenses that you actually incur. You need to keep records of these expenses to (1) know for sure how much you actually spent; and (2) prove to the IRS that you really spent the money you deducted on your tax return, in case you are audited. (Accounting and bookkeeping are discussed in detail in Chapter 18.)

Start-Up Expenses

The first money you will have to shell out will be for your practice's start-up expenses. These include most of the costs of getting your practice up and running, like license fees, advertising costs, attorney and accounting fees, travel expenses, market research, and office supplies expenses. Start-up costs are not currently deductible—that is, you cannot deduct them all in the year in which you incur them. However, you can deduct up to $5,000 in start-up costs in the first year you are in business. You must deduct amounts that exceed the first-year threshold amount over the next 15 years. (See Chapter 10 for a detailed discussion of deducting start-up expenses.)

> EXAMPLE: Cary, an optometrist who recently graduated from optometry school, decides to open his own practice. Before Cary's optometry office opens for business in August, he has to rent space, hire and train employees, and obtain all necessary optometric equipment. These start-up expenses cost Cary $50,000. Cary may deduct $5,000 of this amount the first year he's in business. The remainder may be deducted over the first 180 months that he's in business—$2,500 per year for 15 years.

Operating Expenses

Operating expenses are the ongoing day-to-day costs a business incurs to stay in business. They include such things as rent, utilities, salaries, supplies, travel expenses, car expenses, and repairs and maintenance. These expenses (unlike start-up expenses) are currently deductible—that is, you can deduct them all in the same year in which you pay them. (See Chapter 3.)

> EXAMPLE: After Cary's optometry office opens, he begins paying $5,000 a month for rent and utilities. This is an operating expense that is currently deductible. When Cary does his taxes, he can deduct from his income the entire amount he paid for rent and utilities for the year.

Capital Expenses

Capital assets are things you buy for your practice that have a useful life of more than one year, such as land, buildings, equipment, vehicles, books, furniture, and patents you buy from others. These costs, called capital expenses, are considered to be part of your investment in your business, not day-to-day operating expenses.

Large businesses—those that buy at least several hundred thousand dollars of capital assets in a year—must deduct these costs by using depreciation. To depreciate an item, you deduct a portion of the cost in each year of the item's useful life. Depending on the asset, this could be anywhere from three to 39 years (the IRS decides the asset's useful life).

Small businesses can also use depreciation, but they have other options available for deducting many capital expenses. They can deduct items that cost less than $2,500 in a single year using the de minimis safe harbor deduction. They can also currently deduct a substantial amount of long-term asset purchases in a single year using bonus depreciation or a provision of the tax code called Section 179. Section 179 and bonus depreciation are discussed in detail in Chapter 9.

> **EXAMPLE:** Cary spent $1,000 on a new office chair for his office and $10,000 on new optometry equipment. Because the chair and equipment have a useful life of more than one year, they are capital assets. He can deduct the chair in a single year using the de minimis safe harbor. He can deduct the cost of the equipment in one year using Section 179 or depreciate it over several years using bonus and regular depreciation.

Certain capital assets, such as land and corporate stock, never wear out. Capital expenses related to these costs are not deductible; the owner must wait until the asset is sold to recover the cost. (See Chapter 9 for more on this topic.)

Inventory

Inventory is merchandise that a business makes or buys to resell to customers. It doesn't matter whether you manufacture the merchandise yourself or buy finished merchandise from someone else and resell the items to customers. Inventory doesn't include tools, equipment, or other items that you use in your practice; it refers only to items that you buy or make to sell.

Whether professionals sell inventory for tax purposes can be a tricky question. Materials that are an indispensable and inseparable part of the rendering of a service are not inventory—for example, gold that a dentist places in patients' teeth is not inventory.

You must deduct inventory costs separately from all other business expenses—you deduct inventory costs as you sell the inventory. Inventory that remains unsold at the end of the year is a business asset, not a deductible expense. (See Chapter 12 for more on deducting inventory.)

EXAMPLE: In addition to providing optometric services, Cary stocks and sells eyeglasses to his patients. In his first year in practice, Cary spent $15,000 on his inventory of eyeglasses, but sold only $10,000 worth of them. He can deduct only $10,000 of the inventory costs for the year.

Choice of Business Entity

This chapter is about how your tax life is affected by the form of business entity you use to conduct your professional practice. If you're already in practice, you will learn the pros and cons of the business form you have chosen—and you may decide to convert to another type of entity or tax treatment. If you're just starting your practice, you will need to figure out which business entity and tax treatment is best for you.

Types of Business Entities

Every business has a legal form, including a professional practice. If you're in practice right now, your business almost certainly falls into one of the following categories:

- sole proprietorship
- partnership
- corporation
- limited liability company (LLC), or
- limited liability partnership (LLP).

The sole proprietorship and partnership are the default business entities—they come into existence automatically unless a business's owners take the steps necessary to form one of the other entities.

The following chart gives you an idea of the breakdown for the types of business entities professionals use. (It does not include professionals who provide health services—doctors, dentists, and so on.)

Tax Returns Filed by Professionals—2013	
Type of Entity	**Number of Tax Returns Filed in 2013**
Sole proprietors	3,274,649
Partnerships (including LLPs)	122,248
LLCs	173,842
C corporations	199,431
S corporations	702,282

Sole Proprietorship

The majority of professionals who practice by themselves are sole proprietors. Many have attained this legal status without even realizing it. Quite simply, if you start running a professional practice by yourself and do not incorporate or form an LLC or LLP, you are automatically a sole proprietor.

A sole proprietorship is a one-owner business. Unlike a corporation, an LLC, a general partnership, or an LLP, it is not a separate legal entity. The business owner (proprietor) personally owns all the assets of the business and is in sole charge of its operation. Most sole proprietors run small operations, but a sole proprietor can hire employees and nonemployees, too. Indeed, some sole proprietors have large operations with many employees.

You don't have to do anything special or file any papers to set up a sole proprietorship, other than the usual license, permit, and other regulatory requirements your state and/or locality imposes on any business. Of course, if you're in a profession that requires a license to practice, you must comply with the applicable requirements or the state may force you to close your proprietorship.

Sole proprietorships are the most common form of business entity used by professionals. One big reason for their popularity is that they are by far the simplest and cheapest way to organize a one-owner business.

If you practice by yourself, a sole proprietorship may well be your best bet. As far as taxes are concerned, it's an excellent choice because it provides pass-through taxation, which most professionals prefer. You also won't have to file a separate tax return for your practice, which saves time and money.

Sole proprietorships do have one big drawback: They offer no limited liability. Corporations, LLCs, and LLPs provide limited liability, which is the main reason why many professionals use them. However, when you practice by yourself, the limited liability you'll obtain by forming a corporation, an LLC, or an LLP is often more illusory than real.

Thus, sticking with the unflashy, simple, and cheap sole proprietorship is a perfectly rational choice. Remember, however, that if you stop practicing by yourself and form a group practice, you can no longer be a sole proprietor. You'll automatically become a partner in a partnership unless you form an LLC, an LLP, or a corporation—which is highly advisable.

RESOURCE

For detailed guidance about how to form and run a sole propri-etorship, refer to *Working for Yourself: Law & Taxes for Independent Contractors, Freelancers & Consultants,* by Stephen Fishman (Nolo).

Limited Liability Company (LLC)

The limited liability company, or LLC, is the newest type of business form in the United States. The LLC is a unique hybrid: a cross between a partnership and corporation. It provides the flexibility, informality, and tax attributes of a partnership and the limited liability of a corporation. However, a few states (California, Oregon, and Rhode Island) bar most types of professionals from using them. In these states, professionals seeking the desirable attributes of an LLC will usually choose either an LLP or an S corporation instead.

In most states, professionals who form LLCs must adhere to restrictions similar to those for professional corporations. All the owners must be licensed to perform the professional services carried on by the LLC and ownership cannot be transferred to unlicensed individuals. Thus, for example, all the owners of a dental LLC must be licensed dentists, and no dentist-owner may transfer his or her LLC ownership to a nondentist.

To form an LLC, one or more people must file articles of organization with their state's business filing office. Although not required by all states, it is highly desirable to adopt a written LLC operating agreement laying out how the LLC will be governed. If you don't prepare an operating agreement, the default provisions of your state's LLC laws will apply.

LLCs provide limited liability and partnership tax treatment—an ideal combination for many professionals. If you're in a group practice, the LLC should be on the top of your list when choosing your business entity.

On the other hand, if you are in solo practice, you won't gain much by forming an LLC. As far as taxes go, you'll still be treated like a sole proprietorship by the IRS. More importantly, the limited liability a solo practitioner obtains by using an LLC may prove to be more mythical than real.

 **RESOURCE**

For a complete discussion on how to form limited liability companies, see *Form Your Own Limited Liability Company,* by Anthony Mancuso (Nolo).

Limited Liability Partnership (LLP)

Professionals in all states now have the option of forming a special type of partnership called a limited liability partnership, or LLP (also called a "registered limited liability partnership"). LLPs are much the same as regular general partnerships except for one crucial advantage—they limit the partners' liability for malpractice claims and, in some states, debts incurred by the partnership.

Professionals in some states—California, for example—use LLPs because state law prohibits them from forming LLCs, another popular entity that provides limited liability. LLPs are limited to professionals in certain occupations—typically people who work in the medical, legal, and accounting fields, and a few other professions in which a professional-client relationship exists. In some states, engineers, veterinarians, and acupuncturists are also allowed to form LLPs. Not all categories of licensed professionals can form an LLP—it depends on your state.

At least two partners are needed to form an LLP, and the partners must usually be licensed in the same or related professions. LLPs don't come into existence automatically like general partnerships. In most states, creating an LLP requires registration with the state government, annual filings, and administrative fees.

Form an LLP if you want to have an LLC, but your state doesn't allow people in your profession to use them. If your state allows you to use either an LLC or LLP, don't choose an LLP without first carefully checking your state's laws to see if LLPs provide the same degree of limited liability protection as LLCs. If they don't, form an LLC.

Corporation

A corporation is a legal form in which you can organize and conduct a business and share in the profits or losses. In the past, most states prohibited many types of professionals—for example, doctors and lawyers—from forming a corporation because they feared they would be used to limit their liability for malpractice. Now, all states permit professionals to form a special kind of corporation called a professional corporation or professional service corporation. The professional corporation has the basic attributes of a regular corporation with certain restrictions about ownership and the type of work it can do. (All further references to corporations include professional corporations and professional service corporations.)

The list of professionals who must form professional corporations varies from state to state, but usually includes:

- accountants
- engineers
- lawyers
- psychologists
- social workers
- veterinarians, and
- health care professionals, such as doctors, dentists, nurses, physical therapists, optometrists, opticians, and speech pathologists.

Most states impose restrictions on who may own a professional corporation and the work it can do. Typically, a professional corporation must be organized for the sole purpose of performing professional services, and all shareholders must be licensed to render that service. For example, in a medical corporation, all the shareholders must be licensed physicians.

CAUTION

A professional corporation is a state law classification: It has nothing to do with the IRS or taxes. A professional corporation can be either a C or an S corporation for tax purposes, as described below. A professional corporation is also not the same as a personal service corporation (PSC). A PSC is an IRS classification that has nothing to do with the professional corporation rules of your state (see "Personal Service Corporations," below, for more on PSCs).

Although the word corporation tends to conjure up images of huge business corporations (like Google or Microsoft), in reality, most corporations—especially those owned by professionals—are small operations. In fact, in many professional corporations, there is only one shareholder who is also often the sole employee—that is, a single person directs and runs the corporation and owns all the corporate stock.

A corporation has a legal existence completely separate from its owners—indeed, it is considered to be a person for legal purposes. It can hold title to property, sue and be sued, have bank accounts, borrow money, hire employees, and do anything else in the business world that a human being can do. If you incorporate your practice, the corporation becomes the owner of the business, and you own the corporation in the form of stock ownership and ordinarily work as its employee.

You create a corporation by filing the necessary forms with and paying the required fees to your appropriate state agency—usually the office of the secretary of state or corporations commissioner. Each state specifies the forms to use and the filing cost. You will need to check your state law to determine whether you must form a professional corporation and to make sure you meet any special requirements for professional corporations. You'll also need to choose a name for your corporation, adopt corporate bylaws, set up your corporate records, and "capitalize" your corporation—issue stock in return for money, property, and/or services provided to the corporation.

Many professionals, particularly those in the health care field, have incorporated their practices. Many of these corporations were formed before LLCs became widely available and corporations were the only game in town if a professional wanted limited liability. Even if they want to, the shareholders of many of these corporations can't convert them to another type of entity because the tax costs would be prohibitive.

Although their popularity has diminished somewhat since the advent of the LLC, professionals nevertheless continue to form corporations. S corporations are especially popular because they can provide savings on Social Security and Medicare taxes. C corporations are often chosen because they provide the best deductions for fringe benefits—a very important consideration for many high-income professionals. However, you can obtain these same benefits by forming an LLC and electing to have it taxed as an S or C corporation.

Perhaps the most important reason corporations continue to be used is habit. People like what they're used to, and everyone is used to corporations. They have been around for over 100 years and are well understood by businesspeople, courts, lawyers, and tax professionals. LLCs are much newer and have more legal uncertainties.

RESOURCE

For more information on corporations and how to incorporate, refer to *Incorporate Your Business: A Step-by-Step Guide to Forming a Corporation in Any State,* by Anthony Mancuso (Nolo). You can also check for online incorporation services (see Nolo's website at www.nolo.com).

Partnership

In the past, almost all professionals who practiced with others were partners in a general partnership. However, most professionals abandoned the general partnership form when other types of business entities (like professional corporations, LLCs, and LLPs) were created that limited their personal liability for malpractice claims and debts—something a partnership does not do.

A partnership is a form of shared ownership and management of a business. A general partnership automatically comes into existence whenever two or more people enter into a venture together to earn a profit and don't choose to form some other business entity. As with sole proprietorships, it is not necessary to file any papers to form a general partnership. The partners contribute money, property, and/or services to the partnership and in return receive a share of the profits it earns. The partnership form is extremely flexible because the partners may agree to split the profits and manage the business in virtually any way they want. (We refer to general partnerships simply as partnerships.)

Unlike a sole proprietorship, a partnership has a legal existence distinct from its owners (the partners). It can hold title to property, sue and be sued, have bank accounts, borrow money, hire employees, and do anything else in the business world that a human being can do. Because a partnership is a separate legal entity, property acquired by a partnership is property of the partnership and not of the partners individually. This differs from a sole proprietorship where the proprietor-owner individually owns all the sole proprietorship property.

Because partnerships provide no limited liability to their owners, professionals abandoned them in droves when professional corporations and LLCs became available. Indeed, the partnership has become nearly extinct among professionals.

If you are in a partnership right now, you should seriously think about forming an LLC, an LLP, or a corporation so that you can limit your personal liability for acts by the other people in your group practice. However, if limited liability is not important to you—for example, because you have plenty of insurance—a partnership is just as good for a group practice as an LLC or LLP.

 RESOURCE
For a detailed discussion of partnerships including how to write partnership agreements, see *Form a Partnership: The Complete Legal Guide*, by Denis Clifford and Ralph Warner (Nolo).

Limiting Your Liability

The most important consideration in choosing your business structure (or deciding whether or not to stick with what you have) is usually liability—that is, the extent a business's owners are personally responsible for paying for their business's debts and business-related lawsuits. Indeed, this issue is seen as so important that the corporation, LLC, and LLP were created for the express purpose of limiting their owners' liability.

It's likely that you're as concerned about your liability as anybody else. For this reason, you might think that you should form a corporation or limited liability company. After all, these business forms are supposed to provide limited liability—protection from debts and lawsuits. Indeed, many people seem to believe that forming a corporation, an LLP, or an LLC is like having a magic shield against liability. However, the sad truth is that there are many holes in the limited liability shield offered by the corporation, LLP, and LLC.

What Is Liability?

Liability means being legally responsible for a debt or for doing something that injures someone, such as committing professional malpractice or injuring someone in a traffic accident. If you are personally liable for a debt or wrong and a person sues you and obtains a judgment against you, you'll have to pay the judgment yourself. If you don't pay, the person who obtained the judgment can take your personal property to pay it (subject to certain limits). Thus, you could end up losing your personal bank accounts, personal property (like your car), and even your house.

On the other hand, if only your business is liable for a debt or wrongdoing, you have no legal obligation to use personal funds to pay a person who obtains a judgment against your business. But, of course, your business assets can by taken to satisfy a judgment against your business.

Obviously, business owners, including professionals, don't want to put their personal assets at risk if they get sued for malpractice or other alleged wrongdoing, or if their practice incurs debts. It was to help avoid personal liability and encourage people to invest in businesses that the corporation was created. Much later, the limited liability company was established to provide the same degree of limited liability without the expense and bother of forming and running a corporation. LLPs were also established to give professionals limited liability. Corporations, LLCs, and LLPs are all limited liability entities.

The default business entities—the sole proprietorship and partnership—provide no limited liability at all—you are personally liable for your business's debts and wrongdoing by you or anyone else who works in your practice. If you want limited liability, you must take the necessary steps to form a corporation, or an LLC or LLP under your state law.

> ⓘ **CAUTION**
> **Liability has nothing to do with taxation or the way a business entity is taxed.** For example, the owners of a partnership will have unlimited liability even if they choose to have their partnership taxed as a corporation. You must actually form a limited liability business entity under the applicable state law to benefit from its limited liability attributes.

Liability for Professional Malpractice

The single greatest liability exposure most professionals face is for malpractice. A single medical malpractice lawsuit, for example, can result in a judgment for millions. Even if you're innocent, defending a malpractice lawsuit can cost hundreds of thousands of dollars. Can a limited liability entity help you avoid personal liability for malpractice? Yes, but not as much as you might think.

Your Own Malpractice

No limited liability entity—whether corporation, LLC, or LLP—protects you against personal liability for your own malpractice, or other personal wrongdoing. If your business doesn't have enough assets to pay a judgment obtained against you, your personal assets can be taken. Thus, your personal assets will always be on the line if you are sued for malpractice. This is why professionals should always have malpractice insurance.

> **EXAMPLE:** Janet, a civil engineer, forms a professional corporation of which she is the sole shareholder. She helps design a bridge that collapses, killing dozens of commuters. Even though Janet is incorporated, she could be held personally liable (along with her corporation) for any damages caused by her alleged malpractice in designing the bridge. Both Janet's personal assets and those of her corporation are at risk.

Malpractice by Others

What if somebody else in your practice gets sued for malpractice? If your practice is a partnership, each partner is personally liable for any wrongful acts committed by another partner in the ordinary course of partnership business. Thus, you will be personally liable for malpractice claims against your partners, even if you were not personally involved. This makes the partnership a bad choice for professionals who practice together. It is by far the most important reason that most professionals don't practice as regular partnerships.

In contrast, if your practice is a corporation, or an LLC or LLP, you won't be personally liable for malpractice by your fellow co-owners (or employees) as long as you weren't personally involved in the alleged wrongdoing. Many states require that certain types of professionals have malpractice insurance to obtain this limited liability. The rules vary from state to state—you should learn yours.

> **EXAMPLE:** Louis is a doctor involved in an incorporated medical practice with Susan and Florence. One of Louis's patients claims he committed malpractice and sues Louis personally and also sues the group. While both the group and Louis can be held liable, the other doctors in the group, Susan and Florence, cannot be held personally liable for Louis's malpractice. This means their personal assets are not at risk.

Thus, if you're involved in a group practice with other professionals, it's *highly advisable* to form a limited liability entity. You don't want to be held personally liable for someone else's malpractice.

On the other hand, if you practice alone, a limited liability entity won't help you at all when it comes to malpractice liability, because there is no co-owner whose malpractice you need to be insulated from.

Liability for Business Debts

In addition to liability for malpractice, you could be personally liable for debts incurred by your practice.

Sole Proprietors and Partnerships

When you're a sole proprietor, you are personally liable for all the debts of your business. This means that a business creditor—a person or company to whom you owe money for items you use in your business—can go after all your assets, both business and personal. This may include, for example, your personal bank accounts, stocks, your car, and even your house. Similarly, a personal creditor—a person or company to whom you owe money for personal items—can go after your business assets, such as business bank accounts and equipment.

Partners are personally liable for all partnership debts and lawsuits, the same as sole proprietors. However, partnership creditors are required to proceed first against the partnership property. If there isn't enough to satisfy the debts, they can then go after the partners' personal property.

In addition, each partner is deemed to be the agent of the partnership when conducting partnership business in the usual way. This means you'll be personally liable for partnership debts your partners incur while carrying on partnership business, whether you knew about them or not.

Limited Liability Entities

Corporations and LLCs were created to enable people to invest in businesses without risking all their personal assets if a business failed or became unable to pay its debts. (In some states, LLPs provide no protection at all against partnership debts; in others, they provide the same protection as an LLC or a corporation.)

If you're talking about a large corporation or LLC, then limited liability for debts really does exist. For example, if you buy stock in Microsoft, you don't have to worry about Microsoft's creditors suing you. But it usually doesn't work that way for small corporations or small LLCs— especially newly established ones without a track record of profits and good credit history.

Major creditors, such as banks, don't want to be left holding the bag if your business goes under. To help ensure payment, they will want to be able to go after your personal assets as well as your business assets. As a result, if you've formed a corporation or an LLC, they will typically demand that you personally guarantee business loans, credit cards, or other extensions of credit—that is, sign a legally enforceable document pledging your personal assets to pay the debt if your business assets fall short. This means that you will be personally liable for the debt, just as if you were a sole proprietor or partner.

Not only do banks and other lenders universally require personal guarantees, other creditors do as well. For example, you may be required to personally guarantee payment of your office lease and even leases for expensive equipment. Standard forms used by suppliers often contain personal guarantee provisions making you personally liable when your company buys equipment and similar items.

You can avoid having to pledge a personal guarantee for some business debts. These will most likely be routine and small debts. But, of course, once someone gets wise to the fact that your business is not paying its bills, they won't extend you any more credit. If you don't pay your bills and obtain a bad credit rating, no one may be willing to let you buy things for your business on credit. Only careless creditors might not require a personal guarantee in these circumstances.

Piercing the Corporate Veil

Another way you can be personally liable even though you've formed a corporation is through a legal doctrine called "piercing the corporate veil." Under this legal rule, courts disregard the corporate entity and hold its owners personally liable for any harm done by the corporation *and* for corporate debts. Corporate owners are in danger of having their corporation pierced if they treat the corporation as their alter ego, rather than as a separate legal entity—for example, they fail to contribute money to the corporation or issue stock, they take corporate funds or assets for personal use, they commingle corporate and personal funds, or they fail to observe corporate formalities, such as keeping minutes and holding board meetings. The same type of piercing can probably be used against LLC owners.

Other Types of Liability

Malpractice and business debts aren't the only type of liability you need to worry about. Other forms of liability include:

- premises liability: responsibility for injuries or damages that occur at your office or other place of business
- infringement liability: when someone claims that you have infringed on a patent, copyright, trademark, or trade secret, and
- employer liability: liability for injuries or damages caused by an employee while he or she was working for you.

If you're a sole proprietor or partner in a partnership, you'll be personally liable for these types of lawsuits. Theoretically, you're not personally liable if you form a corporation or an LLC. (In some states, LLPs are also supposed to provide protection from these types of liability; in others, they protect only against malpractice liability by others in your practice.)

However, remember that you're always personally liable for your own negligence or intentional wrongdoing. You can be personally liable under a negligence theory for all the different types of lawsuits outlined above. Here are some examples of how you could be sued personally even though you've formed a corporation, or an LLC or LLP:

- An employee accidentally injures someone while running an errand for you. The injured person sues you personally for damages claiming you negligently hired, trained, and/or supervised the employee.
- Someone sues you, claiming you've infringed upon a patent, trade secret, or copyright. Even if you've formed a corporation or an LLC, you can be personally liable for such claims.
- The person in charge of your payroll fails to properly withhold and pay income and Social Security taxes for your employees. You can be personally liable even if you weren't personally involved.

In all these cases, forming a corporation or an LLC or LLP will prove useless to protect you from personal liability.

The Role of Insurance

If incorporating or forming an LLC or LLP won't relieve you of all your personal liability, what are you supposed to do to protect yourself from business-related lawsuits? There's a very simple answer: Get insurance. Your insurer will defend you in such lawsuits and pay any settlements or damage awards up to your policy limits. This is what all wise business owners do, whether they are sole proprietors, partners, LLP owners, LLC members, or corporation owners. Liability and many other forms of business insurance are available to protect you from the types of lawsuits described above. Liability insurance premiums are deductible as a business expense.

Note carefully, however, that insurance won't protect you from liability for business debts—for example, if you fail to pay back a loan or default on a lease. This is where bankruptcy comes in.

Type of Entity	Limited Liability Against Lawsuits?	Limited Liability Against Debts?
Sole proprietorship	No	No
Partnership	No	No
LLC	Yes	Yes
LLP	Yes	Maybe
Corporation	Yes	Yes

The Four Ways Business Entities Are Taxed

Businesses are not all taxed alike. There are four different types of tax treatment available:

- sole proprietorship tax treatment
- partnership tax treatment
- S corporation tax treatment, and
- C corporation tax treatment.

You get to choose which type of tax treatment you want. This is one of the most important business decisions you'll ever make because there are big differences among the available choices. For example, if you choose S or C corporation treatment, you'll be your practice's employee and have to have your income and Social Security taxes withheld from your salary. In contrast, you're not an employee if your practice receives sole proprietorship or partnership tax treatment. Nothing is withheld from your pay, so you'll have to pay estimated taxes four times a year. There are also important differences as to how profits can be allocated among a group practice's owners, how losses can be deducted, and even the likelihood of an IRS audit. These and other differences are compared below. But first, you need to understand how the different forms of tax treatment work.

Tax Treatment Choices

Whenever a business entity is created or comes into existence, it automatically receives a form of tax treatment by default. However, except for sole proprietorships, business entities have some leeway to change from their default treatment to another type of tax treatment.

A multiowner LLC, LLP, or partnership is automatically taxed as a partnership by default, but may choose to be taxed as a C corporation or an S corporation. This is easily accomplished by filing a document called "an election" with the IRS. Once this is done, as far as the IRS is concerned, the LLC, LLP, or partnership is now the same as a corporation and it files the tax forms for that type of entity. However, the great majority of LLCs, LLPs, and partnerships stick with their default partnership tax treatment.

Corporations are taxed as C corporations by default, but may change to S corporation tax treatment by filing an S corporation election. This is extremely common. A single-owner LLC is taxed as a sole proprietorship by default but can elect to be taxed as a C or an S corporation by filing an election. This is not common. The sole proprietorship is the only entity that can't change its tax treatment—it must retain the sole proprietorship taxation treatment that it receives by default.

The table below shows all the choices available for each type of entity.

Type of Entity	Tax Treatment Choices
Sole proprietorship	Sole proprietorship taxation (default treatment)
Partnership, LLP, multiowner LLC	Partnership taxation (default treatment) C corporation taxation S corporation taxation
Single-owner LLC	Sole proprietorship taxation (default treatment) C corporation taxation S corporation taxation
Corporation	C corporation taxation (default treatment) S corporation taxation

Sole Proprietorship Taxation

When you're a sole proprietor (or single-member LLC with sole proprietor tax treatment), you and your business are one and the same for tax purposes. Sole proprietorships don't pay taxes or file tax returns. Instead, you must report the income you earn or losses you incur on your own personal tax return (IRS Form 1040). If you earn a profit, the money is added to any other income you have—for example, interest income or your spouse's income if you're married and file a joint tax return—and that total is taxed.

Although you are taxed on your total income regardless of its source, the IRS still wants to know about the profitability of your business. To show whether you have a profit or loss from your sole proprietorship, you must file IRS Schedule C, *Profit or Loss From Business*, with your tax return. On this form, you list all your business income and deductible expenses. If you have more than one business, you must file a separate Schedule C for each one.

> **EXAMPLE:** Irina is a sole proprietor dentist with no one else in her practice. This year, she had $250,000 in dental income and $150,000 in expenses, giving her a $100,000 profit. She files Schedule C with her personal tax return (IRS Form 1040) listing the expenses and income from her practice. She reports her $100,000 profit on her Form 1040 and pays personal income tax on it, as well as Social Security and Medicare taxes. To figure her taxes, she adds her dental income to any other taxable income she has for the year—for example, investment income—and pays taxes on it at personal tax rates.

Sole proprietors must use the sole proprietor form of taxation. If a sole proprietor wants a different type of tax treatment, he or she must form a business entity, such as a corporation or an LLC.

In addition, LLCs with single owners are automatically treated like sole proprietorships for tax purposes. However, they have the option of switching to C or S corporation taxation.

Partnership Taxation

The next basic form of business taxation is partnership taxation. This form of taxation applies to partnerships, LLPs, and multi-member LLCs. When they are first formed, these entities all automatically use partnership taxation; and the great majority continue to use it throughout their existence. However, they have the option to switch to other forms of taxation.

Under partnership tax treatment, the business entity is a pass-through entity for tax purposes—that is, it ordinarily pays no taxes itself. Instead, the profits, losses, deductions, and tax credits of the business are passed through the business to the owner's individual tax returns. If the business has a profit, the owners pay income tax on their ownership share on their individual returns at their individual income tax rates. If the business incurs a loss, it is likewise shared among the owners who may deduct it from other income on their individual returns, subject to certain limitations.

Unlike a sole proprietorship, a partnership is considered to be separate from the partners for the purposes of computing income and deductions. The partnership files its own tax return on IRS Form 1065, *U.S. Return of Partnership Income.* Form 1065 is not used to pay taxes; rather, it is an information return that informs the IRS of the partnership's income, deductions, profits, losses, and tax credits for the year. Form 1065 also includes a separate part called Schedule K-1 in which the partnership lists each partner's share of the items listed on Form 1065. A separate Schedule K-1 must be provided to each partner. Each partner reports on his or her individual tax return (Form 1040) the partner's share of the partnership's net profit or loss as shown on Schedule K-1. Ordinary business income or loss is reported on Schedule E, *Supplemental Income and Loss.* However, certain items must be reported on other schedules—for example, capital gains and losses must be reported on Schedule D and charitable contributions on Schedule A.

> EXAMPLE: Irina decides to join her dental practice with her friend Leo's dental practice. They practice together as general partners. The partnership earns $500,000 in income in one year and has $200,000 in deductible

expenses. The $300,000 annual profit the partnership earns is passed through the partnership to Leo's and Irina's individual tax returns—each gets 50% of the profit, or $150,000. Each must pay personal income tax on his or her share of the profits. These profits are added to any other income they have and are taxed at their individual tax rates.

S Corporation Taxation

S corporations are taxed much like partnerships. Like a partnership, an S corporation is a pass-through entity—income and losses pass through the corporation to the owners' personal tax returns.

S corporations also report their income and deductions much like partnerships. An S corporation files an information return (Form 1120S) reporting the corporation's income, deductions, profits, losses, and tax credits for the year. Like partners, each shareholder must be provided a Schedule K-1 listing his or her shares of the items on the corporation's Form 1120S. The shareholders file Schedule E with their personal tax returns (Form 1040) showing their shares of corporation income or losses.

No business entity starts out with the S corporation form of taxation. Instead, you must obtain it by filing an election with the IRS. The most common way to obtain S corporation taxation is to form a regular C corporation and then file an election to be taxed as an S corporation with the IRS. This simply involves filing IRS Form 2553 with the IRS. However, S corporation status is allowed only if all of the following apply:

- The corporation has no more than 100 shareholders.
- None of the corporation's shareholders are nonresident aliens— that is, noncitizens who don't live in the United States.
- The corporation has only one class of stock—for example, there can't be preferred stock giving some shareholders special rights.
- None of the corporation's shareholders are members of other corporations or partnerships.

These restrictions apply whether you form a C corporation and change it to an S corporation, or form an LLC, an LLP, or a partnership and elect S corporation tax treatment. They do not pose a problem for the vast majority of professionals.

The other way to obtain S corporation status is to form a partnership or an LLP or LLC and file an S corporation election with the IRS. This isn't usually done because professionals who have LLCs, LLPs, or partnerships usually prefer their default partnership tax treatments. However, if you already have an LLC, an LLP, or a partnership, and S corporation tax treatment sounds attractive to you, you should consider filing an S corporation election. But see a tax professional before making this important decision. (See "Should You Change Your Business Entity or Tax Treatment?" below.)

C Corporation Taxation

Under the C corporation form of taxation, the business is treated as a separate taxpaying entity. Profits and losses do not pass through to the owners' individual tax returns as they do with the sole proprietorship, partnership, and S corporation forms of taxation. Instead, C corporations must pay income taxes on their net income and file their own tax returns with the IRS using Form 1120 or Form 1120-A.

In effect, when one or more professionals form a C corporation, they create two or more separate taxpayers—the corporation and themselves, the shareholders. This separate tax identity has both advantages and disadvantages.

A C corporation pays income tax only on its net profit for the tax year, and it pays this at its own corporate tax rates, not the personal tax rates of its owners. It gets to deduct from its income all of its ordinary and necessary business expenses, including employee salaries, most fringe benefits, bonuses, and operating expenses like office rent. However, dividends distributed to the shareholders are not deductible (which, in theory, can lead to double taxation—see "Double Taxation," below).

C corporation shareholders don't pay personal income tax on income the incorporated business earns until it is distributed to them (as individual income) in the form of salary, bonuses, or dividends. They also don't get to deduct the corporation's business expenses on their personal returns. These deductions belong to the corporation.

> EXAMPLE: Bill forms a C corporation—Bill, Inc.—to own and operate his medical practice. He owns all the stock in the corporation. The corporation takes in $500,000 in income. It pays out $300,000 in operating expenses and salaries for Bill's employees, and pays Bill a $100,000 salary. Bill, Inc., had a net profit for the year of $100,000 ($500,000 income − $400,000 expenses = $100,000 net profit). It must pay taxes on its profit at the applicable corporate tax rate. Bill, Inc., files its own tax return and pays the tax from its own funds. Bill, the individual and employee of Bill, Inc., must file his own personal income tax return and pay income taxes on his $100,000 salary at individual income tax rates. If Bill, Inc., distributes any of its $100,000 profit to Bill, the individual, as a dividend, Bill, the individual, will have to pay tax on that amount as well at capital gains rates.

All corporations are initially taxed as C corporations and stay that way unless they file elections to be taxed as S corporations with the IRS. In addition, partnerships, LLPs, and LLCs can elect to be taxed like C corporations. This is not commonly done, but is an option you should consider if you already have an LLC or LLP, or a partnership and would like to obtain the benefits of C corporation tax treatment without going to the trouble of actually forming a corporation. See a tax professional first, however, because once you choose C corporation treatment it may be prohibitively expensive to switch back.

Comparing Tax Treatments

No single type of tax treatment is best for every professional. To help you intelligently choose the tax treatment for your practice, this section compares how the four tax treatments differ in nine crucial areas:

- tax deductions
- tax rates
- owners' employment status
- fringe benefits
- allocating profits and losses
- deducting business losses
- retaining earnings in the business, and
- state taxes.

Tax Deductions

Does your form of taxation change the type of tax deductions you may take for your practice? Mostly, no. Tax deductions are largely the same no matter how a business is taxed. Any business may deduct the ordinary and necessary expenses it incurs, as well as take depreciation for long-term business assets. This covers almost all the deductions in this book.

However, some deductions differ for C and S corporations, as compared with sole proprietor and partnership taxation:

- C and S corporations need not pay tax on all or part of the dividends they receive from stock they own in other corporations.
- C and S corporations get much better treatment for charitable deductions, inventory, or scientific property (see Chapter 13).
- There are major differences in the way capital gains and losses are taxed (see IRS Publication 544, *Sales and Other Dispositions of Assets,* for details).

In addition, C corporation employees need not pay tax on many types of fringe benefits, including health insurance and other medical benefits (see Chapter 16).

Tax Rates

When it comes to income tax rates, sole proprietorships, S corporations, partnerships, and LLCs are all the same. Sole proprietors pay tax on their net self-employment income at their individual personal income tax rates. The profits earned by S corporations, partnerships, and LLCs are passed through to their owners and likewise taxed at their owners' personal rates. Individual personal income tax rates are shown in the chart below.

2017 Federal Personal Income Tax Brackets

Tax Bracket	Income If Single	Income If Married Filing Jointly
10%	Up to $9,325	Up to $18,650
15%	$9,326 to $37,950	$18,651 to $75,900
25%	$37,951 to $91,900	$75,901 to $153,100
28%	$91,901 to $191,650	$153,101 to $233,350
33%	$191,651 to $416,700	$233,351 to $416,700
35%	$416,701 to $418,400	$416,701 to $470,700
39.6%	All over $418,400	All over $470,700

In contrast, C corporations pay corporate income taxes on their net income at their own tax rates shown below. You can see that the top individual tax rate of 39.6%, which went into effect in 2013, now exceeds the top C corporation tax rate of 35%. C corporation rates are also lower than individual rates at some lower income levels. For example, a single individual must pay a combined 19.5% tax rate on the first $75,000 of income, while a corporation pays 18.3%.

Regular C Corporation Income Tax Rates

Taxable Income	Tax Rate
Up to $50,000	15%
$50,001 to $100,000	25%
$100,001 to $335,000	34%
$335,001 to $10,000,000	39%
$10,000,001 to $15,000,000	35%
$15,000,001 to $18,333,333	38%
All over $18,333,333	35%

Does this mean you can save on taxes by using C corporation tax treatment? Usually, the answer is no. There are two reasons for this:

- the 35% flat tax rate for personal service corporations, and
- double taxation.

Both issues are discussed in detail below.

Personal Service Corporations

Special tax rules apply to C corporations (or LLCs, LLPs, or partnerships that elect to be taxed as C corporations) owned by people engaged in occupations involving professional services. The IRS calls such corporations personal service corporations, or PSCs. These corporations pay corporate tax at a flat rate of 35% on all their net income. The reasoning behind this rule is that professionals who form C corporations shouldn't have a tax advantage over professionals who have other types of business entities. Therefore, they must pay tax on all their income at the second highest individual tax rate.

Personal Service Corporation Income Tax Rates	
Taxable Income	Tax Rate
All over $0	35%

EXAMPLE: The Walter Marvin Professional Corporation is a C corporation owned by Marvin. His company has a $100,000 profit for the year. It must pay corporate income tax on the whole $100,000 at the flat 35% rate because his corporation is a personal service corporation.

A C corporation will be classified as a personal service corporation if substantially all the stock is owned by corporate employees engaged in the following activities or professions:

- health services
- law
- accounting (including bookkeeping and tax return preparation; *Rainbow Tax Service v. Comm'r*, 128 T.C. 5 (2007))
- engineering

- architecture
- consulting
- actuarial science, or
- performing arts.

Health services include medical services provided by physicians, nurses, dentists, physical therapists, and other similar health care professionals. Veterinarians are included as well. (Rev. Rul. 91-30.) Consulting means getting paid to give a client your advice or counsel. You're not a consultant if you get paid only if the client buys something from you or from someone else through you. Thus, consulting does not include sales or brokerage services.

These categories include the great majority of C corporations formed by professionals. Fortunately, the vast majority of PSCs make sure their corporation has no net profit for the year by taking out any profits in the form of salary or bonuses (on which they pay tax on their personal returns at individual rates). Or, they have their corporation provide them with fringe benefits which are not taxable at all. Thus, few PSCs actually pay income taxes at the 35% rate. In fact, they usually don't pay any taxes at all.

The IRS can disregard your PSC status altogether if it determines that your principal purpose for forming the PSC was to obtain corporate tax benefits. (IRC § 269A(a).) If this occurs, the IRS can treat you as if you never incorporated for tax purposes and may reallocate income to you. You could also lose tax benefits you obtained by forming the PSC, such as tax savings from health and accident insurance plans, medical reimbursement plans, and employer pension plans.

This IRS rule is intended to prevent professionals from forming PSCs solely to obtain tax benefits, and it applies only to PSCs that perform services for just one client or patient. Thus, it's usually not an issue because most PSCs are formed to provide services to a large number of patients or clients.

EXAMPLE: Sally is a medical doctor employed by Acme Hospital. Sally wants to obtain the benefit of a medical reimbursement plan, but Acme doesn't have one. So, she forms a professional corporation that she wholly owns and has it provide her, its only employee, with a plan. Sally has Acme hire her corporation, Sally, Inc., to work for it, instead of hiring her as an individual. Acme pays Sally, Inc., which then pays Sally, its employee. Sally works only for Acme Hospital. If Sally is audited, the IRS could disregard her corporation and treat her as a sole proprietor, thereby denying her the tax benefits she obtained through her corporation's medical reimbursement plan.

The rule may also apply to a professional who is a member of a partnership, an LLC, an LLP, or a corporation and who forms a PSC to substitute for the professional in the entity.

> **EXAMPLE:** Andre is a dentist who practices in an LLC with Tom and Mike. Andre wants to obtain tax-advantaged benefits that he can get only as an employee of a professional corporation. He forms a professional corporation and becomes its only employee. He then transfers his interest in the LLC to his corporation. The corporation, not Andre personally, is now part owner of the LLC. As Andre's employer, the corporation has Andre provide dental services to the LLC, and pays him a salary and benefits, such as a medical reimbursement plan. Because Andre is an employee, he need not pay income tax on these fringe benefits, and they may be deducted as a business expense by his corporation—making them tax free. This all sounds great, but the IRS could disregard Andre's corporation because (1) it's a PSC, (2) it performs all its services for one entity (the LLC), and (3) its principal purpose was to give Andre tax benefits he couldn't get otherwise (such as a medical reimbursement plan).

You can avoid any risk of having the IRS disregard your PSC status if you perform your services for more than one client or patient. For example, Sally from the first example above would have been safe had her PSC performed services for two or more hospitals at the same time. You can also avoid the rule if you can show the IRS you had a significant nontax reason for forming your PSC—for example, to obtain limited liability.

CAUTION

For PSCs, don't go it alone. Be sure to consult your tax adviser before forming a professional corporation if it will be a PSC and you'll perform substantially all your services for one client or entity.

Avoiding PSC Status

To be classified as a PSC for IRS purposes, a C corporation must have:
- employees who spend 95% or more of their time on health, law, engineering, architecture, accounting, actuarial science, performing arts, or consulting services, and
- stock that is at least 95% (by value) owned by employees who perform such professional services for the corporation. (Temp. Reg. § 1.448-1T(e)(4),(5).)

One way to avoid having your C corporation classified as a PSC is to engage in more than one line of business. The corporation won't be a PSC if the second business requires at least 5% of the corporation's employees' time and doesn't involve one of the PSC services listed above. For example, one CPA firm avoided PSC status by purchasing its office building and carefully documenting that more than 5% of its employees' time was spent managing the building.

Double Taxation

If you're the owner of a C corporation (or choose that method of taxation for your LLC, LLP, or partnership), any direct payment of your corporation's profits to you will be considered a dividend by the IRS and taxed twice. First, the corporation will pay corporate income tax on the profit at corporate rates on its own return, and then you'll pay personal income tax on what you receive from the corporation. This is called "double taxation."

C corporation dividends are usually taxed at capital gains rates. These rates have gone up for 2013 and later, particularly for high-income taxpayers who are subject to the 3.8% Medicare tax on net dividend and investment income (see below). Dividends from stock owned more than one year are taxed at the long-term capital gains rate shown in the chart below.

2017 Income If Married Filing Jointly	Tax Rate on Qualified Dividends
$75,900 or less	0
$75,901 to $250,000	15%
$250,001 to $470,700	18.8% (15% long-term capital gains rate + 3.8% Medicare tax)
All over $470,700	23.8% (20% long-term capital gains rate + 3.8% Medicare tax)

2017 Income If Single	Tax Rate on Qualified Dividends
$37,950 or less	0
$37,951 to $200,000	15%
$200,001 to $416,701	18.8% (15% long-term capital gains rate + 3.8% Medicare tax)
All over $416,701	23.8% (20% long-term capital gains rate + 3.8% Medicare tax)

The Medicare Net Investment Income Tax

As part of the Obamacare health reforms, a brand new Medicare Net Investment Income Tax went into effect in 2013. This is a 3.8% tax on net dividend and investment income earned by taxpayers whose adjusted gross incomes exceed a threshold amount. The tax must be paid on the lower of:

- the amount that a taxpayer's adjusted gross income (investment income plus other taxable income) exceeds $200,000 for single taxpayers, or $250,000 for married couples filing jointly, or
- the taxpayer's total net investment income.

Thus, the tax applies only to people with relatively high incomes—singles must pay the tax only if their AGI is over $200,000; married taxpayers filing jointly must have an AGI over $250,000 to be subject to the tax.

The Medicare Net Investment Income Tax applies to all dividends issued by regular C corporations to their shareholders. Thus, a professional who has formed a professional corporation taxed as a C corporation is subject to the tax. (See "C Corporation Tax Treatment," below.)

When you add the personal tax on dividends to the 35% corporate income tax rate most professional C corporations must pay, you have a total tax of as much as 58.8%. Ouch!

Professionals who have C corporations can often avoid the double taxation problem by ensuring that the corporations have no net profits at the end of the year that they must pay tax on. Ordinarily, you'll be an employee of your corporation and the salary, benefits, and bonuses you receive will be deductible expenses for corporate income tax purposes. If large enough, your employee compensation will eat up all or most of the corporate profits so there's little or no taxable income left on which your corporation will have to pay income tax. In accounting parlance, the corporation's income is "zeroed out." You'll only pay income tax once—personal income tax on your employee compensation.

When you own your C corporation, whether alone or with one or more co-owners, you get to decide how much to pay yourself, and what form your payments will take. Obviously, you'll want to pay yourself enough to avoid double taxation. However, your decision about how much to pay yourself is subject to review by the IRS in the event of an audit. The IRS allows corporate owner-employees to pay themselves only a reasonable salary for work they actually perform. Any amounts that are deemed unreasonable are treated as disguised dividends by the IRS and are subject to double taxation. With the substantial rise in capital gains rates that went into effect in 2013, the IRS may scrutinize the amount of compensation C corporations pay their shareholder-employees more closely than ever before. (See Chapter 15 for a detailed discussion of how much you can pay yourself when you are an incorporated professional-employee.)

Double taxation can become all too real for C corporations (or LLCs, LLPs, or partnerships taxed that way) that own assets that appreciate in value over time, such as real estate or patents. If a C corporation with such assets liquidates (goes out of business), the property must be treated as if it were sold by the corporation for its fair market value. The corporation must pay income taxes on the gain—that is, on the amount the property's fair market value exceeds its basis (cost). Moreover, if the property is distributed to the shareholders on liquidation, they will have to pay tax on the amount that the property's fair market value exceeds the tax basis of their shares. The same holds true if the property is sold and the money distributed to the shareholders.

> **EXAMPLE:** Charles, Inc., is a C corporation solely owned by Charles, a podiatrist. The corporation has owned a small office building for over ten years. The building is worth $250,000, but has only a $50,000 basis. Charles liquidates his corporation and has it transfer ownership of the building to him. Charles's basis in his corporate stock is $75,000. He has a $175,000 capital gain he must pay personal income tax on ($250,000 building value – $75,000 corporate basis = $175,000 gain). His corporation has a $200,000 gain it must pay income tax on ($250,000 building value – $50,000 building basis = $200,000 gain). Thus, there is a double tax—to Charles and his corporation.

In contrast, the owners of an entity taxed as a partnership or an S corporation can ordinarily distribute appreciated assets to themselves tax free upon liquidation. This makes these tax treatments far superior for businesses that own assets that appreciate in value over time.

If you're a sole proprietor, you already personally own all your business assets, so the issue of asset distributions does not arise.

Owners' Employment Status

Should you be an employee of your practice or a self-employed business owner? The answer to this question has important consequences because employees and self-employed people are treated differently for many tax purposes. Each type of employment status has its pros and cons; neither is better for every professional. You choose your employment status when you choose your tax treatment. If you choose S or C corporation tax treatment, you'll be an employee. If you choose any other tax treatment, you'll be self-employed. You should understand the ramifications of this decision before you make it.

Sole Proprietor and Partnership Tax Treatment

If your practice is taxed as a sole proprietorship or partnership, you are not an employee of your business entity. Instead, you are a business owner— also called self-employed. Your business doesn't have to pay payroll taxes on your income or withhold income tax from your pay. It need not file employment tax returns, or pay state or federal unemployment taxes. You need not be covered by workers' compensation insurance. All this can save hundreds of dollars per year.

However, you do have to pay self-employment taxes—that is Social Security and Medicare taxes—on your business income, called self-employment income by the IRS. Self-employment taxes consist of a 12.4% Social Security tax on income up to an annual ceiling. In 2017, the annual Social Security ceiling was $127,200. Medicare taxes consist of a 2.9% tax up to an annual ceiling—$200,000 for single taxpayers and $250,000 for married taxpayers filing jointly. All income above the ceiling is taxed at a 3.8% rate. This combines to a total 15.3% tax on employment or self-employment income up to the Social Security tax ceiling. The Social Security tax ceiling is adjusted annually for inflation. These taxes must be paid four times a year (along with income taxes) in the form of estimated taxes. Self-employment taxes are equivalent to the total Social Security and Medicare tax (FICA tax) paid for an employee.

> **EXAMPLE:** Mel is a sole proprietor dentist who is married and files jointly. In 2017, his net income from self-employment was $400,000. He must pay a 15.3% self-employment tax on the first $127,200 of his income. The remaining $271,800 of his income is subject only to Medicare taxes, not Social Security tax. He must pay a 2.9% Medicare tax on his income from $127,200 to $250,000. He must pay a 3.8% Medicare tax on his income over $250,000. His total self-employment tax is (15.3% x $127,200) + (2.9% x $122,800) + (3.8% x $150,000) = $28,723.

S Corporation Tax Treatment

As far as employment status goes, things work very differently for professionals who choose S corporation status. Although an S corporation is taxed much like a partnership, it is still a corporation—a separate legal entity. An S corporation shareholder who performs more than minor services for the corporation will be its employee for tax purposes, as well as a shareholder. In effect, an active shareholder in a corporation wears at least two hats: as a shareholder (owner) of the corporation, and as an employee of that corporation. If the corporation is small, as most professional corporations are, the shareholder-employee normally serves as an officer and director of the corporation as well. So, one person can be wearing four hats.

A shareholder-employee must be compensated for his or her services to the practice with a reasonable salary and any other employee compensation the corporation wants to provide. The shareholder-employee must report the S corporation's earnings on his or her personal income tax return, and pay the employee share of Social Security and Medicare taxes on any employee salary he or she is paid. The corporation must withhold federal income and employment tax from the shareholder-employee's pay, and pay state and federal unemployment taxes and Social Security and Medicare taxes on the employee's behalf.

The Social Security and Medicare tax rate for an employee is the same as for a self-employed business owner; however, it's paid differently. Half the total tax is deducted by the employer from the employee's pay, and half is paid by the employer itself. When you own the business that is paying these taxes, it makes no practical difference that half is paid by the employer—you are the employer.

> **EXAMPLE:** Assume that Mel (from the above example) has formed an S corporation of which he's the sole shareholder. Because he performs dental services for the corporation, he is its employee for tax purposes. In one recent year, the corporation paid Mel $400,000 in employee salary. The corporation withholds half of Mel's Social Security and Medicare taxes from his wages and pays the other half itself. The total tax is $28,723, just like when Mel was a sole proprietor.

Also, most states require that each employee be provided with workers' compensation insurance coverage. However, some states dispense with this requirement if the corporation has only a few employees. Unemployment insurance and workers' compensation coverage costs at least several hundred dollars per employee.

Clearly, being classified as an S corporation employee has many disadvantages for a professional. But it also has two big potential advantages: S corporation treatment can provide a way to take money out of your corporation without having to pay employment tax or the new Medicare Net Investment Income Tax. This can make S corporation tax treatment very attractive for professionals.

You do not have to pay employment tax on distributions (dividends) from your S corporation—that is, on earnings and profits that pass through the corporation to you as a shareholder, not as an employee in compensation for your services. The larger your distribution, the less employment tax you'll pay. The S corporation is the only business form that makes it possible for its owners to save on taxes. This is the main reason S corporations have been, and remain, popular with professionals.

> **EXAMPLE:** Assume that Mel's S corporation pays him a $200,000 salary. The remaining $200,000 of the corporation's profits are passed through the S corporation and reported as an S corporation distribution on Mel's personal income tax return, not as employee salary. Because it is not viewed as employee wages, neither Mel nor his corporation need to pay employment tax on this amount. Mel and his corporation only pay a total of $21,573 in employment taxes instead of $28,723.

If you took no salary at all, you would not owe any employment taxes. As you might expect, however, this is not allowed. The IRS requires S corporation shareholder-employees to pay themselves reasonable salaries—at least what other businesses pay for similar services. (See "Paying Yourself" in Chapter 15 for a detailed discussion of what constitutes a reasonable salary.)

The S corporation form can also enable you to take money out of your business without having to pay the 3.8% Medicare Net Investment Income Tax. Dividends paid to C corporation shareholders are subject to this tax. But distributions paid to an S corporation shareholder are not, as long as the shareholder "materially participates" in the business. There are several tests for material participation. For example, you materially participate in a business if, during the year, you (and your spouse, if any) are:

- the only people who work in the business
- spend over 500 hours per year working in the business, or
- spend over 100 hours working in the business, and no one else, including employees, puts in more than 100 hours.

Professionals ordinarily materially participate in their businesses as a matter of course.

> **EXAMPLE:** Assume that Mel from the above example is a single taxpayer who materially participates in his S corporation's dental business. The $200,000 dividend his S corporation paid him is not subject to the 3.8% Medicare Net Investment Income Tax. If Mel's business had been organized as a C corporation, he would have had to pay this tax—a 3.8% tax on $200,000, or $7,600. Thus, having an S corporation instead of a C corporation saved Mel $7,100 in employment tax and $7,600 in Medicare Net Investment Income Tax.

C Corporation Tax Treatment

When you form a C corporation (or choose that method of taxation for your LLC, LLP, or partnership) and actively work in the business, you become your corporation's employee, with the same tax consequences as described for an S corporation employee above. However, C corporation shareholder-employees can't save on taxes by paying themselves corporate distributions instead of employee salaries. This is because a C corporation is a taxpaying entity and cannot deduct distributions made to shareholders. Thus, it must pay corporate income tax on the distributions—ordinarily at a 35% rate. Moreover, the shareholders must pay a capital gains tax on such distributions.

> **EXAMPLE:** Assume that Mel from the above examples has a C corporation. It pays him a $200,000 employee salary and a $200,000 shareholder distribution. Mel and his corporation must pay employment taxes on his salary, just like when Mel had an S corporation. These amount to (15.3% x $127,200) + (2.9% x $72,800) = $21,573. Moreover, because it is a C corporation, Mel's corporation must pay corporate income tax on the $200,000 dividend. It must pay this tax at a flat 35% rate because it is a personal service corporation. Thus, it must pay a $70,000 tax. Mel must pay both the capital gains and Medicare Net Investment Income Tax on his dividend. At his income level, this is an 18.8% tax; thus he owed $37,600. The total tax on the $200,000 dividend is a whopping $107,600.

However, being a C corporation employee, instead of a self-employed business owner or an S corporation employee, has tax advantages when it comes to fringe benefits.

Fringe Benefits

Fringe benefits are things like health, disability, and life insurance; paid vacations; a company car; and reimbursement of medical expenses not covered by insurance. This is the one major area where C corporation tax treatment is far superior to the other tax regimes.

C Corporation Tax Treatment

When you form a C corporation (or elect to have your LLC, LLP, or partnership taxed as a C corporation) and actively work in the business, you become your corporation's employee. Being a corporate employee, instead of a self-employed business owner, has significant tax advantages when it comes to fringe benefits. The tax law allows a C corporation to provide its employees with many types of fringe benefits that it can deduct from the corporation's income as a business expense. But the employees need not include the value of the fringe benefits in their taxable income, effectively making them tax free. This can save many thousands of dollars in taxes. No other business entity can do this.

Possible tax-free employee fringe benefits include:
- health, accident, and dental insurance for you and your family
- disability insurance
- reimbursement of medical expenses not covered by insurance
- deferred compensation plans
- working condition fringe benefits such as company-owned cars, and
- group term life insurance.

EXAMPLE: Marilyn incorporates her optometric practice, of which she is the only employee. Marilyn's corporation provides her with health insurance and a medical reimbursement plan for uninsured medical expenses for her and her family at a cost of $10,000 per year. The entire cost can be deducted from the corporation's income for corporate income tax purposes, but is not included as income on Marilyn's personal tax return. In effect, no tax has to be paid on the $10,000.

Sole Proprietorship, Partnership, and S Corporation Tax Treatment

Professionals taxed as sole proprietors, S corporation owners, and partners, may deduct 100% of their health insurance premiums from their personal income tax. This includes their own health insurance premiums as well as those for their spouses and dependents. But this is a special personal deduction, not a business deduction. Thus, it doesn't reduce their income for Social Security and Medicare tax purposes.

These professionals get no other tax-advantaged fringe benefits. If the entity provides the owner with another type of fringe benefit, its value must be included in the owner's personal tax return and income tax must be paid on it. For example, if an entity taxed as a partnership provides an owner with disability insurance, the owner must include the value of the insurance in his or her taxable income for the year. But there is one way around this: The business owner can hire his or her spouse as an employee and provide the spouse with benefits. (See Chapter 11.)

 RELATED TOPIC

See Chapter 16 for a detailed discussion of fringe benefits for professionals who are taxed as C corporations.

Allocating Profits and Losses

Partnerships, LLPs, and LLCs taxed like partnerships (as most are) have a tax advantage when it comes to allocating profits and losses. Unlike corporations, they have great flexibility on how to allocate profits and losses among the owners. For example, one owner could get 75% of the profits and the other 25%, even though they are each equal owners of the LLC or partnership. Professionals involved in group practices find this flexibility very attractive because it allows them to be creative in fashioning their compensation. For example, partnership or LLC profits can be distributed according to each owner's collections or receipts, shared equally, shared according to each owner's percentage of ownership, based on complex formulas involving points or units, or based on a combination of methods—for example, distributions could be based partly on ownership percentages and partly on collections. Or, they can use a less rational approach: Partners or LLC members can simply get together at the end of the year and decide how much each person should get of the firm's net profits for the year. However, there are limits on how creative LLCs, LLPs, and partnerships can get. Complex IRS rules ("substantial economic effect rules") permit the IRS to disregard a partnership allocation of profits or losses if it's done only to avoid taxes.

You don't have the same flexibility with an S or C corporation. Any profits taken out of a corporation as dividends must be distributed to the shareholders in proportion to their ownership share. For example, if there are two shareholders and each owns 50% of the stock, they must each receive, and pay income tax on, a 50% share of any corporate dividend. The only way to provide disproportionate distributions is to pay some shareholder-employees more salary or other employee compensation than others. But there is a limit on how much employee compensation a C corporation shareholder-employee may reasonably be paid. And, it's preferable to pay S corporation shareholders as little employee compensation as possible to avoid employment taxes. (See Chapter 15.)

Deducting Business Losses

Some professional practices lose money. Though this is not common, it can occur. How you can deduct these losses will depend on what type of tax treatment you have for your business. And though the problem of having losses doesn't occur often with professional businesses, the differences between the tax treatments and how you can deduct the losses is significant.

Sole Proprietorship and Partnership Tax Treatment

Just as income passes through a sole proprietorship or partnership to the owners' personal tax returns, so do losses. Thus, subject to some important limitations, losses from an entity taxed as a sole proprietorship (sole proprietorship or single-member LLC) or an entity taxed as a partnership (LLC, LLP, or partnership) can be deducted from any other income the owners have. They can even be deducted from income earned in prior years that has already been taxed, or saved up to be used in future years. This makes sole proprietorship or partnership tax treatment ideal for a business that expects to lose money, which is sometimes the case with professionals who are just starting out.

> EXAMPLE 1: Lisa holds a full-time job as an engineer. She decides to establish a part-time consulting business she operates as a sole proprietor. During her first year as a sole proprietor, she incurs $11,000 in expenses and earns $1,000 in consulting fees, giving her a $10,000 loss from her consulting business. She reports this loss on IRS Schedule C, which she files with her personal income tax return (Form 1040). Because Lisa is a sole proprietor, she can deduct this $10,000 loss from any income she has, including her $100,000 annual salary from her engineering job. This saves her about $4,000 in taxes for the year.

> EXAMPLE 2: Jack and Johanna are a married couple who file a joint income tax return. Johanna earns $80,000 a year from her job. Jack is a lawyer employed by an insurance company. He quits his job and starts his own legal practice. He forms a one-owner LLC, which is taxed as a sole proprietorship. In his first year in business, his company earns $20,000 and has $40,000 in expenses. The entire $20,000 business loss passes through the LLC to Jack and Johanna's personal joint tax return. They subtract the $20,000 loss from their total taxable income for the year, which consists of Johanna's $80,000 salary. This leaves them with $60,000 in income for the year. Because they are in the 25% income tax bracket, they've saved $5,000 in federal income tax (25% × $20,000 = $5,000).

However, there are some limitations on the amount of losses an owner of an entity taxed as a partnership can deduct on his or her personal tax return. The most important limit is that the deduction for losses cannot exceed the owner's tax basis in a partnership, or an LLP or LLC taxed like a partnership. Basis means your total investment in the business for tax purposes. In general, a business owner cannot deduct a loss that exceeds the owner's cash contribution to the entity, plus income previously realized from the entity, reduced by any losses or deductions that were previously deducted. Importantly, owners of entities taxed as partnerships may also add to their basis their share of all the entity's liabilities—loans and other debts—which can greatly increase their basis and allow them to deduct more losses.

> **EXAMPLE:** Ralph and Norton, both chiropractors, decide they want to join their practices. They form an LLC taxed like a partnership. They each own a 50% interest in the LLC and equally share all partnership profits and losses. They each contribute $10,000 to the LLC. The LLC also obtained a $50,000 bank loan to cover its first-year operating expenses. Ralph and Norton each have a $35,000 basis in the LLC ($10,000 cash contribution + 50% of the $50,000 loan = $35,000). The LLC loses $50,000 the first year. Ralph and Norton may each deduct $25,000 of the loss on their personal returns. This leaves them each with a $10,000 basis. If the LLC loses $50,000 the next year, they will each be able to deduct only $10,000 of the loss, and will end up with a zero basis.

S Corporation Tax Treatment

S corporation shareholders (or owners of LLCs, LLPs, or partnerships taxed that way) may also deduct their share of business losses from their personal incomes. However, unlike owners of partnership tax entities, S corporation shareholders may not add S corporation liabilities to their basis. The only liabilities that may be added to an S corporation shareholder's basis are shareholder loans that the shareholder makes to the corporation. Thus, if Ralph and Norton from the above example had formed an S corporation, they each would have only a $10,000 starting basis and could deduct only that amount of their first year loss. As a result, partnership tax treatment has a big advantage over S corporation tax treatment when it comes to deducting losses.

C Corporation Tax Treatment

If a C corporation has a loss for the tax year, that loss is trapped in the corporation—it stays in the corporation and can only be deducted on the corporation's tax return. Losses do not pass through to the shareholders' personal returns as is the case with pass-through entities. Thus, the shareholders don't get to deduct the losses from their personal income from other sources. This makes the C corporation form of taxation the worst possible for a money-losing business. However, few professionals incur losses, so this factor is usually not so important when choosing their tax treatments.

Retaining Earnings in Your Business

If you want to keep earnings in your business without paying personal income tax on those earnings, you will not want to choose partnership tax treatment. Each owner of a practice that is taxed as a partnership must pay taxes on his or her entire share of profits, even if the entity chooses to reinvest the profits in the business rather than distribute them to the owners. This results in phantom income—income you must pay tax on even though you never received it.

> EXAMPLE: Mario, Paula, and Ralph jointly own a group optometric practice organized as an LLC and taxed like a partnership. This year, they had $300,000 in profits, which they share equally. They would like to keep $100,000 of their profits in the business to help purchase new equipment and a building for their practice. They are free to do this, but they will still all be taxed on their full share of the LLC's $300,000 profit, even though it is not distributed to them. Thus, they each have to pay tax on $100,000—their individual shares of the $300,000 profit—even though they each actually receive only $67,000 from their LLC and the remaining $100,000 is left in the LLC bank account.

The same thing happens to sole proprietors. They pay tax on all their business profits, even those they leave in their businesses.

C corporation tax treatment is the only form of taxation that allows business owners to retain earnings in the business without having to pay personal income taxes on them. This allows you to split the income your business earns with your corporation. Unfortunately, income splitting is not nearly as advantageous for professionals as it is for most other business owners. This is because a professional corporation taxed as a C corporation usually qualifies as a personal service corporation that must pay a flat 35% income tax on all its income. (Of course, this rule also applies to LLCs, LLPs, and partnerships that choose to be taxed as C corporations.)

Tax Savings Through Income Splitting

It is still possible to save some money through income splitting because you don't have to pay Social Security and Medicare taxes on profits you retain in a C corporation. These consist of a 12.4% Social Security tax on income up to an annual ceiling. In 2017, the annual Social Security ceiling was $127,200. Medicare taxes consist of a 2.9% tax up to an annual ceiling—$200,000 for single taxpayers and $250,000 for married couples filing jointly. All income above the ceiling is taxed at a 3.8% rate. This combines to a total 15.3% tax on employment or self-employment income up to the Social Security tax ceiling. Whether you'll save money, and how much, depends on your personal income tax bracket. If you are in the top 39.6% tax bracket, you'll have a combined 43.4% tax on your employee compensation (39.6% income tax + 3.8 Medicare tax = 43.4%). If you keep money in your corporation instead of taking it out as employee compensation, the corporation will just have to pay a 35% corporate income tax, so you save 8.4% in taxes.

> **EXAMPLE:** Betty, a single doctor, owns and operates an incorporated medical practice taxed as a C corporation. In one year, the corporation pays Betty a $450,000 salary, which places her in the top 39.6% income tax bracket. After paying all its annual expenses, Betty's corporation is left with a net profit of $100,000. Rather than pay herself the $100,000 as an employee bonus, Betty decides to leave the money in her corporation and use it for future expansion. The corporation pays 35% corporate income tax on these retained earnings. Had Betty taken the $100,000 as a bonus, she would have had to pay a 39.6% personal income tax on it, plus a 3.8% Medicare tax (or $43,400). Keeping the money in her corporation saved Betty $8,400 in taxes because instead she would owe $35,000 in taxes (the 35% corporate income tax).

Professional corporations in the fields of health, law, accounting, architecture, or consulting may keep up to $150,000 of their C corporation earnings in their corporate bank account without penalty. Professionals who don't practice in these fields may keep up to $250,000 in a C corporation. You can use this money to expand your practice, buy equipment, or pay yourself employee benefits, such as health insurance and pension benefits.

If you keep more than the $150,000 or $250,000 limit, you'll become subject to an extra 15% tax called the "accumulated earnings tax." This tax is intended to discourage you from sheltering too much of your corporation's earnings. However, you can avoid the 15% if you can show the IRS that the excess accumulations are held for reasonably anticipated needs of the business, not just to avoid taxes. In practice, though, few small corporations need to, or are able to, accumulate more than the $150,000 or $250,000 limit.

Personal Holding Company Penalty Tax

If five or fewer professionals own 50% or more of a C corporation's stock, the corporation can become subject to the personal holding company tax. This is an extra 15% penalty tax on the corporation's income. The tax can be imposed if at least 60% of the corporation's undistributed income for the tax year is personal holding company income. This is income derived from passive sources such as interest, royalties, dividends, and rents. Unfortunately for professionals, income from professional services can also be personal holding company income.

Amounts received for professional services are personal holding company income if both of the following are true:

- They are paid under a written or oral contract in which the client (rather than the corporation) can designate (by name or description) the particular employee who is to perform the services.
- The designated employee owns 25% or more of the corporation's stock. (IRC § 543(a)(7).)

EXAMPLE: Sally is the sole owner of her C corporation. Her company is hired by Acme, Inc., to perform consulting services. The contract specifies that Sally, and Sally alone, may perform the services. All the income Sally's company earns from the contract is personal holding company income. If all her corporation's personal holding company income for the year amounts to 60% or more of her company's total income, the 15% personal holding company tax will be triggered.

Many professional corporations meet the five-owner/50% ownership test and thus can be subject to the personal holding company penalty if they are not careful. (You can't get around the ownership test by giving corporate stock to other business entities or relatives.)

Fortunately, it's relatively easy to avoid the personal holding company penalty tax. First, you should make sure that no agreement you make with any client requires that the services be performed by any employee of your corporation who owns 25% or more of the company stock. It's also advisable to include in your client agreement a provision that your corporation, not the client, has the right to designate the person who will perform the services.

If you are considering incorporating your practice (or changing your LLC, LLP, or partnership to C corporation tax treatment), you should be careful about assigning your personal service contracts to your new corporation. It could trigger the personal holding company tax. Fortunately, the IRS permits newly incorporated businesses in this fix to avoid the tax in many cases by paying out a deficiency dividend. However, the corporation will still be subject to interest and other penalty payments. It's wise for any professional who incorporates an existing practice to check with a tax professional to make sure the corporation will not run afoul of the personal holding company tax rule.

State Taxes

Depending on where you practice, state taxes might be an important factor in your choice of business entity. Some states impose higher taxes on businesses than others.

All states except Nevada, South Dakota, Washington, and Wyoming impose corporate income tax based on the amount of taxable income earned in the state by the corporation. The rates vary from state to state. Some states also charge franchise taxes—for example, California exacts a hefty $800 minimum franchise tax per year after the first year a corporation is in business.

Most states tax sole proprietorships, partnerships, LLCs, and LLPs the same way the IRS does. The owners pay taxes to the state on their personal returns, and the entity itself does not pay a state tax. But some states impose special taxes on pass-through entities. For instance, California levies a tax on LLCs that make over $250,000 per year; the tax ranges from about $900 to $11,000. A similar tax is imposed on California S corporations. Illinois and Massachusetts charge LLCs $250 and $500, respectively, as annual report filing fees.

In addition, some states (including California, Delaware, Illinois, Massachusetts, New Hampshire, Pennsylvania, and Wyoming) impose an annual LLC fee that is not income related. This may be called a franchise tax, an annual registration fee, or a renewal fee. In most states, the fee is about $100; but California exacts an $800 minimum franchise tax per year from LLCs and LLPs as well. Before forming any business entity, find out what taxes or fees your state charges. You should be able to find this at the website of your state's secretary of state, department of corporations, or department of revenue or tax.

Should You Change Your Business Entity or Tax Treatment?

Neither your choice of business entity under state law, nor the tax treatment for your business under federal tax law, is engraved in stone. You can always switch to another form of tax treatment, another business entity form, or both. Indeed, many professionals start out as sole proprietors and then switch to either corporations, LLCs, or LLPs when they take on partners and want limited liability.

Whether you should make a change depends on what your goals are and what type of entity and tax treatment you have now. There is no business entity or form of tax treatment that is right for every professional.

The following chart can help you decide if you should convert to a different entity, or simply change your tax treatment (which is easier to do). For example, if you want limited liability, the chart shows that you must have a C or an S corporation or an LLC or LLP (with any type of tax treatment). If you want to combine your limited liability with lower

Social Security and Medicare taxes, you can choose an S corporation, or an LLC or LLP with S corporation tax treatment. If, instead, you want limited liability and maximum deductions for fringe benefits, you'll want a C corporation, or an LLC or LLP with C corporation tax treatment. But no entity will give you limited liability, lower Social Security and Medicare taxes, and maximum deductions for benefits.

The Cost of Converting to Another Business Form

As a general rule, unincorporated professionals will have little tax cost in converting to a sole proprietorship, or partnership or an LLC or LLP. However, there can be exceptions. Thus, before doing such a conversion, you should consult a tax professional.

Converting to a corporation can be tax free if IRS rules are followed. (See IRC § 351.) However, in some cases, there can be serious tax consequences, particularly for professionals whose main business asset is their accounts receivable. Tax will be due if the business liabilities transferred to (or assumed by) the corporation exceed the owner's tax basis in the transferred business assets.

> **EXAMPLE:** Felix is a sole proprietor architect who decides to incorporate his practice. By far his largest business asset is his practice's accounts receivable—the money owed to him by his clients—which amounts to $100,000. However, under standard tax rules, he has a zero basis in such accounts receivable. His only other business asset is $10,000 in cash. He transfers the receivables and cash to the corporation along with $100,000 in liabilities. The amount of transferred liabilities exceeds the basis in his business assets by $90,000. Felix will have to pay tax on the $90,000 excess.

This result can be avoided with careful planning. For example, Felix (from the above example) could retain his accounts receivable and pay personal income tax on them as they are paid. Or, he could lend money to his architecture practice prior to incorporation so that the basis in the transferred assets exceeds the amount of liabilities. Thus, it's essential that your tax adviser approve your incorporation plans before you file articles of incorporation to convert an existing sole proprietorship, partnership, LLC, or LLP to a corporation.

Choice of Business Entity Decision Matrix							
	Limit liability	Maximize deductions for fringe benefits	Reduce Social Security and Medicare taxes	Deduct business losses	Retain earnings in business	Reduce IRS audit chances	Simplicity and low cost
C corporation	✓	✓			✓	✓	
S corporation	✓		✓			✓	
Multiowner LLC or LLP with partnership tax treatment	✓			✓		✓	
LLC or LLP with C corporation tax treatment	✓	✓			✓	✓	
LLC or LLP with S corporation tax treatment	✓		✓	✓		✓	
Partnership with partnership tax treatment						✓	
Partnership with C corporation tax treatment			✓	✓		✓	
Partnership with S corporation tax treatment		✓			✓	✓	
Sole proprietorship				✓			✓
One-owner LLC with sole proprietorship tax treatment	✓			✓			

There are often significant tax costs if you want to convert out of a C corporation. Indeed, if you already have a C corporation, you may be stuck with it. To convert a corporation to a sole proprietorship, an LLC or LLP, or a partnership, it must be dissolved and its assets liquidated. Both the C corporation and its shareholders may end up owing substantial taxes when the corporation is dissolved. For example, the corporation may owe taxes if it owns assets that appreciated over its existence, such as real property. The shareholders may also have to pay income tax if the amount or cash value of the property they receive on liquidation exceeds their individual basis in their shares.

Dissolution isn't necessary when a C corporation is converted to an S corporation. But there could still be substantial tax problems—for example, collection of accounts receivable could be subject to double taxation. In addition, the S corporation may have to pay tax on "built-in gains" if it sells assets within a specified period after electing S status. Built-in gains are the amount by which the fair market value of the corporation's assets exceeds their tax basis when the S election was made. The general rule is that appreciated corporate assets must be owned for five years or more after the conversion to S status to avoid this tax.

Again, consult a tax professional before converting a corporation to another business entity form.

RESOURCE

Refer to *LLC or Corporation? How to Choose the Right Form for Your Business,* by Anthony Mancuso (Nolo), for a good overview of the tax and other consequences of converting to a different business entity.

Changing Your Tax Treatment

As discussed above, it's possible to change the way your business is treated for tax purposes without changing your business form. This can be much cheaper and easier than converting to another business entity.

LLCs, Partnerships, LLPs

Partnerships, multiowner LLCs, and LLPs automatically receive partnership tax treatment when they are created. However, they can change to S or C corporation tax treatment. LLCs with only one owner receive sole proprietorship tax treatment when they are created. They can also switch to S or C corporation treatment. You do this by making an election to receive corporation tax treatment with the IRS.

Most businesses don't make this election because most LLCs, LLPs, and partnerships want to be taxed like partnerships (or sole proprietorships in the case of single-owner LLCs). However, you might choose to be taxed as an S corporation if you want to save on employment taxes. Or, you might want to be taxed like a C corporation because you want maximum deductions for fringe benefits.

If you want to make an election to change your tax treatment, you simply check the appropriate box on IRS Form 8832, *Entity Classification Election,* and file it with the IRS. The election can be made at any time. Once you file the form, your LLC, LLP, or partnership will be treated exactly like a C corporation by the IRS (most states also recognize the election for state tax purposes). You'll have to file corporate tax returns and will have all the benefits and burdens of C corporation tax treatment described above. If you want your LLC, LLP, or partnership to be taxed like an S corporation, you may do so by filing an S corporation election on IRS Form 2553. But you must meet all the conditions for S corporation status to be treated as one (see "S Corporation Taxation" under "The Four Ways Business Entities Are Taxed," above).

Your business will still be an LLC or LLP, or a partnership for all other nontax purposes. Thus, for example, a partnership will not provide limited liability to its owners even if it's taxed like a corporation by the IRS.

EXAMPLE: Tony and Mitch, both Michigan orthodontists, co-own an LLC taxed like a partnership. They both decide they want to take advantage of the tax-free fringe benefits available to C corporations. There are two ways they can do this: (1) They can dissolve their LLC and form a new corporation in Michigan; or (2) they can simply file an election with the IRS to have their LLC taxed like a C corporation. They decide to do it the easy way and file the election. As far the IRS is concerned, the Tony and Mitch LLC is now a C corporation. It is a separate taxpaying entity and must file its own corporate tax returns. Tony and Mitch are now employees of their practice for tax purposes. They must have income and employment taxes withheld from their pay and they will be qualified to receive tax-free employee fringe benefits.

CAUTION

Electing a new tax treatment has the same tax consequences as converting to a different type of business entity. For example, a partnership, an LLP, or a multiowner LLC that elects corporation tax treatment is deemed to have liquidated for tax purposes and contributed all its assets and liabilities to the corporation in exchange for stock. (IRS Reg. § 301.7701-3(g)(1)(i).) This can have costly tax consequences as described above. The moral: Be sure to consult with your tax adviser before making an election to have your LLC, LLP, or partnership taxed like a corporation.

If it turns out you don't like your corporation tax treatment, you can change back to partnership tax treatment by making another election; but, you must ordinarily wait five years to do so. (Treas. Reg. 301.7701-3(c)(1)(iv).) Moreover, electing to change back to partnership tax treatment could result in added taxes because it will be treated as a constructive corporate liquidation for federal income tax purposes and so can be taxable to both the liquidating corporation and its shareholders. Again, consult a tax adviser before making a change.

Corporations

Corporations also have the ability to change how they are taxed. All corporations automatically receive C corporation tax treatment when they are created. But a C corporation that meets the requirements may choose S corporation status by filing an election with the IRS as described above. It's also possible for an S corporation to revoke its S corporation status and return to C corporation tax treatment.

Automatic Conversion of Your Business Entity

In some cases, your business will automatically convert to one of the two default entities: the sole proprietorship or partnership. This can happen without you even knowing it. For example, if a sole proprietor starts to practice with one or more other professionals instead of on his own, he will automatically become a partner in a partnership unless the partners elect to form a corporation, an LLC, or an LLP. The new partnership will automatically receive partnership tax treatment.

Similarly, if a partnership, an LLC, or LLP, or a corporation breaks up and all the former owners start to practice on their own, they will each automatically become sole proprietors and receive sole proprietor tax treatment.

If you don't want to be a sole proprietor or partner in a partnership, you need to take steps to form another entity. Ideally, you should do this before an automatic conversion occurs.

Operating Expenses

This chapter covers the basic rules for deducting business operating expenses—the bread-and-butter expenses virtually every professional incurs for things like rent, supplies, and salaries. If you don't maintain an inventory or buy expensive equipment, these day-to-day costs will probably be your largest category of business expenses (and your largest source of deductions).

Requirements for Deducting Operating Expenses

There are so many different kinds of business operating expenses that the tax code couldn't possibly list them all. Instead, if you want to deduct an item as a business operating expense, you must make sure the expenditure meets certain requirements. If it does, it will qualify as a deductible business operating expense. To qualify, the expense must be:

- ordinary and necessary
- a current expense
- directly related to your business, and
- reasonable in amount. (IRC § 162.)

Your Practice Must Have Begun

You must be *carrying on* a business to have deductible operating expenses. Costs you incur before your practice is up and running are not currently deductible operating expenses, even if they are ordinary and necessary. However, up to $5,000 in start-up expenses may be deducted the first year you're in business, with the remainder deducted over the next 15 years. (See Chapter 10 for a discussion of start-up expenses.)

Ordinary and Necessary

The first requirement is that the expense must be ordinary and necessary. This means that the cost is common and "helpful and appropriate" for your business (*Welch v. Helvering*, 290 U.S. 111 (1933)). The expense doesn't have to be indispensable to be necessary; it need only help your business in some way—even if it's minor. A one-time expenditure can be ordinary and necessary.

> **EXAMPLE:** Connie, a dentist, buys a television set and installs it in her dental office waiting room so patients can watch TV while waiting for their appointments. Although having a TV set in her waiting room is not an indispensable item for Connie's dental business, it is helpful; some patients might choose Connie instead of another dentist because they can watch TV while they wait. Therefore, the TV is an ordinary and necessary expense for Connie's dental practice.

It's usually fairly easy to figure out whether an expense passes the ordinary and necessary test. Some of the most common types of operating expenses include:

- rent for an outside office
- employee salaries and benefits
- equipment rental
- business websites
- legal and accounting fees
- car and truck expenses
- travel expenses
- meal and entertainment expenses
- supplies and materials
- publications
- subscriptions
- repair and maintenance expenses
- business taxes
- interest on business loans
- licenses
- banking fees
- advertising costs
- home office expenses
- business-related education expenses
- postage
- professional association dues

- business liability and property insurance
- health insurance for employees
- office utilities, and
- software used for business.

Generally, the IRS won't second-guess your claim that an expense is ordinary and necessary, unless the item or service clearly has no legitimate business purpose.

> **EXAMPLE:** An insurance agent claimed a business deduction for part of his handgun collection because he had to go to "unsafe job sites" to settle insurance claims, and there was an unsolved murder in his neighborhood. The tax court disallowed the deduction explaining, "A handgun simply does not qualify as an ordinary and necessary business expense for an insurance agent, even a bold and brave Wyatt Earp type with a fast draw who is willing to risk injury or death in the service of his clients." (*Samp v. Comm'r*, T.C. Memo 1981-1986.)

Current Expense

Only current expenses are deductible as business operating expenses. Current expenses are for items that will benefit your practice for less than one year. These are the costs of keeping your business going on a day-to-day basis, including money you spend on items or services that get used up, wear out, or become obsolete in less than one year. A good example of a current expense is your practice's monthly phone bill, which benefits your business for one month. In contrast, buying a telephone for your practice would be a capital expense (not a current expense) because the phone will benefit your business for more than one year. Other common capital expenses include cars, business equipment, computers, and real estate.

Current expenses are currently deductible—that is, they are fully deductible in the year in which you incur them. Because all business operating expenses are current expenses, they are also all currently deductible. However, the annual deductions for some operating expenses (notably home offices) are limited to the amount of profits you earn from the business in that year. (See Chapter 7 for more on the home office deduction.) Items you buy for your practice that last for more than one year (capital expense items) must be depreciated over several years or deducted in one year under Section 179. (See Chapter 9 for more on deducting long-term assets.)

Business Related

An expense must be directly related to your practice to be deductible as a business operating expense. This means that you cannot deduct personal expenses. For example, the cost of a personal computer is a deductible operating expense only if you use the computer for business purposes; it is not deductible if you use it to pay personal bills or play computer games. If you buy something for both personal and business use, you can deduct only the business portion of the expense. For example, if you buy a cellular phone and use it half of the time for business calls and half of the time for personal calls, you can deduct only half of the cost of the phone as a business expense.

Many expenses have both a personal and business component, which can make it difficult to tell if an expense is business related. Because of this, the business-related requirement is usually the most challenging factor in determining whether an expense qualifies as a deductible business operating expense.

Even the most straightforward costs can present difficulties. For example, it's usually easy to tell whether postage is a personal or business expense. If you mail something for your practice, it's a business expense; if you mail something unrelated to your business, it's a personal expense. But even here, there can be questions. For example, should a doctor be allowed to deduct the postage for postcards he sends to his patients while he is on vacation in Europe? (Yes—the tax court said the postage was deductible as an advertising expense; *Duncan v. Comm'r*, 30 T.C. Memo 386 (1958).)

The IRS has created rules and regulations for some of the more common operating expenses that often involve a difficult crossover of personal and business. Some of these rules help by laying out guidelines for when an expense is and isn't deductible. Others impose record-keeping and other requirements to prevent abuses by dishonest taxpayers. Most of the complexity in determining whether an expense is deductible as a business operating expense involves understanding and applying these special rules and regulations.

The expenses that present the most common problems (and are subject to the most comprehensive IRS rules and regulations) include:

- home office expenses (see Chapter 7)
- meals and entertainment (see Chapter 4)
- travel (see Chapters 5 and 6)
- car and truck expenses (see Chapter 5)
- business gifts (see Chapter 13)
- bad debts (see Chapter 13)
- interest payments (see Chapter 13)
- health insurance (see Chapter 11)
- casualty losses (see Chapter 13)
- taxes (see Chapter 13), and
- education expenses (see Chapter 13).

Through these rules and regulations, the IRS provides guidance on the following types of questions:

- If you rent an apartment and use part of one room as a business office, should you be allowed to deduct all or a portion of the rent as a business operating expense? How much of the room has to be used as an office (and for what period of time) for it to be considered used for business rather than personal purposes? (See Chapter 7 for information on the home office deduction.)
- Can you deduct the money you spend on a nice suit to wear to your office? (See Chapter 13 for information about deducting business clothing.)
- Can you deduct the cost of driving from home to your office? (See Chapter 5 for rules about deducting commuting expenses.)
- Can you deduct the cost of a lunch with a former client? Does it matter whether you actually talk about business at the lunch? (See Chapter 4 for rules about deducting meals and entertainment.)

Reasonable

Subject to some important exceptions, there is no limit on how much you can deduct, as long as the amount is reasonable and you don't deduct more than you spend. As a rule of thumb, an expense is reasonable unless there are more economical and practical ways to achieve the same result. If the IRS finds that your deductions were unreasonably large, it will disallow them or at least disallow the portion it finds unreasonable.

Whether a deduction is reasonable depends on the circumstances, but certain areas are hot buttons for the IRS—especially car, entertainment, travel, and meal expenses. There are strict rules requiring you to fully document these deductions. (See Chapters 4, 5, and 6 for more on car, travel, and meal and entertainment expenses.) The reasonableness issue also comes up when a business pays excessive salaries to employees to obtain a large tax deduction. For example, a professional might hire his 12-year-old son to answer phones and pay him $50 an hour—clearly an excessive wage for this type of work.

For some types of operating expenses, the IRS limits how much you can deduct. These include:

- the home office deduction, which is limited to the profit from your business (although you can carry over and deduct any excess amount in future years) (see Chapter 7)
- business meals and entertainment, which are only 50% deductible (see Chapter 4)
- travel expenses, which are limited depending on the length of your trip and the time you spent on business while away (see Chapter 6), and
- business gifts, which are subject to a $25 maximum per individual per year (see Chapter 13).

Operating Expenses That Are Not Deductible

Even though they might be ordinary and necessary, some types of operating expenses are not deductible under any circumstances. In some cases, this is because Congress has declared that it would be morally wrong or otherwise contrary to sound public policy to allow people to deduct these costs. In other cases, Congress simply doesn't want to allow the deduction. These nondeductible expenses include:

- fines and penalties paid to the government for violation of any law—for example, tax penalties, parking tickets, or fines for violating city housing codes (IRC § 162(f))
- illegal bribes or kickbacks to private parties or government officials (IRC § 162(c))
- lobbying expenses or political contributions; however, a business may deduct up to $2,000 per year in expenses to influence local legislation (state, county, or city), not including the expense of hiring a professional lobbyist (such lobbyist expenses are not deductible)
- two-thirds of any damages paid for violation of the federal antitrust laws (IRC § 162(g))
- professional accreditation fees, including bar exam fees, medical and dental license fees paid to get initial licensing, and accounting certificate fees paid for the initial right to practice accounting
- charitable donations by any business other than a C corporation (these donations are deductible only as personal expenses; see Chapter 13)
- country club, social club, or athletic club dues (see Chapter 4)
- federal income taxes you pay on your business income (see Chapter 13), and
- certain interest payments (see Chapter 13).

Tax Reporting

It's very easy to deduct operating expenses from your income taxes. You simply keep track of everything you buy (or spend money on) for your practice during the year, including the amount spent on each item. Then you record the expenses on your tax return. If you are a sole proprietor or owner of a one-person limited liability company (LLC), you do this on IRS Schedule C, *Profit or Loss From Business*. To make this task easy, Schedule C lists common current expense categories— you just need to fill in the amount for each category. For example, if you spend $1,000 for advertising during the year, you would fill in this amount in the box for the advertising category. You add up all of your current expenses on Schedule C and deduct the total from your gross business income to determine your net business income—the amount on which you are taxed.

If you are a member of a limited liability company with more than one owner, a partner in a partnership, or an S corporation owner, the process is very similar, except you don't use Schedule C. Multi-member LLCs and partnerships file IRS Form 1065, *U.S. Return of Partnership Income*, and their owners' share of expenses is reported on Schedule K-1. S corporations use Form 1120-S, *U.S. Income Tax Return for an S Corporation*. Each partner, LLC member, and S corporation shareholder's share of these deductions passes through the entity and is deducted on the owner's individual tax return on Schedule E. Regular C corporations file their own corporate tax returns.

Meal and Entertainment Expenses

professional practice isn't conducted solely in an office. Your most important business meetings, client contacts, and marketing efforts can take place at restaurants, golf courses, or sporting events. The tax law recognizes this and permits you to deduct part of the cost of business-related entertainment. However, taxpayers have abused this deduction in the past, so the IRS has imposed strict rules limiting the types of entertainment expenses you can deduct and the amount of the deduction you can take.

What Is Business Entertainment?

You may deduct only half of the total amount you spend on business entertainment activities. Because ordinary and necessary business activities are usually fully deductible, you want to be able to distinguish between regular business activities and entertainment.

The basic rule is that entertainment involves something fun, such as:

- dining out
- going to a nightclub
- attending a sporting event
- going to a concert, a movie, or the theater
- visiting a vacation spot (a ski area or beach resort, for example), or
- taking a hunting, yachting, or fishing trip.

Although eating out might fall into other categories of business operating expenses depending on the circumstances, it is by far the number one business entertainment expense.

Activities That Aren't Entertainment

Entertainment does not include activities that are for business purposes only and don't involve any fun or amusement, such as:

- providing supper money to an employee working overtime
- paying for a hotel room used while traveling on business, or
- transportation expenses incurred while traveling on business.

In addition, meals or other entertainment expenses related to advertising or promotions are not considered entertainment. As a rule, an expense for a meal or other entertainment item will qualify as advertising if you make it available to the general public—for example, if a dentist provides free coffee and soft drinks to patients in his waiting room, the cost would not be considered an entertainment expense. These kinds of advertising and promotion costs are fully deductible business operating expenses (see Chapter 13).

Meals Can Be Travel or Entertainment

A meal can be a travel expense or an entertainment expense, or both. The distinction won't affect how much you can deduct—both travel (overnight) and entertainment expenses are only 50% deductible. But different rules apply to the two categories.

A meal is a travel expense if eating out is necessary while you are away from your tax home on a business trip (see Chapter 6 for more on your tax home). For example, any meal you eat alone while on the road for business is a travel expense. On the other hand, a meal is an entertainment expense if you treat a client, a customer, or another business associate and the purpose of the meal is to benefit your practice. A meal is both a travel and an entertainment expense if you treat a client or another business associate to a meal while on the road. However, you may deduct this cost only once—whether you choose to do it as an entertainment or a travel expense, only 50% of the cost is deductible.

Who Can Be Entertained?

You must be with one or more people who can benefit your business in some way to claim an entertainment expense. This could include current or potential:

- clients
- customers
- suppliers
- employees (see Chapter 14 for special tax rules for employees)
- independent contractors
- agents
- partners, or
- professional advisers.

This list includes almost anyone you're likely to meet for business reasons. Although you can invite family members or friends along, you can't deduct the costs of entertaining them, except in certain limited situations.

Deducting Entertainment Expenses

Entertainment expenses, like all business operating expenses, are deductible only if they are ordinary and necessary. This means that the entertainment expense must be common, helpful, and appropriate for your practice. Taxpayers used to have to show only that the entertainment wasn't purely for fun, and that it benefited their business in some way. This standard was so easy to satisfy that the IRS imposed additional requirements for deducting these expenses.

Before the IRS made the standard tougher, you could deduct ordinary and necessary entertainment expenses even if business was never discussed. For example, you could deduct the cost of taking a client to a restaurant, even if you spent the whole time drinking martinis and talking about sports (the infamous three-martini lunch). This is no longer the case—now you must discuss business with one or more business associates either before, during, or after the entertainment if you want to claim an entertainment deduction (subject to one exception; see "Entertainment in Clearly Business Settings," below).

> **CAUTION**
>
> **Who's going to know?** The IRS doesn't have spies lurking about in restaurants, theaters, or other places of entertainment, so it has no way of knowing whether you really discuss business with a client or another business associate. You're pretty much on the honor system here. However, be aware that if you're audited, the IRS closely scrutinizes this deduction because many taxpayers cheat when they take it. You'll also have to comply with stringent record-keeping requirements. (See Chapter 18.)

Business Discussions Before or After Entertainment

The easiest way to get a deduction for entertainment is to discuss business before or after the activity. To meet this requirement, the discussion must be "associated" with your practice—that is, it must have a clear business purpose, such as developing new business or encouraging existing client relationships. You don't, however, have to expect to get a specific business benefit from the discussion. Your business discussion can involve planning, advice, or simply exchanging useful information with a business associate.

You automatically satisfy the business discussion requirement if you attend a business-related convention or meeting to further your business. Business activities—not socializing—must be the main purpose for the convention. Save a copy of the program or agenda to prove this.

Generally, the entertainment should occur on the same day as the business discussion. However, if your business guests are from out of town, the entertainment can occur the day before or the day after the business talk.

> **EXAMPLE:** Mary and Jack are a wealthy couple seeking to build a fancy vacation home. They travel from their home in Boston to New York City to meet with Al, a well-known architect. The couple arrives on Tuesday evening and Al treats them to dinner at a nice restaurant that night. The following morning, Mary and Jack go to Al's office to discuss the building project and look at some preliminary designs. Al can deduct the dinner they had the night before as an entertainment expense.

You can get a deduction even if the entertainment occurs in a place like a nightclub, theater, or loud sports arena where it's difficult or impossible to talk business. This is because your business discussions occur before or after the entertainment, so the IRS won't be scrutinizing whether or not you actually could have talked business during your entertainment activity.

> **EXAMPLE:** Following lengthy negotiations at a client's office, you take the client to a baseball game to unwind. The cost of the tickets is a deductible business expense.

The entertainment can last longer than your business discussions, as long as you don't spend just a small fraction of your total time on business. Thus, it's not sufficient simply to ask an associate, "How's business?" You must have a substantial discussion. Also, your business-related discussions don't have to be face-to-face—they can occur over the telephone or even by email. If you have an email discussion, be sure to save the individual emails.

Business Discussions During Meals

Another way you can deduct entertainment expenses is to discuss business during a meal at a restaurant. To get the deduction, you must show all of the following:

- The main purpose of the combined business discussion and meal was the active conduct of business. You don't have to spend the entire time talking business, but the main character of the meal must be business.
- You did, in fact, have a business meeting, negotiation, discussion, or other bona fide business transaction with your guest or guests during the meal.
- You expect to get income or some other *specific business benefit* in the future from your discussions during the meal—thus, for example, a casual conversation where the subject of business comes up won't do; you have to have a specific business goal in mind.

EXAMPLE: Ivan, a sole proprietor consultant, has had ongoing email discussions with a prospective client who is interested in hiring him. Ivan thinks he'll be able to close the deal and get a contract signed in a face-to-face meeting. He chooses a lunch meeting because it's more informal and the prospective client will like getting a free lunch. He treats the client to a $40 lunch at a nice restaurant. During the lunch, they finalize the terms of a contract for Ivan's consulting services and come to a handshake agreement. This meal clearly led to a specific business benefit for Ivan, so he can deduct half of the cost of both his and his client's lunch as an entertainment expense.

You don't necessarily have to close a deal, sign a contract, or otherwise obtain a specific business benefit to get a deduction. But you do have to have a *reasonable expectation* that you can get some specific business benefit through your discussions at the meal—for example, obtaining a new client or investment in your practice.

No Deductions for Business Discussions During Other Kinds of Entertainment

As a general rule, you can't get a business entertainment deduction by claiming that you discussed business during an entertainment activity other than a meal. In the IRS's view, it's usually not possible to engage in serious business discussions at entertainment venues other than restaurants because of the distractions. Examples of places the IRS would probably find not conducive to serious talk include:

- nightclubs, theaters, or sporting events
- cocktail parties or other large social gatherings
- hunting or fishing trips
- yachting or other pleasure boat outings, or
- group gatherings at a cocktail lounge, golf club, athletic club, or vacation resort that includes people who are not business associates.

This means, for example, that you usually can't claim that you discussed business during a golf game, even if your foursome consists of you and three business associates. In the IRS's view, golfers are unable to play and talk business at the same time. On the other hand, you could have a business discussion before or after a golf game—for example, in the clubhouse. This might seem ridiculous, but it is the rule.

Entertaining at Home

The cost of entertaining at your home is deductible if it meets either of the above two tests. However, the IRS will be more likely to believe that you discussed business during home entertainment if only a small number of people are involved—for example, if you have a quiet dinner party. A larger gathering—a cocktail party, for example—will probably qualify as an entertainment expense only if you have business discussions before or after the event. (For example, you sign a contract with a client during the afternoon and invite him to your house for a large party with your business associates and family.) You can't, however, deduct the costs of inviting nonbusiness guests to your house.

Entertainment in Clearly Business Settings

An exception to the general rule that you must discuss business before, during, or after entertainment is when the entertainment occurs in a clearly business setting. For example, this exception applies to:

- entertainment in a hospitality suite or room at a convention where you discuss your services or products, or
- entertainment that occurs under circumstances where there is no meaningful personal relationship between you and the people you entertained—for example, entertaining local business or civic leaders at the opening of a new hotel to get publicity for your practice, rather than to form business relationships with them.

Calculating Your Deduction

Most expenses you incur for business entertainment are deductible, including meals (with beverages, tax, and tips), your transportation expenses (including parking), tickets to entertainment or sporting events, catering costs of parties, cover charges for admission to nightclubs, and rent paid for a room where you hold a dinner or cocktail party.

You are allowed to deduct only 50% of your entertainment expenses, including taxes and tips. For example, if you spend $50 for a meal in a restaurant, you can deduct $25. You must, however, keep track of everything you spend and report the entire amount on your tax return. The only exceptions to the 50% rule are transportation expenses, which are 100% deductible, and certain meals for employees.

If you have a single bill or receipt that includes some business entertainment as well as other expenses (such as lodging or transportation), you must allocate the expense between the cost of the entertainment and the cost of the other services. For example, if your hotel bill covers meals as well as lodging, you'll have to make a reasonable estimate of the portion that covers meals. It's best to try and avoid this hassle by getting a separate bill for your deductible entertainment.

Expenses Must Be Reasonable

Your entertainment expenses must be reasonable—the IRS won't let you deduct entertainment expenses that it considers lavish or extravagant. There is no dollar limit on what is reasonable; nor are you barred from entertaining at deluxe restaurants, hotels, nightclubs, or resorts.

Whether your expenses will be considered reasonable depends on the particular facts and circumstances—for example, a $250 expense for dinner with a client and two business associates at a fancy restaurant would probably be considered reasonable if you closed a business deal during the meal. Because there are no concrete guidelines, you have to use common sense.

Going "Dutch"

You can deduct entertainment expenses only if you pay for the activity. If a client picks up the tab, you obviously get no deduction. If you split the expense, you must subtract what it would have normally cost you for the meal from the amount you actually paid, and then deduct 50% of that difference. For example, if you pay $20 for lunch and you usually pay only $5, you can deduct 50% of $15, or $7.50.

If you go Dutch a lot and are worried that the IRS might challenge your deductions, you can save your grocery bills or receipts from eating out for a month to show what you usually spend. You don't need to keep track of which grocery items you eat for each meal. Instead, the IRS assumes that 50% of your total grocery receipts are for dinner, 30% for lunch, and 20% for breakfast.

Expenses You Can't Deduct

There are certain expenses that you are prohibited from deducting as entertainment.

Entertainment Facilities

An entertainment facility is any property you own, rent, or use for entertainment—for example, a yacht, hunting lodge, fishing camp, swimming pool, car, airplane, apartment, hotel suite, or home in a vacation resort. You may not deduct any expense for the use of an entertainment facility, including expenses for depreciation and operating costs, such as rent, utilities, maintenance, or security.

However, you can deduct out-of-pocket expenses that you incur while providing entertainment at an entertainment facility—for example, costs for food and beverages, catering, gas, and fishing bait—because these expenses are not for the use of an entertainment facility itself. However, these expenses are subject to the requirements discussed in "Who Can Be Entertained?" and "Deducting Entertainment Expenses," above.

> EXAMPLE: Bill, an attorney, takes a valued client on an afternoon fishing trip. He rents a fishing boat and fishing equipment and has a caterer provide a nice lunch for the trip. Bill may not deduct the cost of renting the fishing boat because it is an entertainment facility. But, if he has a business discussion with the client before, during, or after the trip, he may deduct his out-of-pocket expenses, including the cost of the catered lunch, fishing equipment, and bait.

Nonbusiness Guests' Expenses

You may not deduct the cost of entertaining people who are not business associates. If you entertain business and nonbusiness guests at an event, you must divide your entertainment expenses between the two and deduct only the business part.

> EXAMPLE: You take three clients and six friends to dinner. Because there were ten people at dinner, including you, and only four were business related, 40% of this expense qualifies as business entertainment. If you

spend $200 for the dinner, only $80 would be deductible. And because entertainment expenses are only 50% deductible, your total deduction for the event is $40.

Ordinarily, you cannot deduct the cost of entertaining your spouse or the spouse of a business associate. However, there is an exception: You can deduct these costs if you can show that you had a clear business purpose (rather than a personal or social purpose) in having the spouse or spouses join in.

> EXAMPLE: You take a client visiting from out of town to dinner with his wife. The client's wife joins you because it's impractical (not to mention impolite) to have dinner with the client and not include his wife. Your spouse joins the party because the client's spouse is present. You may deduct the cost of dinner for both spouses.

Club Dues and Membership Fees

In the good old days, you could deduct dues for belonging to a country club or another club where business associates gathered. This is no longer possible. The IRS says you cannot deduct dues (including initiation fees) for membership in any club if one of the principal purposes of the club is to:

- conduct entertainment activities for members, or
- provide entertainment facilities for members to use.

Thus, you cannot deduct dues paid to country clubs, golf and athletic clubs, airline clubs, hotel clubs, or clubs operated to provide members with meals. However, you can deduct other expenses you incur to entertain a business associate at a club.

> EXAMPLE: Jack, a doctor, is a member of the Golden Bear Golf Club in Columbus, Ohio. His annual membership dues are $10,000. One night Jack invites another doctor in the community to dinner at the club's dining room where they discuss Jack's buying his practice. Jack pays $100 for the dinner. Jack's $10,000 annual dues are not deductible, but his costs for the dinner are.

You can deduct dues to join business-related tax-exempt organizations or civic organizations as long as the organization's primary purpose isn't to provide entertainment. Examples include professional associations, such as a medical or bar association, as well as organizations like the Kiwanis or Rotary Club, business leagues, chambers of commerce, and trade associations.

Entertainment Tickets

You can deduct only the face value of an entertainment ticket, even if you paid a higher price for it. For example, you cannot deduct service fees that you pay to ticket agencies or brokers, or any amount over the face value of tickets that you buy from scalpers. However, you can deduct the entire amount you pay for a ticket if it's for an amateur sporting event run by volunteers to benefit a charity.

Ordinarily, you or an employee must be present at an entertainment activity to claim it as a business entertainment expense. This is not the case, however, with entertainment tickets. You can give tickets to clients or other business associates rather than attending the event yourself, and still get a deduction. If you don't go to the event, you have the option of treating the tickets as a gift. You can get a bigger deduction this way sometimes. Gifts of up to $25 are 100% deductible (see Chapter 13), so with tickets that cost less than $50, you get a bigger deduction if you treat them as a gift. If they cost more, treat them as an entertainment expense.

You may also deduct the cost of season tickets at a sports arena or a theater. But, if you rent a skybox or another private luxury box, your deduction is limited to the cost of a regular nonluxury box seat. The cost of season tickets must be allocated to each separate event.

Meals for Employees

Ordinarily, meal and entertainment expenses for your employees are only 50% deductible, just like your own meal and entertainment expenses. However, you or your practice may take a 100% deduction for employee meals:

- provided as part of a company recreational or social activity—for example, a picnic for your employees
- provided on business premises for your convenience—for example, you provide lunch because your employees must remain in the office to be available to work, or
- if the cost is included as part of the employee's compensation and reported as such on his or her W-2.

Expenses Reimbursed by Clients

If a client reimburses you for entertainment expenses, you don't need to count the reimbursement that you receive as income as long as you give the client an adequate accounting of your expenses and comply with the accountable plan rules. Basically, this requires that you submit all your documentation to the client in a timely manner, and return any excess payments. Accountable plans are covered in detail in Chapter 16.

If you comply with the rules, the client gets to deduct 50% of the expenses and you get 100% of your expenses paid for by the client. This is a lot better than getting only a 50% entertainment expense deduction. The reimbursement should not be listed by the client on any Form 1099-MISC a client is required to send to the IRS showing the amount paid to you for your services during the year.

> EXAMPLE: Philip, a sole proprietor marketing consultant, takes several people out to lunch to discuss ways to obtain publicity for a client. He bills his client $500 for the lunches and provides all the proper documentation. The client reimburses Philip $500. Philip gets no deduction for the lunches, but he also doesn't have to include the $500 reimbursement in his income for the year; his client may deduct 50% of the expense as a business entertainment expense.

On the other hand, if you don't properly document your expenses, any reimbursement you obtain from your client must be reported as income on your tax return and should be included in any 1099-MISC form the client provides the IRS reporting how much you were paid (see Chapter 14). The client can still deduct the reimbursement as compensation paid to you. The client's deduction is not subject to the 50% limit because the payment is classified as compensation, not reimbursement of entertainment expenses. You may deduct the expenses on your own return, but your deduction will be subject to the 50% limit.

> **EXAMPLE:** Assume that Philip from the above example fails to make an adequate accounting of his meal expenses to his client, but the client still reimburses him for the full $500. The client may deduct the entire $500, and must include this amount in the 1099-MISC form it provides the IRS reporting how much it paid Philip during the year. Philip must include the $500 as income on his tax return and pay tax on it. He may list the $500 as an entertainment expense on his personal tax return, but his deduction is limited to $250.

If you obtain no reimbursement from your client, you can deduct the cost as a business entertainment expense on your own tax return, but your deduction will be subject to the 50% limit. You must keep adequate records of your entertainment expenses even if your client doesn't reimburse you for them.

Car and Local Travel Expenses

That expensive car parked in your garage not only looks great—it could also be a great tax deduction. This chapter shows you how to deduct expenses for local transportation—that is, business trips that don't require you to stay away from home overnight. These rules apply to local business trips using any means of transportation, but this chapter focuses primarily on car expenses, the most common type of deduction for local business travel.

Overnight trips, whether by car or other means, are covered in Chapter 6.

> **CAUTION**
>
> **Transportation expenses are a red flag for the IRS.** Transportation expenses are the number one item that IRS auditors look at when they examine small businesses. These expenses can be substantial—and it is easy to overstate them—so the IRS will look very carefully to make sure that you're not bending the rules. Your first line of defense against an audit is to keep good records to back up your deductions. This is something no accountant can do for you—you must develop good record-keeping habits and follow them faithfully to stay out of trouble with the IRS.

Deductible Local Transportation Expenses

Local transportation costs are deductible as business operating expenses if they are ordinary and necessary for your business, trade, or profession. The cost must be common, helpful, and appropriate for your business. (See Chapter 3 for a detailed discussion of the ordinary and necessary requirement.) It makes no difference what type of transportation you use to make the local trips—car, van, SUV, limousine, motorcycle, taxi, bus, or train—or whether the vehicle you use is owned or leased. You can deduct these costs as long as they are ordinary and necessary and meet the other requirements discussed below.

Travel Must Be for Business

You can only deduct local trips that are for business—that is, travel to a business location. Personal trips—for example, to the supermarket or the gym—are not deductible as business travel expenses. A business location is any place where you perform business-related tasks, such as:

- the place where you have your principal place of business, including a home office
- other places where you work, including temporary work sites
- places where you meet with clients or patients
- the bank where you do business banking
- a local college where you take professional continuing education classes
- the store where you buy business supplies, or
- the place where you keep business inventory.

Commuting Is Not Deductible

Most professionals have an outside office where they work on a regular basis. Unfortunately, you can't deduct the cost of traveling from your home to your regular place of business. These are commuting expenses, which are a nondeductible personal expense.

Commuting occurs when you go from home to a permanent work location—either your:

- office or another principal place of business, or
- another place where you have worked or expect to work for more than one year.

EXAMPLE: Kim, a consultant, runs her business from an office in a downtown office building. Every day, she drives 20 miles from her suburban home to her office and back. None of this commuting mileage is deductible. But she may deduct trips from her office to a client's office, or any other business-related trip that starts from her office.

Even if a trip from home has a business purpose—for example, to deliver important papers to your office—it is still considered commuting and is not deductible. (You may, however, deduct the cost of renting a trailer or any other extraordinary expenses you incur to haul inventory or supplies from your home.)

Nor can you deduct a commuting trip because you make business calls on your cell phone, listen to work-related tapes, or have a business discussion with an associate or employee during the commute. Also, placing an advertising display on your vehicle won't convert a commute to a business trip.

Because commuting is not deductible, where your office or other principal workplace is located has a big effect on the amount you can deduct for local business trips. You will get the fewest deductions if you work solely in an outside office. You lose out on many potential business miles this way because you can't deduct any trips between your home and your office.

As explained below, you can get the most deductions for local business trips if you have a home office.

You Have a Home Office

If you have a home office that qualifies as your principal place of business, you can deduct the cost of any trips you make from your home to another business location. For example, you can deduct the cost of driving from home to your outside office, a client's office, or to attend a business-related seminar. The commuting rule doesn't apply if you work at home because, with a home office, you never commute to work (you're there already).

Your home office will qualify as your principal place of business if it is the place where you earn most of your income or perform the administrative or management tasks for your practice. (See Chapter 7 for more on the home office deduction.) If your home office qualifies as your principal place of business, you can vastly increase your deductions for business trips.

> EXAMPLE: Kim (from the above example) maintains a home office where she does the administrative work for her consulting practice; she also has an outside office where she does her other work. She can deduct all her

business trips from her home office, including the 20-mile daily trip to her outside office. Thanks to her home office, she can now deduct 100 miles per week as a business trip expense, all of which was a nondeductible commuting expense before she established her home office.

You Go to a Temporary Business Location

Travel between your home and a temporary work location is not considered commuting and is therefore deductible. A temporary work location is any place where you realistically expect to work less than one year.

> **EXAMPLE:** Sally is a sole proprietor engineer. Her office is in a downtown office building, and she does not have a home office. She is hired by Acme Corp. to perform consulting work. This requires that she drive to Acme's offices, 50 miles away from her home. The project is expected to last three months. Sally may deduct the cost of driving from home to Acme Corporation's offices.

A temporary work location is any place where you perform services on an irregular basis with the reasonable expectation that the work there will last one year or less—for example:

- a restaurant where you meet a client for a business discussion
- a weekend-long continuing education seminar in your town that you attend each day and then go home each night, or
- a client's office.

Places like the bank and supply stores do not qualify as temporary work locations because you don't perform work there. You're a customer at those locations.

You can convert a nondeductible commute into a deductible local business trip by making a stop at a temporary work location on your way to your office. Stopping at a temporary work location converts the entire trip into a deductible travel expense.

> **EXAMPLE:** Eleanor's business office is in a downtown building. She has no home office. One morning, she leaves home, stops at a client's office for a one-hour meeting, and then goes to her office. The entire trip is deductible because she stopped at a temporary work location on her way to her office.

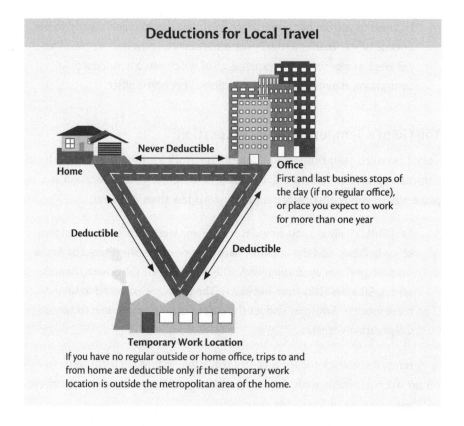

Deductions for Local Travel

Home

Never Deductible

Office
First and last business stops of
the day (if no regular office),
or place you expect to work
for more than one year

Deductible

Deductible

Temporary Work Location
If you have no regular outside or home office, trips to and
from home are deductible only if the temporary work
location is outside the metropolitan area of the home.

Keep in mind, though, that making such stops is necessary only
if you don't have a home office. If Eleanor had a home office, the
commuting rule wouldn't apply and the trip would be deductible with
or without the stop.

The Standard Mileage Rate

If you drive a car, an SUV, a van, or a pickup for business (as most people
do), you have two options for deducting your vehicle expenses: You can
use the standard mileage rate or you can deduct your actual expenses.

Let's start with the easy one: the standard mileage rate. This method
works best for people who don't want to bother with a lot of record
keeping or calculations. But this ease comes at a price—it often results
in a lower deduction than you might otherwise be entitled to using the
actual expense method.

However, this isn't always the case. The standard mileage rate may give you a larger deduction if you drive many business miles each year, especially if you drive an inexpensive car. But, even if the standard mileage rate does give you a lower deduction, the difference is often so small that it doesn't justify the extra record keeping you will have to do using the actual expense method.

How the Standard Mileage Rate Works

Under the standard mileage rate, you deduct a specified number of cents for every business mile you drive. The IRS sets the standard mileage rate each year. For 2017, the standard mileage rate is 53.5 cents per mile. To figure out your deduction, simply multiply your business miles by the applicable standard mileage rate.

> EXAMPLE: Ed, an attorney, drove his car 10,000 miles for business during 2017. To determine his car expense deduction, he simply multiplies his business mileage by 53.5 cents. His deduction for 2017 is $5,350 (53.5 cents x 10,000 =$5,350).

The big advantage of the standard mileage rate is that it requires very little record keeping. You only need to keep track of how many business miles you drive, not the actual expenses for your car, such as gas, maintenance, or repairs.

If you choose the standard mileage rate, you cannot deduct actual car operating expenses—for example, maintenance and repairs, gasoline and its taxes, oil, insurance, and vehicle registration fees. All of these items are factored into the rate set by the IRS. And you can't deduct the cost of the car through depreciation or Section 179 expensing because the car's depreciation is also factored into the standard mileage rate (as are lease payments for a leased car).

The only expenses you can deduct (because these costs aren't included in the standard mileage rate) are:
- interest on a car loan
- parking fees and tolls for business trips (but you can't deduct parking ticket fines or the cost of parking your car at your place of work), and

- personal property tax that you paid when you bought the vehicle, based on its value—this is often included as part of your auto registration fee.

When You Can Use the Standard Mileage Rate

Not everyone can use the standard mileage rate. You won't be able to use it (and will have to use the actual expense method instead) if you can't meet the following requirements.

First-Year Rule

You must use the standard mileage rate in the first year you use a car for business or you are forever foreclosed from using that method for that car. If you use the standard mileage rate the first year, you can switch to the actual expense method in a later year, and then switch back and forth between the two methods after that, provided the requirements listed below are met. For this reason, if you're not sure which method you want to use, it's a good idea to use the standard mileage rate the first year you use the car for business. This leaves all your options open for later years. However, this rule does not apply to leased cars. If you lease your car, you must use the standard mileage rate for the entire lease period if you use it in the first year.

There are some restrictions on switching back to the standard mileage rate after you have used the actual expense method. You can't switch back to the standard mileage rate after using the actual expense method if you took accelerated depreciation, a Section 179 deduction, or bonus depreciation on the car. You can switch back to the standard mileage rate only if you used the straight-line method of depreciation during the years you used the actual expense method. This depreciation method gives you equal depreciation deductions every year, rather than the larger deductions you get in the early years using accelerated depreciation methods.

However, these restrictions on depreciation are often academic. Because of the severe annual limits on the depreciation deduction for passenger automobiles, it often makes no difference which depreciation method you use—you'll get the same total yearly deduction. So using straight-line depreciation poses no hardship. Keep in mind, however, that if you switch to the actual expense method after using the standard mileage rate, you'll have to reduce the tax basis of your car by a portion of the standard mileage rate deductions you already received. This will reduce your depreciation deduction. (See "Vehicle Depreciation Deductions," below.)

Five-Car Rule

You can't use the standard mileage rate if you have five or more cars that you use for business simultaneously. When the IRS says "simultaneously," it means simultaneously. You're barred from using the standard mileage rate only if you operate five or more cars for business at the exact same time.

The Actual Expense Method

Instead of using the standard mileage rate, you can deduct the actual cost of using your car for business. This requires much more record keeping, but it can result in a larger deduction. However, because of the very low caps on depreciation deductions for automobiles, the increase in the amount of the deduction you get by using the actual expense method is often quite small. You may well conclude that it does not justify the additional record keeping required.

How the Actual Expense Method Works

As the name implies, under the actual expense method, you deduct the actual costs you incur each year to operate your car, plus depreciation. If you use this method, you must keep careful track of all the costs you incur for your car during the year, including:
- gas and oil
- repairs and maintenance
- depreciation of your original vehicle and improvements
- car repair tools
- license fees
- parking fees for business trips
- registration fees
- tires
- insurance
- garage rent

- tolls for business trips
- car washing
- lease payments
- interest on car loans
- towing charges, and
- auto club dues.

When you do your taxes, add up the cost of all these items. For everything but parking fees and tolls, multiply the total cost of each item by your car's business use percentage. You determine your business use percentage by keeping track of all the miles you drive for business during the year and the total mileage driven. You divide your business mileage driven by your total mileage driven to figure your business use percentage. For parking fees and tolls that are business related, include (and deduct) the full cost. The total is your deductible transportation expense for the year.

> **EXAMPLE:** In one recent year, Laura drove her car 8,000 miles for her consulting practice and 8,000 miles for personal purposes. Her business use percentage is 50%. She can deduct 50% of the actual costs of operating her car, plus the full cost of any business-related tolls and parking fees. Her expenses amount to $10,000 for the year, so she gets a $5,000 deduction, plus $500 that she paid in tolls and parking for business.

Watch Those Tickets

You may not deduct the cost of driving violations or parking tickets, even if you were on business when you got the ticket. Government fines and penalties are never deductible as a matter of public policy.

Record-Keeping Requirements

When you deduct actual car expenses, you must keep records of all the costs of owning and operating your car. This includes not only the number of business miles and total miles you drive, but also gas, repairs, parking, insurance, tolls, and any other car expenses. Record keeping for car expenses is covered in Chapter 18.

Vehicle Depreciation Deductions

Using the actual expense method, you can deduct the cost of your vehicle. However, you can't deduct the entire cost in the year when you purchase your car. Instead, you must deduct the cost a portion at a time over several years, using a process called depreciation. (For more on depreciation generally, see Chapter 9.) Although the general concept of depreciation is the same for every type of property, special rules apply to depreciation deductions for cars. These rules give you a lower annual deduction for cars than you'd be entitled to using the normal depreciation rules.

This section focuses on the depreciation rules for passenger automobiles, as defined by the IRS. To understand the depreciation rules discussed in this section, you will need to be familiar with the general depreciation rules covered in Chapter 9.

Is Your Vehicle a Passenger Automobile?

First, you must figure out whether your vehicle is a passenger automobile as defined by the IRS. A passenger automobile is any four-wheeled vehicle made primarily for use on public streets and highways that has an unloaded gross weight of 6,000 pounds or less. The vehicle weight includes any part or other item physically attached to the automobile or usually included in the purchase price of an automobile. This definition includes virtually all automobiles.

However, if your vehicle is classified as a truck or van by the manufacturer, it is a passenger automobile only if it has a gross loaded vehicle weight of 6,000 pounds or less. The truck or van classification can apply not only to traditional trucks or vans, but to other vehicles such as SUVs, minivans, and crossover vehicles. This is based on Department of Transportation rules that all car manufacturers must follow. The gross loaded weight is based on how much the manufacturer says the vehicle can carry and is different from unloaded weight—that is, the vehicle's weight without any passengers or cargo.

You can find out your vehicle's gross loaded and unloaded weight by looking at the metal plate in the driver's side door jamb, looking at your owner's manual, checking the manufacturer's website or sales brochure, or asking an auto dealer. The gross loaded weight is usually called the gross vehicle weight rating (GVWR for short). The gross unloaded weight is often called the "curb weight."

Passenger Automobiles Are Listed Property

All passenger automobiles are listed property—property that is often used for personal purposes. As explained in Chapter 9, the IRS imposes more stringent requirements on deductions for listed property to discourage fraudulent deduction claims. Because passenger automobiles are listed property, you must keep mileage records showing how much you use your car for business and personal purposes and you must file IRS Form 4562, *Depreciation and Amortization*, with your annual tax return.

What You Can Depreciate

Your depreciation deductions are based on your total investment in your car or other vehicle (also called your basis). You multiply the basis amount by the percentage of business use of the car to determine the total amount you may depreciate. For example, if you use a car 100% for business, you may depreciate its entire basis. If you use it 50% for business, you may depreciate only 50% of its basis. How you determine your car's basis depends on how you acquired it. If you buy a passenger automobile and use it for business that same year, your basis is its cost. You include the entire cost, even if you financed part of the purchase with a car loan. The cost also includes sales taxes, destination charges, and other fees the seller charges. It does not, however, include auto license and registration fees.

If you trade in your old car to a dealer to purchase a new car, your basis in the car you purchase is equal to the adjusted basis of the trade-in car, plus the cash you pay (whether out of your own pocket or financed with a car loan).

> EXAMPLE: Brenda buys a new car for her consulting practice. The car has a $20,000 sticker price. She trades in her old car and pays the dealer $15,000, all of which she finances with a car loan from her bank. Her trade-in has an adjusted basis of $7,000. Her basis in the new car is $22,000 ($7,000 + $15,000), even though the sticker price on the new car was only $20,000.

If you convert a car that you previously owned for personal use to a business car, your basis in the car is the lower of what you paid for it (at the time you purchased it for personal use) or its fair market value at the time you convert it to business use. Your basis will usually be its fair market value, as this is usually the lower number. You can determine the fair market value by checking used car value guides, such as the *Kelley Blue Book*.

Annual Depreciation Limits for Passenger Automobiles

Passenger automobiles have a five-year recovery period (but it takes six calendar years to depreciate a car; see Chapter 9). As a result, you'd think it would take at most six years to fully depreciate a car. Unfortunately, this is usually not the case. Depreciating a passenger automobile is unique in one very important way: The annual depreciation deduction for automobiles is limited to a set dollar amount each year. The annual limit applies to all passenger vehicles, no matter how much they cost. Because the limits are so low, it can take many years to fully depreciate a car, far longer than the six years it takes to depreciate other assets with a five-year recovery period.

There are two different sets of deduction limits for passenger automobiles: one for passenger automobiles other than trucks and vans, and slightly higher limits for trucks and vans that qualify as passenger automobiles. This includes any vehicle that is (1) classified as a truck or van by the manufacturer, and (2) has a gross loaded weight of 6,000 pounds or less.

The charts below show the maximum annual depreciation deduction allowed for passenger automobiles and trucks and vans placed in service in 2017. The second chart shows the limits for passenger automobiles that are trucks and vans as defined above. You can find all the deduction limits in IRS Publication 946, *How to Depreciate Property*, and Publication 463, *Travel, Entertainment, Gift, and Car Expenses*.

Depreciation Limits for Passenger Automobiles (Must be reduced by percentage of personal use)				
Year Placed in Service	1st Tax Year	2nd Tax Year	3rd Tax Year	4th and Later Years
2017	$3,160 ($11,160 if $8,000 bonus depreciation is used)	$5,100	$3,050	$1,875

Depreciation Limits for Trucks and Vans (Must be reduced by percentage of personal use)				
Year Placed in Service	1st Tax Year	2nd Tax Year	3rd Tax Year	4th and Later Years
2017	$3,560 ($11,560 if $8,000 bonus depreciation is used)	$5,700	$3,450	$2,075

Both charts assume 100% business use of the vehicle. If you use the vehicle for personal use as well as business use, the limits are reduced by the percentage of personal use. For example, if you use the vehicle 40% of the time for personal use, your annual deductions are reduced by 40%.

The depreciation limits are not reduced if a car is in service for less than a full year. This means that the limit is not reduced when the automobile is either placed in service or disposed of during the year.

For the past several years, businesses that purchase personal property have been able to use bonus depreciation. Bonus depreciation enables you to deduct a substantial amount of an asset's cost the first year it is placed in service. For assets other than passenger vehicles, the bonus amount is 50% through 2017. Bonus depreciation may be applied to vehicles, but the bonus amount is fixed at $8,000, no matter how much the vehicle costs. Thus, by using bonus depreciation, you can depreciate $11,160 for a passenger vehicle the first year it is placed in service instead of $3,160 ($11,560 for trucks and vans). However, you may use bonus depreciation only for new vehicles you use more than 50% of the time for business purposes. If your business use falls below 51% anytime during the six-year recovery period, you must give back the extra deductions you took, a process called recapture.

You may combine Section 179 expensing with bonus and regular depreciation, in that order. However, your total deduction cannot exceed the annual limits listed in the charts above. You reduce the depreciable basis in the auto after each deduction is taken.

However, there is usually no point in using Section 179 for a vehicle, because you'll likely reach the annual limit the first year using bonus depreciation and/or accelerated depreciation. It's best to avoid using Section 179 because it is subject to an annual income limit.

Heavy Deductions for Heavy Metal: Expensing SUVs and Other Weighty Vehicles

The depreciation limits discussed above apply only to passenger automobiles—that is, vehicles with a gross unloaded weight of less than 6,000 pounds. However, in the case of trucks and vans, the 6,000-pound weight limit is based on gross loaded weight. (See "Is Your Vehicle a Passenger Automobile?" above.) Vehicles that weigh more than this are not subject to the limits. Using bonus depreciation and/or Section 179, you may be able to deduct all or most of the cost of such a vehicle in a single year—a potentially enormous deduction for businesspeople who purchase heavy SUVs and similar vehicles for their business.

Bonus Depreciation

If you place an over 6,000-pound vehicle into service during 2017, it will qualify for bonus depreciation. This means you'll be able to deduct 50% of the cost in one year if you use the vehicle 100% for business.

Section 179

Until 2004, people who purchased SUVs and other heavy vehicles they used over 50% for business could claim the full Section 179 deduction. However, allowing these huge deductions for Hummers and other SUVs bought for business purposes caused such an uproar that Congress limited the Section 179 deduction for SUVs to $25,000. The limit applies to any SUV placed in service after October 22, 2004. For these purposes, an SUV is any four-wheeled vehicle primarily designed or used to carry passengers over public streets, roads, or highways that has a gross vehicle weight of 6,000 to 14,000 pounds.

Auto Repairs and Improvements

Auto repairs and maintenance costs are fully deductible in the year they are incurred. You add these costs to your other annual expenses when you use the actual expense method. (You get no extra deduction for repairs when you use the standard mileage rate.) If you fix your car yourself, you may deduct the cost of parts and depreciate or deduct tools, but you get no deduction for your time or labor.

Unlike repairs, improvements to your car are capital expenses and must be depreciated over several years, not deducted all in the year when you pay for them. What's the difference between a repair and an improvement? Good question. Unlike a repair, an improvement:

- makes the vehicle much better than it was before
- restores it to operating condition after it has fallen into disrepair, or
- adapts it to a new use.

> EXAMPLE 1: Doug spends $100 to flush the carburetor on his business car. This expense simply keeps the vehicle in good running order: It does not make the car substantially better, restore it, or adapt it to a new use. Thus, the expense is a repair that he may currently deduct that year.

> EXAMPLE 2: Doug spends $2,500 for a brand-new engine for his car. This is an improvement because it makes the vehicle much better than it was before. Doug may not deduct the expense in a single year. Instead, he must depreciate it over five years.

Leasing a Car

If you lease a car that you use in your practice, you can use the actual expense method to deduct the portion of each lease payment that reflects the business percentage use of the car. You cannot deduct any part of a lease payment that is for commuting or personal use of the car.

> EXAMPLE: John pays $400 a month to lease a Lexus. He uses it 50% for his dental sales practice and 50% for personal purposes. He may deduct half of his lease payments ($200 a month) as a local transportation expense for his sales business.

Leasing companies typically require you to make an advance or down payment to lease a car. You can deduct this cost, but you must spread the deduction out equally over the entire lease period.

You always have the option of using the standard mileage rate instead of the actual expense method to deduct your business use of a leased car. If you choose the standard mileage method, you deduct a set amount per business mile. You don't get to deduct your lease payments. Whichever method you choose, you must stick with it for the entire term of your lease plus any extensions. You cannot switch.

Other Local Transportation Expenses

You don't have to drive a car or another vehicle to get a tax deduction for local business trips. You can deduct the cost of travel by bus or other public transit, taxi, train, ferry, motorcycle, bicycle, or any other means. However, all the rules limiting deductions for travel by car discussed in "Commuting Is Not Deductible," above, also apply to other transportation methods. This means, for example, that you can't deduct the cost of commuting from your home to your office or other permanent work location. The same record-keeping requirements apply as well.

Reporting Transportation Expenses on Schedule C

If you're a sole proprietor, you will list your car expenses on Schedule C, *Profit or Loss From Business*. Schedule C asks more questions about this deduction than almost any other deduction (reflecting the IRS's general suspicion about auto deductions).

Part IV of Schedule C is reproduced below. If you answer "yes" to Question 46, you cannot claim to use your single car 100% for business. If you answer "no" to Questions 47a or 47b, you do not qualify for the deduction.

Part IV   **Information on Your Vehicle.** Complete this part **only** if you are claiming car or truck expenses on line 9 and are not required to file Form 4562 for this business. See the instructions for line 13 on page C-4 to find out if you must file Form 4562.

43   When did you place your vehicle in service for business purposes? (month, day, year) ▶ ..../......./.......

44   Of the total number of miles you drove your vehicle during 2007, enter the number of miles you used your vehicle for:

   a   Business ....   **b**   Commuting (see instructions) ....   **c**   Other ....

45   Do you (or your spouse) have another vehicle available for personal use?. . . . . ☐ Yes   ☐ No

46   Was your vehicle available for personal use during off-duty hours?   . . . . ☐ Yes   ☐ No

47a   Do you have evidence to support your deduction?   . . . . ☐ Yes   ☐ No

   b   If "Yes," is the evidence written? .   . . . ☐ Yes   ☐ No

---

Report Your Interest Expenses Separately

If you deduct the interest you pay on a car loan, you have the option of reporting the amount in two different places on your Schedule C: You can lump it in with all your other car expenses on Line 9 of the schedule titled "Car and truck expenses," or you can list it separately on Line 16b as an "other interest" cost. Reporting your interest expense separately from your other car expenses reduces the total car expense shown on your Schedule C. This can help avoid an IRS audit.

When Clients Reimburse You

Professionals who undertake local travel while performing services for clients often have their expenses reimbursed by the clients. You need not include such reimbursements in your income if you provide an adequate accounting of the expenses to your client and comply with the accountable plan rules. Basically, this requires that you submit all your documentation to the client in a timely manner, and return any excess payments. Accountable plans are covered in detail in Chapter 16. Record-keeping rules for business driving are covered in Chapter 18.

If you do not adequately account to your client for these expenses, you must include any reimbursements or allowances in your income. They should also be included in any 1099-MISC form the client provides the IRS reporting how much you were paid (see Chapter 14). The client can still deduct the reimbursement as compensation paid to you. You may deduct the expenses on your own return, but you'll need documentation to back them up in the event of an audit.

Professionals With Business Entities

If your practice is legally organized as a corporation, a multi-member LLC, a partnership, or an LLP, there are special complications when it comes to deducting car expenses. Moreover, you have the option of having your practice own (or lease) the car you use, instead of using your personal car for business driving.

> **SKIP AHEAD**
> **This section doesn't apply to professionals who are sole proprietors or owners of one-person LLCs taxed as sole proprietorships.** There is no separate legal entity to get between them and their business expense deductions. Moreover, sole proprietors don't have company cars because they personally own all their business assets.

Using Your Own Car

If you use your own car for business driving, how your expenses may be deducted depends on whether your practice is a corporation, an LLC, a partnership, or an LLP.

LLCs, Partnerships, and LLPs

If you have organized your practice as a multi-member LLC, a partnership, or an LLP, it is probably taxed as a partnership (see Chapter 2). Usually, you'll seek reimbursement for your deductible car and other local travel expenses from your business entity. You can use either the standard mileage rate or actual expense method to calculate your expenses.

As long as you comply with the record-keeping rules for car expenses and your reimbursement is made under an accountable plan, any reimbursement you receive will not be taxable income. Basically, you must submit all your documentation to the practice in a timely manner and return any excess payments. Accountable plans are covered in detail in Chapter 16.

The practice can deduct the amount of the reimbursed car expenses on its tax return (IRS Form 1065) and reduce its taxable profit for the year. Or, in many cases, the practice will obtain reimbursement from the client on whose behalf you did your local business travel (see "When Clients Reimburse You," above).

> **EXAMPLE:** Rick, a partner in a CPA firm organized as a multi-member LLC, uses his personal car for local business driving. He uses the standard mileage rate and keeps careful track of all of his business mileage. He submitted a request for reimbursement to the firm, along with his mileage records. He was entitled to a $4,050 reimbursement from his firm. This money is not taxable income to Rick, and the firm may list it on its tax return as a business expense, or seek reimbursement from Rick's clients.

Instead of seeking reimbursement, you can deduct car expenses on your personal tax return, provided either of the following is true:

- You have a written partnership agreement or LLC operating agreement that provides that the expense will not be reimbursed by the partnership or LLC.
- Your practice has an established routine practice of not reimbursing the expense.

Absent such a written agreement or established practice, *no personal deduction may be taken.* You must seek reimbursement from the partnership, LLP, or LLC instead. If you take a personal deduction for your car expenses, your practice does not list them on its tax return, and they do not reduce your practice's profits. But they will reduce your taxable income. (See Chapter 16.)

You deduct your unreimbursed car expenses (and any other unreimbursed business expenses) on IRS Schedule E (Part II) and attach it to your personal tax return. You must attach a separate schedule to Schedule E listing the car and other business expenses you're deducting.

> EXAMPLE: Assume that Rick's CPA firm has a written policy that all the partners must personally pay for their own car expenses. Instead of seeking reimbursement, Rick lists his $4,050 car expense on his own tax return, Schedule E, reducing his taxable income by that amount. The CPA firm does not list the expense on its return; thus Rick's expense does not reduce the firm's income.

Corporations

If your practice is legally organized as a corporation (whether a C or an S corporation), you are probably working as its employee. Special rules govern all business expense deductions by employees. Your best option is to have your corporation reimburse you for your car expenses. You get reimbursement in the same way as described above for LLCs and partnerships. You must comply with all the documentation rules for car expenses and the accountable plan requirements. If you do, your corporation gets to deduct the expense and you don't have to count the reimbursement as taxable income. If you fail to follow the rules, any reimbursements must be treated as employee income subject to tax (but you may deduct your expenses as described below). (See Chapter 16.)

Using a Company Car

If your business entity buys a car for you to use (that is, your business, not you personally, holds the title to the car), the dollar value of your business driving is a tax-free working condition fringe benefit provided to you by your practice. In addition, the practice gets to deduct all of its actual car expenses on its tax return—for example, depreciation, interest on a car loan, maintenance, fuel it pays for, and insurance costs.

You get no personal deduction for these expenses; but, of course, if your practice is a pass-through entity, the deduction on its return will reduce the amount of taxable profit passed on to your tax return. However, you can personally deduct the actual cost of fuel or maintenance you pay for yourself, and the cost of anything else you buy for the car. You can't use the standard mileage rate to figure your costs; you must keep track of your mileage using one of the methods described in Chapter 18. And, if you personally buy fuel or other items for the car, you must comply with all the documentation rules for car expenses covered in that chapter.

EXAMPLE: John, a veterinarian, is a one-third owner of a group practice organized as an LLC. This year, the LLC buys a $20,000 car that John uses 100% for business driving. He keeps careful track of his mileage and can show that he drove the car 6,000 miles. The LLC may deduct on its tax return all the expenses it incurs from owning the car:

Interest on car loan	$ 1,100
Depreciation	11,160
Fuel	1,200
Maintenance	1,000
Insurance	1,000
Total	$ 15,460

John's LLC lists the $15,460 as a deduction on its tax return. As a result, instead of reporting a $300,000 annual profit, it has a $284,540 profit. John pays income and self-employment tax on his distributive share of this amount, which is one-third. John gets no personal deduction for these expenses, but he may personally deduct as a business expense the cost of fuel he paid for with his own money. This gives him a $400 deduction. John need not pay any tax on the value of having the car because it is a tax-free working condition fringe benefit provided to him by the LLC.

Things get more complicated if, as is often the case, you use a company car for both business and personal driving. The dollar value of your personal use of the car is treated as a taxable fringe benefit. The amount must be added to your annual compensation and income, Social Security, and Medicare taxes must be paid on it.

EXAMPLE: Assume that John (from the above example) uses his company car 60% for business driving and 40% for personal driving. His LLC still gets the $15,460 deduction for its car expenses. However, the dollar value of John's personal driving is a taxable fringe benefit that must be added to his annual compensation. If the value of his personal driving was $5,000, he has to pay income and self-employment tax on this amount. He still gets to deduct the cost of fuel he paid for when he drove the car for business.

Here's the key question: How do you place a dollar value on your personal use of a company car? This determines how much money must be added to your income for such use. You can use three different methods to figure this out, and they may yield very different results. You can either determine the fair market value of your use of the car, use the standard mileage rate, or use an annual lease value created by the IRS. For more information, refer to IRS Publication 15-B, *Employer's Tax Guide to Fringe Benefits*.

Long-Distance Travel Expenses

f you travel overnight for business, you can deduct your airfare, hotel bills, and other expenses. If you plan your trip right, you can even mix business with pleasure and still get a deduction. However, IRS auditors closely scrutinize these deductions. Many taxpayers claim them without complying with the stringent rules the IRS imposes. To avoid unwanted attention, you need to understand the limitations on this deduction and keep proper records.

What Is Business Travel?

For tax purposes, business travel occurs when you travel away from your tax home for your business on a temporary basis. You don't have to travel any set distance to get a travel expense deduction. However, you can't take this deduction if you just spend the night in a motel across town. You must travel outside your city limits. If you don't live in a city, you must go outside the general area where your business is located.

You must stay away overnight or at least long enough to require a stop for sleep or rest. You cannot satisfy the rest requirement by merely napping in your car.

> EXAMPLE: Phyllis, an engineer with her own firm based in Los Angeles, flies to San Francisco to meet potential clients, spends the night in a hotel, and returns home the following day. Her trip is a deductible travel expense.

If you don't stay overnight (or long enough to require sleep or rest), your trip will not qualify as business travel and your expenses will not be deductible as business travel expenses subject to one exception for lodging expenses—see "New IRS Rule on Deducting Lodging Expenses," below. This does not necessarily mean that you can't take a tax deduction. Local business trips, other than commuting, are deductible. However, you may only deduct your transportation expenses—the cost of driving or using some other means of transportation. You may not deduct meals or other expenses the way you can when you travel for business and stay overnight.

EXAMPLE: Philip drives from his office in Los Angeles to a client meeting in San Diego and returns the same day. His 200-mile round trip is a deductible local business trip. He may deduct his expenses for the 200 business miles he drove, but he can't deduct the breakfast he bought on the way to San Diego.

 RELATED TOPIC

For a detailed discussion of tax deductions for local business travel, see Chapter 5.

New IRS Rule on Deducting Lodging Expenses

For decades, the rule has been that you can deduct business travel expenses, such as hotel or other lodging expenses, only when you travel away from your tax home overnight for your business. However, the IRS has created an exception to this rule. It now allows local lodging expenses—that is, hotel or other lodging expenses while an individual is not away from his or her tax home—to be deducted if:

- the lodging is necessary for the person to participate fully in, or be available for, a bona fide business meeting, conference, training activity, or other business function
- the lodging lasts for no more than five calendar days and does not recur more than once per calendar quarter
- in the case of an employee, the employer requires the person to remain at the activity or function overnight, and
- the lodging is not lavish or extravagant and does not provide any significant element of personal pleasure, recreation, or benefit. (IRS Reg. § 1.162-32(a).)

EXAMPLE: Jane, a lawyer with her own practice, attends a weekend certification program on mediation at a hotel near her office. The program provider requires all attendees (most of whom come from out-of-town) to remain at the hotel overnight, at their own expense, for the bona fide purpose of facilitating the mediation training. Jane may deduct the cost as a business expense.

Where Is Your Tax Home?

Your tax home is the entire city or general area where your principal place of business is located. This is not necessarily the place where you live.

The IRS doesn't care how far you travel for business. You'll get a deduction as long as you travel outside your tax home's city limits and stay overnight. Thus, even if you're just traveling across town, you'll qualify for a deduction if you manage to stay outside your city limits.

> EXAMPLE: Pete, a tax adviser, has his office in San Francisco. He travels to Oakland for an all-day meeting with a client. At the end of the meeting, he decides to spend the night in an Oakland hotel rather than brave the traffic back to San Francisco. Pete's stay qualifies as a business trip even though the distance between his San Francisco office and the Oakland client meeting is only eight miles. Pete can deduct his hotel and meal expenses.

If you don't live in a city, your tax home covers the general area where you are located. This general area is anywhere within about 40 miles of your tax home.

Multiple Work Locations

If you work in more than one location, your tax home is your main place of business. To determine this, consider:

- the total time you spend in each place
- the level of your business activity in each place, and
- the amount of income you earn from each place.

> EXAMPLE: Lee, a dentist, has his own dental office in Houston, Texas. In addition, he works in his father's dental office in Dallas, Texas. He spends three weeks a month in Houston and one week in Dallas. He makes $150,000 per year from his Houston practice and $50,000 per year from his work in Dallas. Houston—where he spends more time and makes more money—is his tax home.

Temporary Work Locations

You may regularly work at your tax home and also work at another location. It may not always be practical to return from this other location to your tax home at the end of each workday. Your overnight stays at these temporary work locations qualify as business travel as long as your work there is truly temporary—that is, it is reasonably expected to last no more than one year. If that is the case, your tax home does not change and you are considered to be away from home for the entire period you spend at the temporary work location.

> **EXAMPLE:** Betty is a self-employed sexual harassment educator. She works out of her home office in Chicago, Illinois. She is hired to conduct sexual harassment training and counseling for a large company in Indianapolis, Indiana. The job is expected to last three months. Betty's assignment is temporary, and Chicago remains her tax home. She may deduct the expenses she incurs traveling to and staying in Indianapolis.

Even if the job ends up lasting more than one year, the job location will be treated as temporary and you can still take your travel deductions, if you reasonably expected the job to last less than one year when you took it. However, if at some later point the job is expected to last more than one year, the job location will be treated as temporary only until the earlier of when your expectations changed, or 12 months.

> **EXAMPLE:** Dominic, a self-employed computer expert who lived in Louisiana, took on a project as an independent contractor for a company located in Houston, about 320 miles away from his home. The project was expected to last nine to ten months, although Dominic was hired on a month-to-month basis. Due to technological delays, the project ended up taking 13 months. Nevertheless, the tax court held that Houston was a temporary work location for Dominic because he reasonably expected the project to last less than one year when he took it. Thus, the court held he was entitled to deduct his travel expenses from Louisiana to Houston for the first 12 months. (*Senulis v. Comm'r*, T.C. Summ. Op. 2009-97 (2009).)

On the other hand, if you reasonably expect your work at the other location to last more than one year, that location becomes your new tax home and you cannot deduct your expenses while there as travel expenses.

> **EXAMPLE:** Carl, a CPA who is a partner in an accounting firm with several offices in the Northwest, ordinarily works from the firm's Seattle office and lives in Seattle. However, the firm's Boise, Idaho, office is short-staffed, so Carl goes there to help handle the workload. He expects he'll have to work out of the Boise office for at least 12 months. He lives in a Boise hotel. Boise is now Carl's tax home and he may not deduct his expenses while staying there as travel expenses, even though he lives in Seattle. Thus, he may not deduct his hotel or food expenses. However, he may deduct his travel expenses if he travels back and forth between Boise and Seattle for a business purpose.

If you go back to your tax home from a temporary work location on your days off, you are not considered away from home while you are in your hometown. You cannot deduct the cost of meals and lodging there. However, you can deduct your expenses, including meals and lodging, while traveling between your temporary work location and your tax home. You can claim these expenses up to the amount it would have cost you to stay at your temporary work location. In addition, if you keep your hotel room during your visit home, you can deduct that cost.

Your Trip Must Be for Business

Your trip must be primarily for business to be deductible, and you must have a business intent and purpose before leaving on the trip. You have a business purpose if the trip benefits your business in some way. Examples of business purposes include:

- finding new clients, patients, or new markets for your services
- dealing with existing clients or patients
- learning new skills to help in your practice
- contacting people who could help your practice, such as potential investors, or
- checking out what the competition is doing.

It's not sufficient merely to claim that you had a business purpose for your trip. You must be able to prove this by showing that you spent at least part of the time engaged in business activities while at your destination. Acceptable business activities include:

- visiting or working with existing or potential clients or patients, and
- attending professional seminars or conventions where the agenda is clearly connected to your practice.

On the other hand, business activities do not include:

- sightseeing
- recreational activities that you attend by yourself or with family or friends, or
- attending personal investment seminars or political events.

Use common sense when deciding whether to claim that a trip is for business. If you're audited, the IRS will likely question any trip that doesn't have some logical connection to your existing professional practice.

Travel for a New Business or Location

You must actually be in business to have deductible business trips. Trips you make to investigate a potential new business or to actually start or acquire a new business are not currently deductible business travel expenses. However, they may be deductible as business start-up expenses, which means you can deduct up to $5,000 of these expenses the first year you're in business if your total start-up expenses are less than $50,000). (See Chapter 10 for more on start-up expenses.)

Travel as an Education Expense

You may deduct the cost of traveling to an educational activity directly related to your business.

> EXAMPLE: Louis, an architect, travels from his home in Philadelphia to a conference in London on how to make buildings bombproof. The cost is a deductible travel expense.

However, you can't take a trip and claim that the travel itself constitutes a form of education and is therefore deductible.

EXAMPLE: Assume that Louis travels from Philadelphia to London just to see the sights and become more familiar with British architecture. This trip is not a deductible travel expense. (See Chapter 13 for more on education expenses.)

Visiting Professional Colleagues

Visiting professional colleagues or competitors may be a legitimate business purpose for a trip. But you can't just socialize with them. You must use your visit to learn new skills, check out what your competitors are doing, seek investors, or attempt to get new clients or patients.

What Travel Expenses Are Deductible

Subject to the limits discussed in "How Much You Can Deduct," below, virtually all of your business travel expenses are deductible. These fall into two broad categories: your transportation expenses and the expenses you incur at your destination.

 CAUTION

Attorneys may be barred from deducting advanced client costs. Your travel costs might not be deductible if they constitute advanced client costs you incur while performing legal services for a client. (See Chapter 16.)

Transportation expenses are the costs of getting to and from your destination—for example:
- fares for airplanes, trains, or buses
- driving expenses, including car rentals
- shipping costs for your personal luggage, equipment, or other things you need for your practice, and
- 50% of meals and beverages, and 100% of lodging expenses you incur while en route to your final destination.

If you drive your personal car to your destination, you may deduct your costs by using the standard mileage rate or your actual expenses. You may also deduct your mileage while at your destination. (See Chapter 5 for more on deducting car expenses.)

You may also deduct the expenses you incur to stay alive (food and lodging) and do business while at your destination. Destination expenses include:

- hotel or other lodging expenses for business days
- 50% of meal and beverage expenses (see "How Much You Can Deduct," below)
- taxi, public transportation, and car rental expenses at your destination
- telephone, Internet, and fax expenses
- computer rental fees
- laundry and dry cleaning expenses, and
- tips you pay on any of the other costs.

You may deduct 50% of entertainment expenses if you incur them for business purposes. You can't deduct entertainment expenses for activities that you attend alone because this solo entertainment obviously wouldn't be for business purposes. If you want to deduct the cost of a nightclub or ball game while on the road, be sure to take a business associate along. (See Chapter 4 for a detailed discussion of the special rules that apply to deductions for entertainment expenses.)

Traveling First Class or Steerage

To be deductible, business travel expenses must be ordinary and necessary. This means that the trip and the expenses you incur must be helpful and appropriate for your business, not necessarily indispensable. You may not deduct lavish or extravagant expenses, but the IRS gives you a great deal of leeway here. You may, if you wish, travel first class, stay at four-star hotels, and eat at expensive restaurants. On the other hand, you're also entitled to be a cheapskate—for example, you could stay with a friend or relative at your destination to save on hotel expenses and still deduct meals and other expenses.

Taking People With You

You may deduct the expenses you pay for a person who travels with you only if he or she:

- is your employee
- has a genuine business reason for going on the trip with you, and
- would otherwise be allowed to deduct the travel expenses.

These rules apply to your family as well as to nonfamily. This means you can deduct the expense of taking your spouse, child, or other relative only if the person is your employee and has a genuine business reason for going on a trip with you. Typing notes or assisting in entertaining clients is not enough to warrant a deduction; the work must be essential to your practice.

However, this doesn't mean that you can't take any deductions at all when you travel with your family. You may still deduct your business expenses as if you were traveling alone—and you don't have to reduce your deductions, even if others get a free ride with you. For example, if you drive to your destination, you can deduct the entire cost of the drive, even if your family rides along with you. Similarly, you can deduct the full cost of a single hotel room even if you obtain a larger, more expensive room for your whole family.

> EXAMPLE: Yamiko, an engineer, travels from New Orleans to Sydney, Australia, to meet with a client. She takes her husband and young son with her. The total airfare expense for her and her family is $2,500. She may deduct the cost of a single ticket: $1,000. She spends $250 per night for a two-bedroom hotel suite in Sydney. She may deduct the cost of a single room for one person: $100 per night.

How Much You Can Deduct

If you spend all of your time at your destination on business, you may deduct 100% of your expenses (except meal expenses, which are only 50% deductible). However, things are more complicated if you mix business and pleasure. Different rules apply to your transportation expenses and the expenses you incur while at your destination ("destination expenses").

Travel Within the United States

Business travel within the United States is subject to an all or nothing rule: You may deduct 100% of your transportation expenses only if you spend more than half of your time on business activities while at your destination. If you spend more time on personal activities than on business, you get no transportation deduction. In other words, your business days must outnumber your personal days. You may also deduct the destination expenses you incur on the days you do business. Expenses incurred on personal days at your destination are nondeductible personal expenses. (See "Calculating Time Spent on Business," below, for the rules used to determine what constitutes a business day.)

> **EXAMPLE:** Tom works in Atlanta. He takes the train for a business trip to Houston. He spends six days in Houston, where he spends all his time on business and spends $400 for his hotel, meals, and other living expenses. On the way home, he stops in Mobile for three days to visit his parents and spends $100 for lodging and meals there. His round-trip train fare is $250. Tom's trip consisted of six business days and three personal days, so he spent more than half of the trip on business. He can deduct 100% of his train fare and the entire $400 he spent while on business in Houston. He may not, however, deduct the $100 he spent while visiting his parents. His total deduction for the trip is $650.

If your trip is primarily a vacation—that is, you spend over half of your time on personal activities—the entire cost of the trip is a non-deductible personal expense. However, you may deduct any expenses you have while at your destination which are directly related to your business. This includes such things as phone calls or faxes to your office, or the cost of renting a computer for business work. It doesn't include transportation, lodging, or food.

> **EXAMPLE:** Tom (from the above example) spends two days in Houston on business and seven days visiting his parents in Mobile. His entire trip is a nondeductible personal expense. However, while in Houston he spends $50 on long distance phone calls to his office—this expense is deductible.

As long as your trip is primarily for business, you can add a vacation to the end of the trip, make a side trip purely for fun, or go to the theater and still deduct your entire airfare. What you spend while having fun is not deductible, but you can deduct all of your business and transportation expenses.

> EXAMPLE: Bill, an engineer, flies to Miami for a four-day trial. He spends three extra days in Miami swimming and enjoying the sights. Because he spent over half his time on business—four days out of seven—the cost of his flight is entirely deductible, as are his hotel and meal costs during the trial. He may not deduct his hotel, meal, or other expenses during his vacation days.

Travel Outside the United States

Travel outside the United States is subject to more flexible rules than travel within the country. The rules for deducting your transportation expenses depend on how long you stay at your destination.

Trips of up to Seven Days

If you travel outside the United States for no more than seven days, you can deduct 100% of your airfare or other transportation expenses, as long as you spend part of the time on business. You can spend a majority of your time on personal activities, as long as you spend at least some time on business. Seven days means seven consecutive days, not counting the day you leave but counting the day you return to the United States. You may also deduct the destination expenses you incur on the days you do business. (See "Calculating Time Spent on Business," below, for the rules used to determine what constitutes a business day.)

> EXAMPLE: Billie, a urologist, flies from Portland, Oregon, to Vancouver, Canada. She spends four days sightseeing in Vancouver and one day at a seminar on urologic surgery. She may deduct 100% of her airfare, but she can deduct her lodging, meal, and other expenses from her stay in Vancouver only for the one day she attended the seminar.

Trips for More Than Seven Days

The IRS does not want to subsidize foreign vacations, so more stringent rules apply if your foreign trip lasts more than one week. For these longer trips, the magic number is 75%: If you spend more than 75% of your time on business at your foreign destination, you can deduct what it would have cost to make the trip if you had not engaged in any personal activities. This means you may deduct 100% of your airfare or other transportation expense, plus your living expenses while you were on business and any other business-related expenses.

> **EXAMPLE:** Sean, an international business consultant, flies from Boston to Dublin, Ireland. He spends one day sightseeing and nine days in client meetings. He has spent 90% of his time on business, so he may deduct 100% of his airfare to Dublin and all of the living and other expenses he incurred during the nine days he was in Dublin on business. He may not deduct any of his expenses (including hotel) for the day he spent sightseeing.

If you spend more than 50%—but less than 75%—of your time on business, you can deduct only the business percentage of your transportation and other costs. You figure out this percentage by counting the number of business days and the number of personal days to come up with a fraction. The number of business days is the numerator (top number), and the total number of days away from home is the denominator (bottom number). For ease in determining the dollar amount of your deduction, you can convert this fraction into a percentage.

> **EXAMPLE:** Sam flies from Las Vegas to London, where he spends six days on business and four days sightseeing. He spent 6/10 of his total time away from home on business. The fraction 6/10 converts to 60% (6 ÷ 10 = 0.60). He therefore spent 60% of his time on business. He can deduct 60% of his travel costs—that is, 60% of his round-trip airfare, hotel, and other expenses. The trip cost him $3,000, so he gets an $1,800 deduction.

If you spend less than 51% of your time on business on foreign travel that lasts more than seven days, you cannot deduct any of your costs.

Side Trips

Expenses you incur if you stop at a nonbusiness (personal) destination en route to, or returning from, your business destination are not deductible. For example, if you stop for three vacation days in Paris on your way to a weeklong client meeting in Bangladesh, you may not deduct your expenses from your Paris stay.

Determining how much of your airfare or other transportation costs are deductible when you make side trips is a three-step process:

1. Determine the percentage of the time you spent on vacation.
2. Multiply this vacation percentage by what it would have cost you to fly round-trip from your vacation destination to the United States.
3. Subtract this amount from your total airfare expense to arrive at your deductible airfare expense.

> EXAMPLE: Jason, a psychotherapist, lives in New York. On May 5, he flew to Paris to attend a psychotherapy conference that began that same day. The conference ended on May 14. That evening, he flew from Paris to Dublin to visit friends until May 21, when he flew directly home to New York. The entire trip lasted 18 days, 11 of which were business days (the nine days in Paris and the two travel days) and seven of which were vacation days. He spent 39% of his time on vacation (7 ÷ 18 = 39%). His total airfare was $2,000. Round-trip airfare from New York to Dublin would have been $1,000. To determine his deductible airfare, he multiplies $1,000 by 39% and then subtracts this amount from his $2,000 airfare expense: 1,000 × 39% = 390; $2,000 − $390 = $1,610. His deductible airfare expense is $1,610.

Conventions

Your travel to, and stay at, a convention is deductible in the same manner as any other business trip, as long as you satisfy the following rules.

Conventions Within North America

You may deduct the expense of attending a convention in North America if your attendance benefits your practice. You may not, however, deduct any expenses for your family.

How do you know if a convention benefits your practice? Look at the convention agenda or program (and be sure to save a copy). The agenda does not have to specifically address what you do in your practice, but it must be sufficiently related to show that your attendance was for business purposes. Examples of conventions that don't benefit your practice include those for investment, political, or social purposes.

Foreign Conventions

More stringent rules apply if you attend a convention outside of North America. You can take a deduction for a foreign convention only if it:

- is directly related to your practice (rather than merely benefiting it), and
- could as reasonably be held outside of North America as in North America.

To determine if it's reasonable to hold the convention outside of North America, the IRS looks at the purposes of the meeting and the sponsoring group, the activities at the convention, where the sponsors live, and where other meetings have been or will be held.

The sponsors of conventions for professionals held outside the United States usually try to come up with a reason justifying the location—for example, the American Bar Association held a convention in London during which the American lawyers studied the British legal system by attending trials at the famed Old Bailey Courthouse.

Travel by Ship

You can deduct travel by ship if a convention or another business event is conducted on board a ship, or if you use a ship as a means of transportation to a business destination. The following additional rules apply to travel by sea.

Forget about getting a tax deduction for a purely pleasure cruise. You may, however, be able to deduct part of the cost of a cruise if you attend a convention, seminars, or similar meetings directly related to your practice while on board. Personal investment or financial planning seminars don't qualify.

But there is a major restriction: You must travel on a U.S.-registered ship that stops only in ports in the United States or its possessions, such as Puerto Rico or the U.S. Virgin Islands. If a cruise sponsor promises you'll be able to deduct your trip, investigate carefully to make sure it meets these requirements.

If you go on a cruise that is deductible, you must file with your tax return a signed note from the meeting or seminar sponsor listing the business meetings scheduled each day aboard ship and certifying how many hours you spent in attendance. Make sure to get this statement from the meeting sponsor. Your annual deduction for attending conventions, seminars, or similar meetings on ships is limited to $2,000.

Calculating Time Spent on Business

To calculate how much time you spend on business while on a business trip, you must compare the number of days you spend on business with the number you spend on personal activities. All of the following are considered business days:

- any day in which you work for more than four hours
- any day in which you must be at a particular place for your practice—for example, to attend a client meeting—even if you spend most of the day on personal activities
- any day in which you spend more than four hours on business travel—travel time begins when you leave home and ends when you reach your hotel, or vice versa
- any day in which you drive 300 miles for business (you can average your mileage); for example, if you drive 1,500 miles to your destination in five days, you may claim five 300-mile days, even if you drove 500 miles on one of the days and 100 miles on another
- any day in which your travel and work time together exceeds four hours
- any day in which you are prevented from working because of circumstances beyond your control—for example, a transit strike or terrorist act, and

- any day sandwiched between two work days if it would have cost more to go home than to stay where you are—this rule can let you count weekends as business days. (See "Maximizing Your Business Travel Deductions," below.)

EXAMPLE: Mike, a sole proprietor architect who hates flying, travels by car from his home in Reno, Nevada, to Cleveland, Ohio, for a meeting with a potential client. He makes the 2,100-mile drive in six days, arriving in Cleveland on Saturday night. He has his meeting with the client for one hour on Monday. The investor is intrigued with Mike's ideas, but wants him to come up with a preliminary design. Mike works on this for five hours on Tuesday and three hours on Wednesday, spending the rest of his time resting and sightseeing. He has his second client meeting, which lasts two hours, on Thursday. He sightsees the rest of the day and then drives straight home on Friday. Mike's trip consisted of 15 business days: 11 travel days, one sandwiched day (the Sunday before his first meeting), two meeting days, and one day when he worked more than four hours. He had one personal day—the day when he spent only three hours working.

Be sure to keep track of your time while you're away. You can do this by making simple notes on your calendar or travel diary. (See Chapter 18 for a detailed discussion of record keeping while traveling.)

50% Limit on Meal Expenses

The IRS figures that whether you're at home or away on a business trip, you have to eat. Because home meals ordinarily aren't deductible, the IRS won't let you deduct all of your food expenses while traveling. Instead, you can deduct only 50% of your meal expenses while on a business trip. There are two ways to calculate your meal expense deduction: You can keep track of your actual expenses or use a daily rate set by the federal government.

Deducting Actual Meal Expenses

If you use the actual expense method, you must keep track of what you spend on meals (including tips and tax) en route to and at your business destination. When you do your taxes, you add these amounts together and deduct half of the total.

> **EXAMPLE:** Frank goes on a business trip from Santa Fe, New Mexico, to Reno, Nevada. He gets there by car. On the way, he spends $200 for meals. While in Reno, he spends another $200. His total meal expense for the trip is $400. He may deduct half of this amount, or $200.

If you combine a business trip with a vacation, you may deduct only those meals you eat while on business—for example, meals you eat while attending client meetings or doing other business-related work. Meals that are part of business entertainment are subject to the rules on entertainment expenses covered in Chapter 4.

You do not necessarily have to keep all your receipts for your business meals, but you need to keep careful track of what you spend, and you should be able to prove that the meal was for business. (See Chapter 18 for a detailed discussion of record keeping for meal expenses.)

Using the Standard Meal Allowance

When you use the actual expense method, you must keep track of what you spend for each meal, which can be a lot of work. So the IRS provides an alternative method of deducting meals: Instead of deducting your actual expenses, you can deduct a set amount for each day of your business trip. This amount is called the standard meal allowance. It covers your expenses for business meals, beverages, tax, and tips. The amount of the allowance varies depending on where and when you travel.

The good thing about the standard meal allowance is that you don't need to keep track of how much you spend for meals and tips. You only need to keep records to prove the time, place, and business purpose of your travel. (See Chapter 4 for more on meal and entertainment expenses.)

The bad thing about the standard meal allowance is that it is based on what federal workers are allowed to charge for meals while traveling, and is therefore relatively modest. In 2017, the daily rates for domestic travel ranged from $51 per day for travel in the least expensive areas to up to $74 for high-cost areas, which includes most major cities. While it is possible to eat on $74 per day in places like New York City or San Francisco, you won't have a very good time. If you use the standard meal allowance and spend more than the allowance, you get no deduction for the overage.

Not Everyone Can Use the Standard Meal Allowance

The standard meal allowance may not be used by an employer to reimburse an employee for travel expenses if the employee:
- owns more than 10% of the stock in an incorporated practice, or
- is a close relative of a 10% or more owner—a brother, sister, parent, spouse, grandparent, or another lineal ancestor or descendent.

In these instances, the employee must deduct actual meal expenses for business-related travel to be reimbursed by the employer. Thus, if you've incorporated your business and work as its employee, you must keep track of what you spend on meals when you travel for business and are reimbursed for your expenses by your corporation.

The rates are generally higher for travel outside the continental United States—that is, Alaska, Hawaii, and foreign countries. For example, in 2017, the allowance for Tokyo, Japan, was $219. In contrast, travelers to Baghdad were permitted only $11 per day.

The standard meal allowance includes $5 per day for incidental expenses—tips you pay to porters, bellhops, maids, and transportation workers. If you wish, you can use the actual expense method for your meal costs and the $5 incidental expense rate for your tips. However, you'd have to be a pretty stingy tipper for this amount to be adequate.

The standard meal allowance is revised each year. You can find the current rates for travel within the United States on the Internet at www. gsa.gov (look for the link to "Per Diem Rates") or in IRS Publication 1542. The rates for foreign travel are set by the U.S. State Department and can be found at www.state.gov. When you look at these rate listings, you'll see several categories of numbers. You want the "M & IE Rate"—short for meals and incidental expenses. Rates are also provided for lodging, but these don't apply to nongovernmental travelers.

You can claim only the standard meal allowance for business days. If you travel to more than one location in one day, use the rate in effect for the area where you spend the night. You are allowed to deduct 50% of the standard meal allowance as a business expense.

> EXAMPLE: Art travels from Los Angeles to Chicago for a three-day business conference. Chicago is a high-cost locality, so the daily meal and incidental expense rate (M&IE) is $74. Art figures his deduction by multiplying the daily rate by five and multiplying this by 50%: 5 days × $74 = $370; $370 × 50% = $185.

If you use the standard meal allowance, you must use it for all of the business trips you take during the year. You can't use it for some trips and then use the actual expense method for others. For example, you can't use the standard allowance when you go to an inexpensive destination and the actual expense method when you go to a pricey one.

Because the standard meal allowance is so small, it's better to use it only if you travel exclusively to low-cost areas or if you are simply unable or unwilling to keep track of what you actually spend for meals.

Maximizing Your Business Travel Deductions

Here are some simple strategies you can use to maximize your business travel deductions.

Plan Ahead

Plan your itinerary carefully before you leave to make sure your trip qualifies as a business trip. For example, if you're traveling within the United States, you must spend more than half of your time on business for your transportation to be deductible. If you know you're going to spend three days on business, arrange to spend no more than two days on personal activities so this rule is satisfied. If you're traveling overseas for more than 14 days, you'll have to spend at least 75% of your time on business to deduct your transportation—you may be able to do this by using strategies to maximize your business days. (See "Maximize Your Business Days," below.)

Make a Paper Trail

If you are audited by the IRS, there is a good chance you will be questioned about business travel deductions. Of course, you'll need to have records showing what you spent for your trips. (See Chapter 18 for a detailed discussion on record keeping.) However, you'll also need documents proving that your trip was for your existing business. You can do this by:

- making a note in your calendar or daily planner of every client meeting you attend or other business-related work you do, being sure to note the time you spend on each business activity
- obtaining and saving business cards from anyone you meet while on business
- noting in your calendar or daily planner the names of all the people you meet for business on your trip
- keeping the program or agenda from a convention or training seminar you attend, as well as any notes you made
- after you return, sending thank-you notes to the business contacts you met on your trips, being sure to keep copies, and
- keeping copies of business-related correspondence or emails you sent or received before the trip.

Maximize Your Business Days

If you mix business with pleasure on your trip, you have to make sure that you have enough business days to deduct your transportation costs. You'll need to spend more than 50% of your days on business on domestic trips and more than 75% for foreign trips of more than seven days.

You don't have to work all day for that day to count as a business day: Any day in which you work at least four hours is a business day, even if you goof off the rest of the time. The day will count as a business day for purposes of determining whether your transportation expenses are deductible, and you can deduct your lodging, meal, and other expenses during the day, even though you only worked four hours.

You can easily maximize your business days by taking advantage of this rule. For example, you can:

- work no more than four hours in any one day whenever possible
- spread your business over several days—for example, if you need to be present at three meetings, try to spread them over two or three days instead of one, and
- avoid using the fastest form of transportation to your business destination—travel days count as business days, so you'll add business days to your trip if you drive instead of fly. Remember, there's no law that says you have to take the quickest means of transportation to your destination.

Take Advantage of the Sandwich Day Rule

IRS rules provide that days when you do no business-related work count as business days when they are sandwiched between workdays, as long as it was cheaper to spend that day away than to go back home for the off days. If you work on Friday and Monday, this rule allows you to count the weekend as business days, even though you did no work.

> EXAMPLE: Kim, an optometrist, flies from Houston to Honolulu, Hawaii, for an optometrist convention. She arrives on Wednesday and returns the following Wednesday. She does not attend any convention activities during the weekend and goes to the beach instead. Nevertheless, because it was cheaper for her to stay in Hawaii than to fly to Houston just for the weekend and then back to Hawaii, she may count Saturday and Sunday as business days. This means she can deduct her lodging and meal expenses for those days (but not the cost of renting a surfboard).

Converting a Vacation Into a Business Trip

Here are three strategies you can use to legally convert a nondeductible personal vacation into a deductible business trip:

- **Combine your vacation with a continuing professional education program.** Travel to take continuing education courses required for your profession is deductible. Sign up for a program in a desirable location and take the family along with you.
- **Visit a colleague.** Travel to attend meetings with professional colleagues for business purposes—not to socialize—is tax deductible. Document your visit with letters and email.
- **Hold a board meeting.** If your practice is incorporated, you can hold your annual board meeting in a desirable location and deduct your travel expenses. You must really hold a board meeting and have documentation to prove it—corporate minutes and a written agenda.

If you use any of these strategies and take your family with you, your family's expenses are not deductible, unless a family member provides essential services to your practice. However, your travel expenses are deductible, provided you follow the rules covered above. For example, if you travel within the United States, you must spend at least 51% of your total days on business to deduct your transportation expenses. If you spend over half your days on nonbusiness activities, virtually none of your expenses are deductible. (The rules differ for foreign travel.)

EXAMPLE: Ralph, a Chicago surgeon, attends an educational program on new surgical techniques in Miami and takes his wife and two children with him. He and his family spend seven days in Miami. While his family has fun, Ralph attends the surgery seminar for four hours a day for four days. He spends the other three days relaxing with his family. Ralph spent four of seven days on business, which is more than 50% of his total time in Miami. Thus, he gets to deduct his airfare to and from Miami and his hotel and meal expenses for his four business days. He and his family stayed in a two-bedroom hotel suite, but he can deduct only what it would have cost for a single room.

Travel Expenses Reimbursed by Clients

Professionals who travel while performing services for clients often have their expenses reimbursed by the clients. You need not include such reimbursements in your income if you provide an adequate accounting of the expenses to your client and comply with the accountable plan rules. Basically, this requires that you submit all your documentation to the client in a timely manner and return any excess payments. Accountable plans are covered in detail in Chapter 16. Record-keeping rules for long-distance travel are covered in Chapter 18.

> EXAMPLE: Farley, an architect, incurs $5,000 in travel expenses while working on a new shopping center for a client. He keeps complete and accurate records of his expenses which he provides to his client. His client reimburses him the $5,000. Farley need not include the $5,000 in his income for the year and Farley's client may deduct the reimbursement as a business expense.

If you do not adequately account to your client for these expenses, you must include any reimbursements or allowances in your income, and they should also be included in any 1099-MISC form the client is required to provide the IRS reporting how much you were paid (see Chapter 16). The client can still deduct the reimbursement as compensation paid to you. You may deduct the expenses on your own return, but you'll need documentation to back them up in the event of an audit.

The Home Office Deduction

The federal government helps out business owners by letting them deduct their home office expenses from their taxable income. If, like many professionals, you regularly work at home, you may be able to claim the home office deduction. Even if you have an outside office where you do the bulk of your work, you still may be able to use this deduction. However, if you plan on taking the deduction, you need to learn how to do it properly. There are strict requirements you must follow and how you claim the deduction will depend in part on what type of business entity you have.

Qualifying for the Home Office Deduction

To take the home office deduction, you must have a home office—that is, an office or other workplace in your home that you use regularly and exclusively for business. Your home may be a house, an apartment, a condominium, a mobile home, or even a boat. You can also take the deduction for separate structures on your property that you use for business, such as an unattached garage, workshop, studio, barn, or greenhouse. If you qualify, you can deduct your expenses for your home office.

> **EXAMPLE:** Rich is a sole proprietor attorney who rents a law office in a downtown office building. However, he also regularly performs law-related work in the basement of his San Francisco rental home, which he has converted into a home office. If he meets the requirements discussed below, he can deduct his home office expenses, including a portion of his rent, from his law practice income. This saves him over $2,000 per year on his income and self-employment taxes.

Three Threshold Requirements

There are three threshold requirements that everyone must meet to qualify for the home office deduction. You must:
- be in business
- use your home office exclusively for business (unless you store inventory in your home), and
- use your home office for your business on a regular basis.

If you get past this first hurdle, then you must also meet *any one* of the following five requirements:
- You use your home office as your principal place of business.
- You regularly and exclusively use your home office for administrative or management activities for your practice and have no other fixed location where you perform such activities.
- You meet patients, clients, or customers at home.
- You use a separate structure on your property exclusively for business purposes.
- You store inventory or product samples at home.

These rules apply whether you are a sole proprietor, partner in a partnership or an LLP, a limited liability company (LLC) owner, or if you have formed a C or an S corporation. However, if you are an employee of a corporation that you own and operate, or have formed a multi-member LLC, LLP, or partnership, there are some additional requirements (see "How to Deduct Home Office Expenses," below).

You Must Be in Business

You may take the home office deduction only for a business. You can't take the deduction for a hobby or another nonbusiness activity that you conduct out of your home. Nor can you take it if you perform personal investment activities at home—for example, researching the stock market.

You don't have to work full time in a business to qualify for the home office deduction. If you satisfy the requirements, you can take the deduction for a side business that you run from a home office. The side business can even be related to your regular business. For example, a surgeon who established a biopsy lab in his home was able to claim the home office deduction for the lab because the lab was a separate business from his surgical practice. (*Hoye v. Comm'r,* T.C. Memo 1990-57.)

However, you must use your home office regularly, and the total amount you deduct cannot exceed your profit from the business. (See below for more on the profit limitation.)

Exclusive Business Use

You can't take the home office deduction unless you use part of your home exclusively for your business. In other words, you must use your home office *only for your business*. The more space you devote exclusively to your business, the more your home office deduction will be worth. This requirement doesn't apply if you store inventory at home.

If you use part of your home—such as a room or garage—as your business office, but you also use that same space for personal purposes, you won't qualify for the home office deduction.

Regular Business Use

It's not enough to use a part of your home exclusively for business; you must also use it regularly. For example, you can't place a desk in a corner of a room and claim the home office deduction if you almost never use the desk for your practice.

Unfortunately, the IRS doesn't offer a clear definition of regular use. The agency has stated only that you must use a portion of your home for business on a continuing basis—not just for occasional or incidental business. One court has held that 12 hours of use a week is sufficient. (*Green v. Comm'r,* 79 T.C. 428 (1982).) You might be able to qualify with less use—for example, an hour a day—but no one knows for sure. It's a good idea to keep track of how much you use your home office. Your record doesn't have to be fancy—notes in an appointment book are sufficient.

One of Five Additional Requirements

Using a home office exclusively and regularly for business is not enough to qualify for the home office deduction: You also must satisfy any one of the additional five requirements described below. Moreover, if your practice is a corporation, you must meet the convenience of the employer test covered in "Special Requirements for Employees," below.

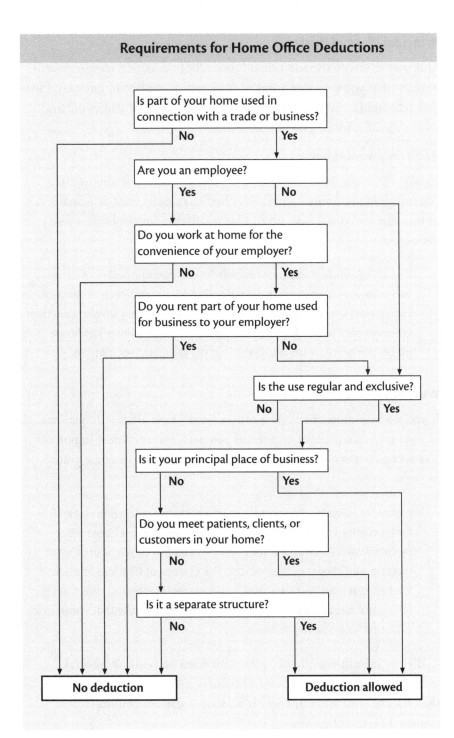

Requirements for Home Office Deductions

Principal Place of Business

One way to satisfy the additional home office deduction requirement is to show that you use your home as your principal place of business. How you accomplish this depends on where you do most of your work and what type of work you do at home.

If you only work at home

If, like a growing number of professionals, you do all or almost all of your work in your home office, your home is clearly your principal place of business and you'll have no trouble qualifying for the home office deduction.

> **EXAMPLE:** Linda, a sole proprietor architect, uses one bedroom of her two-bedroom apartment as the only office for her architecture practice. Except on the relatively rare occasions when she meets with clients in their offices or goes to building sites, she performs all her work in her home office. This office clearly qualifies as her principal place of business.

Working in multiple locations

If you work in more than one location, your home office still qualifies as your principal place of business if you perform your most important business activities—those activities that most directly generate your income—at home.

> **EXAMPLE:** Charles is a consultant who performs marketing research for his clients. He spends 30 to 35 hours per week in his home office performing research and writing reports, and five to ten hours a week meeting with clients in their offices. The essence of Charles's business is marketing research—this is how he generates his income. Therefore, his home qualifies as his principal place of business because that's where he performs his research activities.

If you perform equally important business activities in several locations, your principal place of business is where you spend more than half of your time. If there is no such location, you don't have a principal place of business.

> **EXAMPLE:** Sue is a psychologist who meets with her patients both in an outside office and at home. She spends 25 hours per week in her home office and 15 hours at her outside office. Her home office qualifies as her principal place of business.

Administrative Work

Of course, most professionals spend the bulk of their time working away from home, usually in outside offices. Thus, these home offices cannot qualify as their principal places of business under the test discussed above. Fortunately, legal changes that took effect in 1999 make it possible for such people to qualify for the home office deduction. Under the rules, your home office qualifies as your principal place of business for purposes of the home office deduction, even if you work primarily outside your home, if both of the following are true:

- You use the office regularly and exclusively to perform administrative and/or management activities for your business.
- There is no other fixed location where you conduct substantial administrative or management activities.

Administrative and management activities include, but are not limited to:

- billing clients or patients
- keeping books and records
- ordering supplies
- setting up appointments, and
- writing reports.

This means that you can qualify for the home office deduction even if your home office is not where you generate most of your income. It's sufficient that you regularly use it for the administrative and management activities you perform for your business. As long as you have no other fixed location where you regularly do these activities—for example, an outside office—you'll get the deduction.

You don't have to personally perform at home all the administrative or management activities your business requires to qualify for the home office deduction. Your home office can qualify for the deduction even if:

- You have others conduct your administrative or management activities at locations other than your home—for example, another company does your billing from its place of business.
- You conduct administrative or management activities at places that are not fixed locations for your business, such as in a car or a hotel room.
- You occasionally conduct minimal administrative or management activities at a fixed location outside your home, such as your outside office.

Moreover, you can qualify for the deduction even if you have suitable space to conduct administrative or management activities outside your home, but choose to use your home office for those activities instead.

EXAMPLE: Sally is a sole proprietor attorney with a flourishing criminal defense practice. She has a small office she shares with several other attorneys, but spends most of her work time in court, local jails, and in her car. Sally employs an outside firm to bill her clients and perform the other bookkeeping her practice requires. Sally also has a home office she uses to perform most of the administrative and management tasks she does herself, such as setting up appointments, writing briefs and memos, and ordering supplies. Sally also performs some of these tasks, such as making appointments, while in court or in her car on the way to or from court. She rarely uses her outside office for these tasks. Sally's home office qualifies as her principal place of business for purposes of the home office deduction. She conducts administrative or management activities for her business as an attorney there and has no other fixed location where she conducts substantial administrative or management activities for this business. The fact that she occasionally performs some administrative tasks in her car or in court does not disqualify her for the deduction because they are not fixed locations for her law practice. Likewise, she doesn't lose the deduction because she has an outside company do her billing.

Unfortunately, not all professionals find it convenient, or even possible, to perform all or most of their administrative or management tasks out of their home offices. They must use their outside offices for making appointments, doing record keeping, or similar work. These professionals will not qualify for the home office deduction under the rule described in this section, even if they have home offices they regularly and exclusively use to perform some administrative tasks.

Meeting Clients or Customers at Home

All is not necessarily lost if your home office does not qualify as your principal place of business. You can still take the home office deduction for any part of your home that you use exclusively to meet with clients, customers, or patients. You must physically meet with others in this home location; phoning or emailing them from there is not sufficient. And the meetings must be a regular and integral part of your business; occasional meetings don't qualify.

It's not entirely clear how often you must meet clients at home for those meetings to be considered regular. However, the IRS has indicated that meeting clients one or two days a week is sufficient. Exclusive use means you use the space where you meet clients only for business. You are free to use the space for business purposes other than meeting clients—for example, doing your business bookkeeping or other paperwork. But you cannot use the space for personal purposes, such as watching television.

Many professionals, such as doctors, lawyers, and accountants, can qualify for the home office deduction under this rule because it's easy for them to meet with clients or patients at home. If you want to do this, encourage clients or customers to visit you at home and keep a log or an appointment book showing all of their visits. Also, you should place your home office phone number and address on your business cards and stationery.

Using a Separate Structure

You can deduct expenses for a separate freestanding structure, such as a studio, garage, or barn, if you use it exclusively and regularly for your business. The structure does not have to be your principal place of business or a place where you meet patients, clients, or customers.

Exclusive use means that you use the structure only for business—for example, you can't use it to store gardening equipment or as a guesthouse. Regular use is not precisely defined, but it's probably sufficient to use the structure ten or 15 hours a week.

EXAMPLE: Deborah is a sole proprietor accountant who spends 40 hours per week working in her outside office. This office is her principal place of business, and she does not meet with clients at home or perform most of her administrative and management work there. Nevertheless, Deborah qualifies for the home office deduction: She has a pool house in her back yard that she has converted into a home office that she uses ten to 15 hours per week on her accounting work. Because she uses the separate pool house structure regularly and exclusively for her accounting practice, she gets the home office deduction.

Storing Inventory or Product Samples

You can also take the home office deduction if you sell retail or wholesale products and you store inventory or product samples at home. However, you must meet all of the following tests:

- You sell products at wholesale or retail as your trade or business.
- You keep the inventory or product samples in your home for use in your trade or business.
- Your home is the only fixed location of your trade or business.
- You use the storage space on a regular basis.
- The space you use is a separately identifiable space suitable for storage.

EXAMPLE: Lisa is an optometrist who also maintains a large stock of eyeglasses she sells to her patients, or anyone else who wants to buy them. She rents a home and regularly uses half of her small attached garage to store part of her eyeglass inventory. Lisa can deduct the expenses for the storage space under the home office deduction.

Special Requirement for Employees

If you have formed a corporation to own and operate your practice, you're probably working as its employee. (See Chapter 15.) To qualify for the home office deduction as an employee, you must satisfy all the requirements discussed above. In addition, you must be able to show that you maintain your home office for the convenience of your employer—that is, your corporation. An employee's home office is deemed to be for an employer's convenience if it is:

- a condition of employment
- necessary for the employer's business to properly function, or
- needed to allow the employee to properly perform his or her duties.

The convenience-of-employer test is not met if using a home office is for your convenience or because you can get more work done at home. For example, you won't pass the test if you have an outside office but like to take work home with you.

When you own the business that employs you, you ordinarily won't be able to successfully claim that a home office is a condition of your employment—after all, as the owner of the business, you're the person who sets the conditions for employees, including yourself. Thus, you'll have to satisfy either the necessity or performance tests.

If there is no other office where you do your work, you should be able to successfully claim that your home office is necessary for your business to properly function and/or for you to perform your employee duties.

It will be more difficult to establish necessity if you have an outside office. Nevertheless, business owners in this situation have successfully argued that their home offices were necessary—for example, because their corporate offices were not open or not usable during evenings, weekends, or other nonbusiness hours, or were too far from home to use during off-hours.

Calculating the Home Office Deduction

This is the fun part—figuring out how much the home office deduction will save you in taxes. You can always use the actual expense method discussed below. However, you have the option of using a simplified method of calculating your deduction. (See "Simplified Home Office Deduction Method" below.)

How Much of Your Home Is Used for Business?

To calculate your home office deduction, you need to determine what percentage of your home you use for business. The law says you can use any reasonable method to do this. Obviously, you want to use the method that will give you the largest home office deduction. To do this, you want to maximize the percentage of your home that you claim as your office. There is no single way to do this for every home office. Try both methods described below and use the one that gives you the larger deduction.

Square Footage Method

The most precise method of measuring your office space is to divide the square footage of your home office by the total square footage of your home. For example, if your home is 2,000 square feet and you use 250 square feet for your home office, 12.5% of the total area is used for business (250 divided by 2,000 = 12.5%).

You are allowed to subtract the square footage of common areas, such as hallways, entries, stairs, and landings, from the total area that you are measuring. You can also exclude attics and garages from your total space if you don't use them for business purposes. If you subtract 200 square feet in common areas from the total 2,000 square feet, then your home office percentage will be 14% (250 divided by 1,800 = 14%).

Room Method

Another way to measure is the room method. You can use this method only if all of the rooms in your home are about the same size. Using this method, you divide the number of rooms used for business by the total number of rooms in the home. Don't include bathrooms, closets, or other storage areas. You may also leave out garages and attics if you don't use them for business. For example, if you use one room in a five-room house for business, your office takes up 20% of your home.

TIP

The room method often yields a larger deduction. Even though IRS Form 8829, *Expenses for Business Use of Your Home,* (the form sole proprietors file to claim the home office deduction), seems to require you to use the square footage method, this isn't the case. As long as all of the rooms in your home are about the same size, you can use the room method. Using the room method will often result in a larger deduction.

What Expenses Can You Deduct?

The home office deduction is not one deduction, but many. Most costs associated with maintaining and running your home office are deductible. However, because your office is in your home, some of the money you spend also benefits you personally. For example, your utility bill pays to heat your home office, but it also keeps the rest of your living space warm. The IRS deals with this issue by dividing home office expenses into two categories: direct expenses, which benefit only your home office; and indirect expenses, which benefit both your office and the rest of your home.

Direct Expenses

You have a direct home office expense when you pay for something just for the home office portion of your home. This includes, for example, the cost of painting your home office, carpeting it, or paying someone to clean it. The entire amount of a direct home office expense is deductible.

Virtually anything you buy for your office that becomes obsolete, wears out, or gets used up is deductible. However, you may have to depreciate permanent improvements to your home over 27.5 years, rather than deduct them in the year when you pay for them. Permanent improvements are changes that go beyond simple repairs, such as adding a new room to your home to serve as your office. (See Chapter 9.)

Indirect Expenses

An indirect expense is a payment for something that benefits your *entire home*, including both the home office portion and your personal space. You may deduct only a portion of this expense—the home office percentage of the total.

Most of your home office expenses will be indirect expenses, including:

- **Rent.** If you rent your home or apartment, you can use the home office deduction to deduct part of your rent—a substantial expense that is ordinarily not deductible. Your tax savings will be particularly great if you live in a high-rent area.

- **Mortgage interest and property taxes.** Whether or not you have a home office, you can deduct your monthly mortgage interest and property tax payments as personal itemized income tax deductions on your Schedule A (the tax form where you list your personal income tax deductions). But if you have a home office, you have the option of deducting the home office percentage of your mortgage interest and property tax payments as part of your home office deduction. If you do this, you may not deduct this amount on your Schedule A (you can't deduct the same item twice). The advantage of deducting the home office percentage of your monthly mortgage interest and real estate tax payments as part of your home office deduction is that it is a business deduction, not a personal deduction; as such, it reduces the amount of your business income subject to self-employment taxes, as well as reducing your income taxes.

- **Depreciation.** If you own your home, you're also entitled to a depreciation deduction for the office portion of your home. (See Chapter 9 for a detailed discussion of depreciation.)

- **Utilities.** You may deduct your home office percentage of your utility bills for your entire home. These include electricity, gas, water, heating oil, and trash removal. If you use a disproportionately large amount of electricity for your home office, you may be able to deduct more.

You Can Deduct Business Expenses Even If You Don't Qualify for the Home Office Deduction

Many business owners believe that they can't deduct any expenses they incur while working at home unless they qualify for the home office deduction. This is a myth that has cost many taxpayers valuable deductions. Even if you don't qualify for—or take—the home office deduction, you can still take tax deductions for expenses you incur while doing business at home. The following are expenses that arise from the fact that you are doing business, not from the use of the home itself:

- **Telephone expenses.** You can't deduct the basic cost of a single telephone line into your home, but you can deduct the cost of long-distance business calls and special phone services that you use for your business (such as call waiting or message center). You can also deduct the entire cost of a second phone line that you use just for business, including a cell phone.

- **Business equipment and furniture.** The cost of office furniture, copiers, fax machines, and other personal property you use for your business and keep at home is deductible, whether or not you qualify for the home office deduction. If you purchase these items specifically for your business, you can deduct them using the de minimis safe harbor if they cost less than $2,500, expense them (deduct them in one year) under Section 179, or depreciate them over several years. If you convert personal property you already own to business use, you may depreciate the fair market value. If you're a sole proprietor or owner of a one-person LLC, you deduct these costs directly on Schedule C, *Profit or Loss From Business*. You don't have to list them on the special tax form used for the home office deduction. If you use the property for both business and personal reasons, the IRS requires you to keep records showing when the item was used for business or personal reasons—for example, a diary or log with the dates, times, and reasons the item was used. (See Chapter 18 for a detailed discussion.)

- **Supplies.** Supplies for your business are currently deductible as an operating expense if you elect to use the de minimis safe harbor or the materials and supplies deduction. Otherwise, you must depreciate them or expense them under Section 179.

- **Insurance.** Both homeowners' and renters' insurance are partly deductible as indirect home office expenses. However, special insurance coverage you buy just for your home office—for example, insurance for your computer or other business equipment—is fully deductible as a direct expense.

- **Home maintenance.** You can deduct the home office percentage of home maintenance expenses that benefit your entire home, such as housecleaning of your entire house, roof and furnace repairs, and exterior painting. These costs are deductible whether you hire someone or do them yourself. If you do the work yourself, however, you can deduct only the cost of materials, not the cost of your own labor. Termite inspection, pest extermination fees, and snow removal costs are also deductible. However, the IRS won't let you deduct lawn care unless you regularly use your home to meet clients or customers. Home maintenance costs that don't benefit your home office—for example, painting your kitchen—are not deductible at all.

- **Casualty losses.** Casualty losses are damage to your home caused by such events as fire, floods, or theft. Casualty losses that affect your entire house—for example, a leak that floods your entire home—are deductible in the amount of your home office percentage. Casualty losses that affect only your home office—for example, a leak that floods only the home office area of the house—are fully deductible direct expenses. Casualty losses that don't affect your home office—for example, if only your kitchen floods—are not deductible as business expenses. However, they may be deductible as itemized personal deductions.

- **Condominium association fees.** These fees (often substantial) are partly deductible as an indirect expense if you have a home office.

- **Security system costs.** Security system costs are partly deductible as an indirect expense if your security system protects your entire home. If you have a security system that protects only your home office, the cost is a fully deductible direct expense.

Mileage Deductions for Leaving the House

If your home office is your principal place of business, you can deduct the cost of traveling from your home to other work locations for your business. For example, you can deduct the cost of driving to perform work at a client's or customer's office. If you don't have a home office, these costs are not deductible. The mileage deductions obtained from driving to and from a home office can often exceed the value of the home office deduction itself. (See Chapter 5 for a detailed discussion of the business mileage deduction.)

- **Computer equipment.** Computers and peripheral equipment (such as printers) are deductible whether or not you qualify for the home office deduction. However, if you don't qualify for the home office deduction, you must prove that you use your computer more than half of the time for business by keeping a log of your usage. (See Chapter 18 for more information on this requirement.) If you qualify for the home office deduction, you don't need to keep track of how much time you spend using your computer for business.
- **Supplies and materials.** Office supplies and materials you use for your home business are not part of the home office deduction. They are deductible whether or not you qualify for the home office deduction.

Types of Home Expenses

Expense	Description	Deductibility
Direct	Things you buy only for your home office	Deductible in full
Indirect	Things you buy to keep your entire home up and running	Deductible based on the percentage of your home used as a business office
Unrelated	Things you buy only for parts of your home that are not used for business	Not deductible

Profit Limit on Deductions

You cannot deduct more than the net profit you earn from your home office. If you run a successful business out of your home office, this won't pose a problem. But if your business earns very little or loses money, the limitation could prevent you from deducting part or even all of your home office expenses in the current year.

If your deductions exceed your profits, you can deduct the excess in the following year and in each succeeding year until you deduct the entire amount. There is no limit on how far into the future you can deduct these expenses; you can claim them, even if you no longer live in the home where they were incurred. So, whether or not your business is making money, you should keep track of your home office expenses and claim the deduction on your tax return.

The profit limitation applies only to the home office deduction. It does not apply to business expenses that you can deduct under other provisions of the tax code.

If you're a sole proprietor or the owner of a one-person limited liability company (LLC), your profit (for these purposes) is the gross income you earn from your business minus your business deductions other than your home office deduction. You must also subtract the home office portion of your mortgage interest, real estate taxes, and casualty losses.

If your business is organized as a partnership, a multi-member LLC, or a corporation, the income limit still applies to your home office deduction. Your income when computing your allowable deduction is based on the gross income from your business allocable to your home office, minus all other deductions of the LLC, partnership, or corporation. IRS Publication 587, *Business Use of Your Home*, contains a worksheet you can use to figure this amount.

Special Concerns for Homeowners

Until recently, homeowners who took the home office deduction were subject to a special tax trap: If they took a home office deduction for more than three of the five years before they sold their house, they had to pay capital gains taxes on the profit from the home office portion of their home. For example, if you made a $50,000 profit on the sale of your house, and your home office took up 20% of the space, you would have had to pay a tax on $10,000 of your profit (20% × $50,000 = $10,000).

Fortunately, IRS rules no longer require this. As long as you live in your home for at least two out of the five years before you sell it, the profit you make on the sale—up to $250,000 for single taxpayers and $500,000 for married taxpayers filing jointly—is not taxable. (See IRS Publication 523, *Selling Your Home.*) If you sold your house after May 6, 1997 and paid capital gains tax on the home office portion, you may be entitled to amend your return for the year you sold the house and receive a tax refund from the IRS.

However, you will have to pay a capital gains tax on the depreciation deductions you took after May 6, 1997 for your home office. This is the deduction you are allowed for the yearly decline in value due to wear and tear of the portion of the building that contains your home office. (See Chapter 9 for more information on depreciation deductions.) These "recaptured" deductions are taxed at a 25% rate (unless your income tax bracket is lower than 25%).

Having to pay a 25% tax on the depreciation deductions you took in the years before you sold your house is actually not a bad deal. This is probably no more—and is often less—tax than you would have had to pay if you didn't take the deductions in the first place and instead paid tax on your additional taxable income at ordinary income tax rates.

You can avoid this depreciation recapture if you use the new simplified method of calculating the home office deduction (see "Simplified Home Office Deduction Method," below). When you use this method, you deduct $5 per square foot of your home office and your depreciation deduction for the home office is deemed to be zero for the year. Thus, you have no depreciation recapture when you sell your home. Also, the adjusted basis of your home does not change.

Simplified Home Office Deduction Method

Lots of people who qualify for the home office deduction don't take it because they don't think it's worth the trouble or they are afraid it will result in an IRS audit. In a rare move to simplify life for taxpayers, the IRS has created a new simplified optional home office deduction calculation method. The simplified method went into effect for the 2013 tax year.

It's important to understand that all the regular rules for qualifying for the home office deduction still apply if you use the optional simplified method—that is, you must use a portion of your home regularly and exclusively for business. In addition, the simple method cannot be used by an employee with a home office if the employee receives advances, allowances, or reimbursements for home office expenses from his or her employer.

How the Simple Method Works

The simple method really is simple: You deduct $5 for every square foot of your home office. Thus, all you need to do is measure the square footage of your home office. For example, if your home office is 200 square feet, you'll get a $1,000 home office deduction. That's all there is to it.

You don't need to figure out what percentage of your home your office occupies. You also don't need to keep records of your direct or indirect home office expenses, such as utilities, rent, mortgage payments, real estate taxes, or casualty losses. These expenses aren't deductible when you use the simplified method.

Another big plus: You don't have to complete Form 8829.

Homeowners using the new option cannot claim depreciation deductions for their home offices. However, they can claim allowable mortgage interest, real estate taxes, and casualty losses on the home as itemized deductions on Schedule A. These deductions need not be allocated between personal and business use, as is required under the regular method. Business expenses unrelated to the home, such as advertising, supplies, and wages paid to employees are still fully deductible.

Comparison of Regular and Simplified Home Office Deduction Methods	
Simplified Method	**Regular Method**
Deduction for home office use of a portion of a residence allowed only if that portion is exclusively used on a regular basis for business purposes	Same
Allowable square footage of home used for business (not to exceed 300 square feet)	Percentage of home used for business
Standard $5 per square foot used to determine home business deduction	Actual expenses determined and records maintained
Home-related itemized deductions claimed in full on Schedule A	Home-related itemized deductions apportioned between Schedule A and business schedule (Schedule C or Schedule F)
No depreciation deduction	Depreciation deduction for portion of home used for business
No recapture of depreciation upon sale of home	Recapture of depreciation on gain upon sale of home
Deduction cannot exceed gross income from business use of home less business expenses	Same
Amount in excess of gross income limitation may not be carried over	Amount in excess of gross income limitation may be carried over
Loss carryover from use of regular method in prior year may not be claimed	Loss carryover from use of regular method in prior year may be claimed if gross income test is met in current year

When you use the simplified method, your home office deduction is capped at $1,500 per year. You'll reach the cap if your home office is 300 square feet. Thus, for example, if your home office is 400 square feet, you'll still be limited to a $1,500 home office deduction if you use the simplified method. You can't carry over any part of the deduction to future years.

As with the regular home office deduction, your total annual deduction using the simplified method is limited to the gross income you earned from the business use of your home during the year. Moreover, if you use the simplified method, you can't carry over any excess to a future tax year—something you can do when you use the regular method. Nor can you deduct amounts carried over from past years that you couldn't deduct using the regular method. For this reason, you should never use the simplified method if the profit from your business for the year is less than the amount of your simplified home office deduction.

You may choose either the simplified method or the regular method for any year (2013 or later). You choose your method by using it on your timely filed, original federal income tax return for the year. Once you have chosen a method for a tax year, you cannot later change to the other method for that same year. If you use the simplified method for one year and use the regular method for any subsequent year, you must calculate the depreciation deduction for the subsequent year using the appropriate optional depreciation table. This is true regardless of whether you used an optional depreciation table for the first year the property was used in business.

Is the Simplified Method a Good Deal?

Is it a good idea to use the new simplified home office deduction? Use it only if the deduction you could obtain using the regular method isn't much more than $1,500. Many people with home offices, particularly those who rent their homes, can qualify for home office deductions much larger than $1,500. For example, a person with a 100-square-foot home office in a 1,000-square-foot apartment who pays $1,000 per month in rent and utilities would qualify for a $500 deduction using the simplified method (100 square feet x $5 = $500), and at least a $1,200 deduction using the regular method (10% x $12,000 = $1,200). On the other hand, the simplified method may work out better for homeowners because they have no rent to deduct using the home office deduction and can still deduct their mortgage interest and real estate taxes as itemized personal deductions on Schedule A. Moreover, using the simplified method eliminates having to pay tax on recaptured depreciation deductions for your home office when you sell your home. If you don't plan to live in your home for very long, this can be a substantial benefit.

If you're thinking about using the simplified method, you should figure your deduction using both methods and use the one that gives you the largest deduction. The regular method does require more record keeping than the optional method, but you probably keep these types of records anyway. Doing the required calculations and filling out the form can be challenging, but will be much easier if you use tax preparation software.

How to Deduct Home Office Expenses

How you deduct home office expenses depends on how you've legally organized your practice.

Sole Proprietors

If you are a sole proprietor or have a one-owner LLC taxed as a sole proprietorship (as most are), you deduct your business operating expenses by listing them on IRS Schedule C, *Profit or Loss From Business*. You also list your home office deduction on Schedule C. But, unlike any other operating expense deduction, you must file a special tax form to show how you calculated the home office deduction. This form, Form 8829, *Expenses for Business Use of Your Home*, tells the IRS that you're taking the deduction and shows how you calculated it. You should file this form even if you can't currently deduct your home office expenses because your business has no profits. By filing, you can apply the deduction to a future year in which you earn a profit. For detailed guidance on how to fill out Form 8829, see IRS Publication 587, *Business Use of Your Home*.

LLCs, LLPs, and Partnerships

If your practice is organized as a multi-member LLC, LLP, or partnership and receives partnership tax treatment, you can claim a home office deduction in either of the following ways:

- You can deduct your home office expenses on your personal tax return.
- The LLC, LLP, or partnership can reimburse you for your expenses and list them on its tax return (and the deduction is then passed through to, and shared by, all the business owners).

Personal Deduction

The preferred way for most LLC members or partners in LLPs and partnerships to deduct home office expenses is to claim them on their personal tax returns. In order to do this, however, you must be able to show both that:

- You satisfy all the requirements for the home office deduction covered in "Qualifying for the Home Office Deduction," above.
- Your partnership agreement or LLC operating agreement provides that the expense will *not* be reimbursed by the entity, or there is an established routine practice of not reimbursing the expense.

If there is no written statement or practice prohibiting reimbursement for home office expenses, the IRS will assume that you have the right to be reimbursed for them by the entity. This means you get no personal deduction. Instead, you will have to seek reimbursement of the expenses from the partnership, LLP, or LLC.

If you meet the requirements for claiming the deduction, you can deduct your home office expenses on Part II of IRS Schedule E. They are not miscellaneous itemized deductions (and, therefore, are not subject to a 2% of AGI reduction). You don't have to file Form 8829.

Reimbursement

Instead of taking a personal deduction, an LLC member or a partner in an LLP or partnership can seek reimbursement for home office expenses from the business entity. In this event, the member or partner gets no separate deduction for the expenses on his or her personal return. The LLC or partnership lists the expenses on its return (IRS Form 1065, *U.S. Return of Partnership Income*), combines these expenses with all its other deductible expenses, and then subtracts all its expenses from its income to determine if the practice had a profit or loss for the year. The business's profits or losses then pass through the entity to the owners' individual tax returns. The owners pay individual tax on any profits. Thus, all reimbursed expenses are shared by all the LLC members or partners in a partnership or an LLP.

To obtain reimbursement, you must:

- meet all the requirements for the home office deduction covered in "Qualifying for the Home Office Deduction," above
- document your expenses with receipts and other necessary records, and
- be reimbursed under an accountable plan, an agreement in which the LLC, LLP, or partnership promises to reimburse you only if you provide proper timely substantiation for your expenses. (See Chapter 16 for more on accountable plans.)

If reimbursement is not made under an accountable plan, the money the LLC member or partner receives is treated as a distribution from the LLC, LLP, or partnership and is subject to both income and self-employment taxes. (See Chapter 16 for a detailed discussion of the rules for reimbursing LLC members' or partners' expenses.)

Corporations

If you have formed a corporation to own and operate your practice and work as its employee, there are two ways you can claim a home office deduction: You can take a personal deduction, or your corporation can reimburse you and take the deduction.

Reimbursement

Your corporation can reimburse you directly for your home office expenses and then deduct this amount as an ordinary business expense on its tax return (Form 1120 or 1120S). You get no personal deduction, but you don't need one because your corporation has paid you directly for your home office expenses. Because of the limitations on employees' using the home office personal deduction (see below), this is often the better choice.

To do this you must meet all the requirements for a home office deduction described in "Qualifying for the Home Office Deduction," above. Any reimbursement you receive will not be taxable to you personally if you:

- keep careful track of your home office expenses and can prove them with receipts or other records, and
- have an accountable plan, an agreement in which the corporation promises to reimburse you only if you provide proper timely substantiation for your expenses. (See Chapter 16 for more on accountable plans.)

If you qualify for the deduction but fail to comply with the accountable plan rules, your reimbursement will be treated by the IRS as additional employee compensation and will be subject to income and employment taxes. In this event, you can deduct your home office expenses, but only as a miscellaneous itemized deduction as described below.

Personal Deduction

Corporate employees, including professionals, who qualify for the home office deduction may deduct their home office expenses on their personal tax returns as employee business expenses.

However, this is not a good choice because employees must take the home office deduction as a miscellaneous itemized personal deduction on Schedule A of their personal tax returns. This means you may deduct home office expenses only if you itemize your deductions and only to the extent that your home office expenses, along with your other unreimbursed employee business expenses and other miscellaneous itemized deductions (if any), exceed 2% of your adjusted gross income (AGI).

If your corporation reimburses you for some, but not all, of your home office expenses, you must file Form 2106, *Employee Business Expenses,* to deduct the unreimbursed amount.

Deductions for Outside Offices

The great majority of professionals have outside offices in which they do their work. Most professionals rent their office space, but some own the buildings. Either way, an outside office presents many opportunities for tax deductions.

If You Rent Your Office

Virtually all the expenses you incur for an outside office that you rent for your practice are deductible, including:

- rent
- utilities
- insurance
- repairs
- improvements
- real estate broker fees and commissions to obtain the lease
- fees for option rights, such as an option to renew the lease
- burglar alarm expenses
- trash and waste removal
- security expenses
- parking expenses
- maintenance and janitorial expenses
- lease cancellation fees, and
- attorneys' fees to draft a lease.

If you sign a net lease, you'll have to pay part (or all) of the landlord's maintenance expenses, property taxes, insurance, and maybe even mortgage payments. These payments are treated the same as rent.

A rental deposit is not deductible in the year it is made if it is to be returned at the end of the lease. However, if the landlord applies the deposit to pay rent you owe, make repairs, or because you've breached the lease, you may deduct the amount in that year.

None of the rules applicable to the home office deduction covered in Chapter 7 apply to outside offices. Thus, unlike the home office deduction, there is no profit limit on deductions for outside rental expenses—you get your entire deduction even if it exceeds the profits from your practice. You report rental expenses for an outside office just like any other business expense. You don't have to file IRS Form 8829, which is required when sole proprietors take the home office deduction.

Timing of Deductions

Because you will ordinarily be in your office for more than one year, some of the expenses you pay may benefit your practice for more than a single tax year. In this event, you may have to deduct the expense over more than one year instead of currently deducting it all in a single year. (This discussion assumes that you, like most professionals, are a cash basis taxpayer and use the calendar year as your tax year.)

Current vs. Multiyear Deductions

You may currently deduct any expense you pay for the use of your office during the current tax year.

> EXAMPLE: Leona pays $800 rent each month for the outside office she uses for her psychotherapy practice. In one year, she paid a total of $9,600 in rent. Leona can deduct that total amount ($9,600) on her taxes for that year because the rental payments were a current expense that benefited her for that single tax year.

But if an expense you pay applies beyond the current tax year, the general rule is that you can deduct only the amount that applies to your use of the rented property during the current tax year. You can deduct the rest of your payment only during the future tax year to which it applies.

> EXAMPLE: Steve leased an outside office for three years for $6,000 a year. He paid the entire three-year $18,000 lease amount up front. Each year, Steve can deduct only $6,000—the part of the rent that applies to that tax year.

Subject to the exceptions noted below, these rules apply to office expenses as well, not just rent you pay in advance. For example, they apply to all expenses you pay to get a lease.

12-Month Rule

There is an important exception to the general rule about deducting in the current year. Under the 12-month rule, cash basis taxpayers may currently deduct any expense in the current year so long as it is for a right or benefit that extends no longer than the earlier of:

- 12 months, or
- until the end of the tax year after the tax year in which you made the payment.

> **EXAMPLE:** Stephanie leased an office for five years beginning July 1, 2016. Her rent is $12,000 per year. She paid the first year's rent ($12,000) on June 30. Under the current year rule, Stephanie may deduct in 2016 only the part of her rent payment that applies to that year. Her lease started on July 1 (which is halfway through the year), so she may deduct 50% of the $12,000, or $6,000. However, if Stephanie uses the 12-month rule, her entire $12,000 payment is deductible in 2016. The fact that 50% of her payment was for the following year doesn't matter because the benefit she obtained—the use of her office—lasted for only 12 months.

To use the 12-month rule, you must apply it when you first start using the cash method for your practice. You must get IRS approval if you haven't been using the rule and want to start doing so. Such IRS approval is granted automatically. (See Chapter 18.)

Improvements and Repairs

It's very common for professionals to have permanent improvements made to their offices—for example, they may install new carpeting or new walls. Landlords often give commercial tenants an allowance to make improvements before they move in. You get no deduction in this event. The landlord gets to depreciate improvements it paid for, not you.

However, if you pay for improvements with your own money, you may deduct the cost as a business expense. You have multiple options:

- You can depreciate the improvements.
- You can treat the money you spent for the improvements as rent.

- The improvements may qualify for the Disabled Access Tax Credit or tax deduction for removal of barriers to the disabled.

Improvements may be depreciated over several years as described in "If You Own Your Office," below. They are depreciated over their recovery periods assigned by the IRS, not over the whole term of the lease. For example, the cost of installing new carpeting would be depreciated over five years, even if the lease term is ten years.

If you treat your expenses for improvements as rent, you deduct the cost the same as any other rent. Rent is deductible in a single year unless it is prepaid in advance (see "Timing of Deductions," above). This means you'll get your deduction much more quickly than if you depreciated the improvements over several years. However, if the cost of the improvement is substantial, part of the cost may have to be treated as prepaid rent and deducted over the whole lease term as described above.

Whether an improvement must be depreciated or treated as rent depends on what you and your landlord intended. Your intent should be written into your lease agreement.

In contrast to improvements, repairs may be currently deducted. How to tell the difference between improvements and repairs is discussed in "If You Own Your Office," below.

Cost of Modifying a Lease

You may have to pay an additional rent amount over part of the lease period to change certain provisions in your lease. You must ordinarily deduct these payments over the remaining lease period. You cannot deduct the payments as additional rent, even if they are described as rent in the agreement.

The only exception to this rule is where the 12-month rule can be used. The lease will have to have a short term for the rule to apply.

Cost of Canceling a Lease

Unlike the cost of modifying a lease, you can ordinarily deduct as rent an amount you pay to cancel a business lease.

If You Own Your Office

If you own your outside office, you'll be entitled to most of the same deductions as a renter discussed as above. You'll also get to depreciate the cost of your real estate.

Operating Expenses

Operating expenses are the day-to-day expenses you incur as a result of owning your office. They are currently deductible unless you prepay them for more than one year. Such expenses include those for:

- utilities
- insurance
- repairs
- burglar alarm services
- trash and waste removal
- security services
- parking garage expenses, and
- maintenance and janitorial expenses.

Improvements and Repairs

Provided that they are ordinary, necessary, and reasonable in amount, repairs to your real property are operating expenses that are fully deductible the year in which they are incurred.

However, not all upkeep constitutes a repair for tax purposes. Some changes made to real property are capital improvements. Unlike repairs, improvements cannot be deducted in a single year. Instead, their cost must be depreciated over several years. Improvements to nonresidential real property must be depreciated over an especially long period—39 years.

See Chapter 9 for a detailed discussion of how to tell the difference between a repair and an improvement.

Section 179 Expensing

Section 179 expensing allows you to deduct, in a single year, a substantial amount of tangible personal property you buy for your practice. It may be used for personal property you purchase for your office, except for:

- buildings, or
- building components.

Section 179 is covered in detail in Chapter 9.

Depreciation Deductions

You may deduct the cost of buying your outside office, and improving it, through depreciation. Depreciation is covered in detail in Chapter 9. The following discussion just covers the unique aspects of depreciation for nonresidential real property.

What You Depreciate

Typically, you don't have a single depreciation deduction. Instead, you have many separate depreciation deductions over time.

When your real property is first placed into service, you get to depreciate its tax basis (value for tax purposes). This includes the value of:

- the building and building components
- land improvements, such as landscaping, and
- any personal property items that are not physically part of the building but were included in the purchase price—for example, office furniture.

These items can all be depreciated together. However, you have the option of separately depreciating personal property inside your building, and certain land improvements. This is more complicated, but yields a larger total deduction the first years you own the property.

How Much You Depreciate

You depreciate your property's tax basis—its value for tax purposes. If you've purchased your real property, your starting point in determining its basis is what you paid for the property. Logically enough, this is called cost basis. Your cost basis is the purchase price plus certain other expenses, less the cost of your land.

The following expenses are added to your property's basis:

- abstract fees
- charges for installing utility services
- legal fees
- mortgage commissions
- recording fees
- surveys
- transfer taxes
- title insurance, and
- any amounts the seller owes that you agree to pay, such as back taxes or interest, recording or mortgage fees, charges for improvements or repairs, and sales commissions.

Ordinarily, when you purchase a building with a structure or structures on it, you pay a single lump sum to the seller that includes both the cost of the building (along with its contents) and the land on which it sits. Because you can't depreciate land, you must deduct the value of the land from the purchase price to determine the basis for depreciation of the building. There are several ways to calculate how much your land is worth. Obviously, the less it's worth, the more depreciation you will have to deduct. Land valuation is the single most important factor within your control affecting the amount of your depreciation deductions.

If you construct your building yourself, your basis is the cost of construction. The cost includes the cost of materials and labor, as well as the cost of equipment (including rented equipment). However, you may not add the cost of your own labor to the property's basis. Interest you pay during the construction period must be added to basis; but interest paid before and after construction may be deducted as an operating expense.

Depreciation Period and Method

Nonresidential real property has the longest depreciation period of any business property—39 years. But, in practice, it takes 40 years to fully depreciate a nonresidential building. You don't get a full year's worth of depreciation the first year, so you get some extra depreciation during the 40th year (if you own the building that long).

In addition to having the longest depreciation period, nonresidential real property must be depreciated using the slowest depreciation method: the straight-line method in which you receive equal deductions each year, except the first and last year. You may not use accelerated depreciation, which provides larger deductions in the first few years you own the property, and smaller deductions later on.

Depreciating Improvements

Typically, you'll make additions and improvements to your property after it has been placed into service. These include:

- improvements to the building itself, or to building components— for example, upgrading the heating or air conditioning system
- land improvements, such as planting new trees or shrubbery, and
- adding new personal property to the building—for example, new office furniture.

Such later additions and improvements are depreciated separately from the original property itself.

Recovery period. The general rule is that building improvements are depreciated over 39 years. However, some building improvements made by a landlord or tenant may be depreciated over 15 years.

Depreciation method. Building improvements are depreciated using the straight-line method—the same method as used for the original building (described above). Land improvements are depreciated over 15 years using the 150% declining balance method.

Personal property inside your building is depreciated in the same way as any other personal business property. (See Chapter 9.)

Interest Deductions

Most people, including professionals, borrow money from banks or other financial institutions to purchase real property. Mortgage interest you pay for your outside office is deductible as it is paid each year.

You deduct only the interest you pay on a loan to purchase or improve real property. You may not deduct payments of principal—that is, your repayments of the amount you borrowed. The principal is ordinarily added to the basis of your property and depreciated over 39 years.

In contrast, if you borrow money to repair your rental property, you may deduct the principle amount the year it is incurred as an operating expense.

Expenses you pay to obtain a mortgage on your real property cannot be deducted as interest. Instead, they are added to your basis in the property and depreciated along with the property itself.

Property Taxes

Regular property taxes you pay for your outside office are a deductible business expense. However, real estate taxes imposed to fund specific local benefits, such as streets, sewer lines, and water mains, are not deductible as business expenses. Because these benefits increase the value of your property, you should add what you pay for them to the tax basis (cost for tax purposes) of your property. Water bills, sewer charges, and other service charges assessed against your business property are not real estate taxes, but they are deductible as business expenses.

If You Lease a Building to Your Practice

If your practice is organized as an LLC, LLP, partnership, or corporation, you can realize tax savings if you personally own an office building and lease it to the practice. You'll be the landlord and your practice your tenant. Your practice will pay you rent for the lease. This rent is a deductible expense for the practice as described above in "If You Rent Your Office." You'll have to pay income tax on the rent you receive.

However, you won't have to pay Social Security or Medicare taxes because income from real estate rentals is not subject to these taxes (except in the unlikely event that you are a real estate dealer).

This is a great way to take money out of your business without paying these taxes. Additionally, if your practice is a C corporation, this type of lease arrangement helps you avoid double taxation by reducing your corporation's profits. (See Chapter 15.)

This arrangement is perfectly legitimate so long as you have a real lease (it should be in writing) and charge your practice a reasonable rent. Don't charge more than market rates to obtain greater Social Security and Medicare tax savings.

> **EXAMPLE:** Edna is a doctor whose practice is organized as a multi-member LLC and taxed as a partnership. She personally buys a small building and leases it to her LLC for $5,000 per month, which is the going rate in the area. Edna must pay income tax on the $60,000 in rent she receives each year from her LLC, but not self-employment taxes (Social Security and Medicare taxes). Her LLC deducts the rent as a business operating expense. This reduces by $60,000 the total profit that is passed through the LLC to Edna's personal return. Obviously, if the LLC, not Edna, owned the building, it wouldn't have to pay any rent to Edna and there would be an additional $60,000 to pass through the LLC to her personal return. But this money would be subject to both income and self-employment taxes.

Instead of personally owning the building, you can form another business entity, such as an LLC, to own it and, in turn, own the entity. This gives you a degree of limited liability if something goes wrong on the property. (See Chapter 2.) You still won't have to pay self-employment tax on any income your entity receives from renting real estate.

Moreover, you can have a family member or members own the building instead of you. This will result in a lower income tax burden if the family member is in a lower tax bracket than you. Family members can also own all or part of an LLC or other entity that owns the building.

Deducting Long-Term Assets

This chapter explains how you can deduct long-term property you buy for your practice. You will need to be aware of, and follow, some tax rules that at times may seem complicated. But it's worth the effort. After all, by allowing these deductions, the government is effectively offering to help pay for your equipment and other business assets. All you have to do is take advantage of the offer.

What Is a Long-Term Asset?

Whether an item is a long-term asset or not depends on its useful life. The useful life of an asset is not its physical life, but rather the period during which it may reasonably be expected to be useful in your business—and the IRS, not you, makes this call. Anything you buy that will benefit your business for more than one year is a capital expense. For professionals, this typically includes items such as office furniture, computers, medical and dental equipment, other specialized equipment, buildings, automobiles, and books. These are all long-term assets. Anything you purchase that will benefit your practice for less than one year is a current expense, not a long-term asset.

> EXAMPLE: Reference books you purchase for your professional library that have a useful life of more than one year must be depreciated or expensed under Section 179. However, books and other publications with a useful life of less than one year may be currently deducted as a business operating expense. This includes, for example, publications that are purchased each year that are printed in a loose-leaf format and updated on a regular basis and continuously updated electronic databases. The exception to this would be for items that cost less than $2,500—see "Property Costing $2,500 or Less: The De Minimis Safe Harbor" below.

The difference between current expenses and long-term assets is important for tax purposes because current expenses (also called "operating expenses") can always be deducted in the year you pay for them (assuming you're a cash basis taxpayer). In contrast, the cost of long-term assets may have to be deducted over several years.

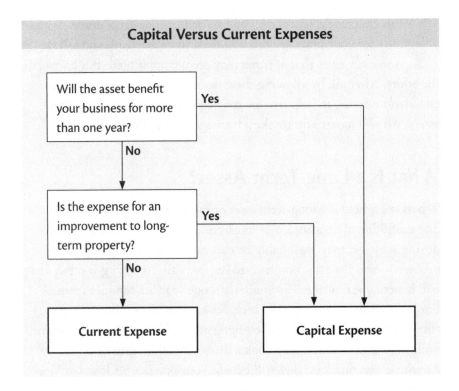

Capital Versus Current Expenses

Will the asset benefit your business for more than one year? — **Yes** → **Capital Expense**

No ↓

Is the expense for an improvement to long-term property? — **Yes** → **Capital Expense**

No ↓

Current Expense

TIP

Inventory is treated differently. This chapter covers the tax treatment of things you buy to use in your business. It does not cover the cost of items you buy or make to sell to others. Such items are called inventory. Inventory is neither a current nor capital expense. Rather, businesses deduct the cost of inventory as it is sold. (See Chapter 12 for more on inventory.)

Repairs Versus Improvements: The New IRS Regulations

The cost of repairs and routine maintenance for long-term assets are operating expenses that can be currently deducted in a single year. Improvements to long-term assets, on the other hand, are capital expenses that must be depreciated over several years.

For example, if you spend $1,000 to repair a business vehicle, you can deduct the entire amount in one year. However, if the $1,000 is for an improvement to the vehicle, you'll have to deduct the amount a little at a time over five years.

It is usually preferable for an expense to be classified as a repair rather than an improvement so you can deduct the entire amount in one year. Unfortunately, telling the difference between a repair and an improvement isn't always easy. Indeed, for decades this issue has resulted in bitter disputes between business owners and the IRS.

In an effort to clarify matters, the IRS issued a massive new set of regulations with complex rules that took full effect on January 1, 2014.

These new regulations are particularly important for business owners who own business real property, such as office buildings or plant or manufacturing facilities, because they require that more expenses for such property be classified as improvements than was often the case in the past. They are also very important to landlords who own residential rental buildings. (For more information, see *Every Landlord's Tax Deduction Guide*, by Stephen Fishman (Nolo).) However, if you operate a small business and only own personal business property, such as office equipment or vehicles, the new regs will likely not make much difference to you. One reason is that small business owners usually don't do much in the way of repairs or improvements to the personal property they use in their business, so the repair versus improvement issue doesn't often arise.

The gist of these new IRS regulations is that, unless a safe harbor or another exception provided by the IRS regulations applies, you must depreciate an expense you incur either to:

- make a long-term asset much better than it was before
- restore the asset to operating condition, or
- adapt the asset to a new use.

Expenses you incur that don't result in a betterment, a restoration, or an adaptation are currently deductible repairs.

EXAMPLE: Daniel, a dentist, owns a malfunctioning film-based X-ray machine. He spends $5,000 to upgrade the machine to a digital X-ray machine. This is a restoration because it restores the machine to operating condition by replacing a major component. It is also a betterment because the digital machine is much better than it was before when it used slower film. Daniel may not deduct the expense in a single year. Instead, he must depreciate it over five years.

Unfortunately, there are no bright-line rules that explain exactly how much an asset must be altered to constitute an improvement. Instead, you have to look at all the facts and circumstances and make a judgment call to determine whether an expense results in the betterment, restoration, or adaptation of a business asset.

EXAMPLE: Instead of upgrading his X-ray machine to digital, Daniel spends $1,000 to replace some parts to get it up and running. This expense simply keeps Daniel's X-ray machine in good running order. It does not make the machine substantially better, restore it, or adapt it to a new use. Thus, the expense is a repair that may be currently deducted in the year it was incurred.

To help you, the IRS has provided detailed definitions of what these terms mean.

Betterments. You incur an expense to make an asset better when you:

- fix a "material condition or defect" that existed before you acquired the asset
- materially add to the asset—for example, physically enlarge, expand, or extend it, or
- materially increase the asset's capacity, productivity, strength, or quality.

Restorations. An expense is for a restoration of an asset if it:

- returns the asset to its "ordinarily efficient operating condition" after it fell into disrepair
- rebuilds the asset to a like-new condition after the end of its economic useful life

- replaces a major component or substantial structural part of the asset, or
- replaces a component of the asset for which the owner has taken a loss.

Adaptations. You must also depreciate amounts you spend to adapt an asset to a new or different use. A use is "new or different" if it is not consistent with your "intended ordinary use" of the asset when you originally placed it in service.

Routine Maintenance Safe Harbor

The IRS repair regulations contain a special safe harbor for routine maintenance. If an expense qualifies as routine maintenance, and is an ordinary and necessary expense, you may automatically treat it as a currently deductible operating expense without having to go through the complexities of the repair regulations outlined above.

Routine maintenance includes two activities:
- inspection, cleaning, and testing, and
- replacing damaged or worn parts with comparable and commercially available replacement parts.

Routine maintenance merely keeps business property in ordinarily efficient operating condition. It doesn't make it better than it originally was or restore used or worn-out property to like-new condition. Maintenance is automatically considered to be routine if, when you placed the asset into service, you reasonably expected to perform such maintenance more than once during its class life—that is, the time period over which it must be depreciated. (See the list of class lives in the "Depreciation Periods" chart later in this chapter.)

For example, an automobile has a class life of five years. If you acquire an automobile for your business, you would reasonably expect to have to change the oil and pay for tune-ups more than once during its class life. Thus, such expenses are currently deductible routine maintenance.

Improvements to Real Property?

There are special rules for real property. For purposes of determining whether an expense is a repair or an improvement, these rules require that buildings be divided up into as many as nine different units (also called units of property): the entire structure and up to eight separate building systems. These include heating, ventilation, and air conditioning (HVAC) systems; plumbing systems; electrical systems; all escalators; all elevators; fire protection and alarm systems; building security systems; and the gas distribution systems.

An improvement to any of these units of property must be depreciated unless a special exception or safe harbor applies. For example, the cost of routine building maintenance expected to be performed at least once every ten years can be currently deducted. There is also a special exception for owners of commercial buildings or residential rentals that cost less than $1 million. They may currently deduct all expenses they incur for repairs, maintenance, or improvements up to an annual ceiling equal to the lesser of 2% of the original cost of the building or $10,000. For a detailed discussion of these rules, refer to *Every Landlord's Tax Deduction Guide*, by Stephen Fishman (Nolo).

Methods for Deducting Business Assets

There are three basic methods that can be used to deduct the cost of long-term business property:

- regular depreciation
- first-year bonus depreciation, and
- Section 179 expensing.

In addition, starting in 2014, the IRS allowed business owners to currently deduct inexpensive tangible property items—those costing no more than $2,500—by making an annual de minimis safe harbor election with their tax returns. Other inexpensive items can be currently deducted as materials and supplies. This has enabled many small business owners to easily currently deduct much of the property they buy for their businesses each year without having to worry about the complex depreciation and Section 179 rules. However, depreciation and/or Section 179 must be used to deduct the cost of more expensive items.

With regular depreciation, you deduct a portion of the cost of long-term business property each year over the asset's useful life. With Section 179 (which is available only for certain eligible property), you currently deduct all or most of the cost of the property in one year. First-year bonus depreciation (if available) allows you to deduct a certain percentage of the cost of qualifying property in the year it is purchased.

You get to decide which depreciation method to use, provided the property meets the applicable eligibility requirements. You don't have to use the same method for all of your business property. (However, as discussed below, bonus depreciation must be used for all property in the same asset class.) Many small business owners choose Section 179 and bonus depreciation when they can because these methods give the largest deduction possible in the first year the asset is purchased. Regular depreciation, on the other hand, forces you to spread your deduction out over several years. Because of inflation and the time value of money, it is usually better to get the largest possible deduction the first year you own an asset. There are some circumstances, however, when it may be more advantageous to use regular depreciation even when you have the option of using Section 179 or bonus depreciation. (See "When to Use Regular Depreciation," below.)

Assuming that bonus depreciation is available, the same asset will often qualify for Section 179 expensing and bonus depreciation. In this event, you decide what method to use or you may choose to combine depreciation methods. If you decide to claim Section 179 expensing and bonus depreciation for the same asset, you must use Section 179 first, then bonus depreciation, and then regular depreciation (if needed). The biggest difference between the two is that Section 179 can be used for both new and used property and bonus depreciation is limited to new property. For this reason, many taxpayers claim Section 179 expensing for their used property and bonus depreciation for their new property.

Section 179 Versus 50% Bonus Depreciation	
Section 179	**Bonus Depreciation**
Limited to annual business profit	No profit limitation
Can use for new and used property	Can use only for new property
Cannot create a net operating loss to be carried back to prior years	Can create a net operating loss to be carried back to prior years and result in an immediate tax refund
$510,000 annual limit	No annual limit: 50% of cost of qualified property placed in service during the year can be deducted in one year (40% for 2018)
Must use property for business more than 50% of the time	No minimum percentage business use of property required (except 51% for listed property)
Recapture of deduction if business use falls below 51%	No recapture (except for listed property where business use falls below 51%)
Does not apply class wide	Applies class wide
Optional	Optional, but must opt out not to take

Rules for Deducting Any Long-Term Asset

There are certain rules that apply when you deduct long-term assets, regardless of which method you use. We will go over those rules and then discuss in more detail the three different methods for deducting long-term business assets and the rules for each.

What Property Is Eligible

You can only depreciate or expense the cost of purchasing long-term business property that wears out, deteriorates, or gets used up over time. You cannot deduct:

- property that doesn't wear out, including land (whether undeveloped or with structures on it), stocks, securities, or gold
- property you use solely for personal purposes

- property purchased and disposed of in the same year
- inventory, or
- collectibles that appreciate in value over time, such as antiques and artwork.

If you use nondepreciable property in your business, you get no tax deduction while you own it. But if you sell it, you get to deduct its tax basis (see below) from the sales price to calculate your taxable profit. If the basis exceeds the sales price, you'll have a deductible loss on the property. If the price exceeds the basis, you'll have a taxable gain.

You also may not depreciate or expense property that you do not own. For example, you get no depreciation or expensing deduction for property you lease. The person who owns the property—the lessor— gets to depreciate it. (However, you may deduct your lease payments as current business expenses.) Leasing may be preferable to buying and depreciating equipment that wears out or becomes obsolete quickly. (See "Leasing Long-Term Assets," below.)

Real Versus Personal Property

You must use regular depreciation to deduct the cost of real property you use in your business. You don't have the option of using any other method. With personal property, you can use Section 179, bonus depreciation, or regular depreciation, provided the item meets the applicable eligibility rules. Personal property consists of virtually any tangible property you buy for your business other than land, land improvements, buildings, and building components.

Mixed-Use Property

In order to deduct a long-term asset, you must have used the property in your business. You can't deduct an asset you use solely for personal purposes.

However, you need not use an asset 100% of the time for business to claim a deduction. You can use it for personal purposes part of the time. In this event, your deduction is reduced by the percentage of your personal use. This will, of course, reduce the amount of your deduction.

You can take a regular or bonus depreciation deduction even if you use an asset only 1% of the time for business, as long as it's not listed property. This is one advantage of depreciation over the Section 179 deduction, which is available only for property you use more than 50% of the time for business.

If you use property for both business and personal purposes, you must keep a diary or log with the dates, times, and reasons the property was used to distinguish business from personal use. Moreover, special rules apply if you use cars and other types of listed property less than 50% of the time for business.

Listed Property

The IRS imposes special rules on certain personal property items that can easily be used for personal as well as business purposes. These items, called "listed property," include cars and other passenger vehicles below 6,000 pounds; motorcycles, boats, and airplanes; computers; and any other property generally used for entertainment, recreation, or amusement—for example, VCRs, cameras, stereos, and camcorders. As long as you use listed property more than 50% of the time for business, you may deduct its cost just like any other long-term business property under Section 179 or by using bonus depreciation or regular depreciation. However, if you use listed property 50% or less of the time for business, you can only use the slowest method of regular depreciation: straight-line depreciation.

When Depreciation Starts and Ends

You begin to depreciate or expense your property when it is placed in service—that is, when it's ready and available for use in your business. As long as it is available for use, you don't have to actually use the property for business during the year to take depreciation.

You stop depreciating property either when you have fully recovered your cost or other basis or when you retire it from service, whichever occurs first. Property is retired from service when you stop using it for business, sell it, destroy it, or otherwise dispose of it.

 CAUTION

You must actually be in business to take depreciation or expensing deductions. In other words, you cannot depreciate or expense an asset until your business is up and running. This is one important reason why it is a good idea to postpone large property purchases until your business has begun. (See Chapter 10 for a detailed discussion of tax deductions for business start-up expenses.)

How Much You Can Deduct

You are allowed to deduct your total investment in a long-term asset you buy for your business, up to your business use percentage of the property. In tax lingo, your investment is called your basis or tax basis. Basis is a word you'll hear over and over again when the subject of depreciation comes up. Don't let it confuse you; it just means the amount of your total investment in the property.

Usually, your basis in long-term property is whatever you paid for it. This includes not only the purchase price, but also sales tax, delivery charges, installation, and testing fees, if any. You may deduct the entire cost, no matter how you paid for the property—in cash, with a credit card, or with a bank loan.

> **EXAMPLE:** Waldo buys a dental X-ray machine for his dental office. He paid $10,000, including $800 in sales tax and $500 for delivery and installation. The basis in the machine is $11,300.

Whenever you use Section 179 expensing or bonus or regular depreciation, you must subtract the amount of your deduction from the property's basis—this is true regardless of whether you actually claimed any depreciation on your tax return. This new basis is called the adjusted basis, because it reflects adjustments from your starting basis. When your adjusted basis is reduced to zero, you can no longer deduct any of the property's cost.

> **EXAMPLE:** Waldo (from the example above) expenses the entire cost of his X-ray machine using Section 179. The machine's adjusted basis is zero, and he gets no more deductions for the property.

Disposing of Long-Term Assets

Depreciable property doesn't last forever, and you probably don't want to use it forever anyway. Sooner or later, you'll get rid of this property. This can be done in a variety of ways—you can:

- sell the property
- trade it in when you buy new property, or
- abandon or destroy it.

Each method has tax consequences.

Sale of Long-Term Assets

If you sell long-term property, your gain or loss on the sale is determined by subtracting the property's adjusted basis from the sales price.

Any depreciation or Section 179 expensing that you claimed is taxed as ordinary income to the extent of your taxable gain. This ordinary income does not go on your Schedule C, where it would be subject to the self-employment tax. Instead, it goes on IRS Form 4797, *Sales of Business Property*, because it is income from the sale of a business asset. Any excess gain—that is, gain over the amount of depreciation and/or expensing claimed—is taxed at capital gains rates, which are usually lower than ordinary income tax rates.

> EXAMPLE: Jack purchased a $10,000 computer system and uses it 100% for his computer security consulting business. He deducts the entire amount using Section 179. This leaves Jack with an adjusted basis of zero. Two years later, Jack sells the system for $5,000, resulting in a taxable gain of $5,000 ($5,000 − zero basis = $5,000). The entire $5,000 gain is taxed as ordinary income, since this is less than the Section 179 expensing Jack claimed.

You can't avoid recapture by not taking a depreciation deduction to which you were entitled. The IRS will treat you as though you took the deduction for recapture purposes, even though you really didn't. Thus, you still have to pay tax on your "gain."

Trade-In of Long-Term Assets

If you trade in a long-term asset for a similar "like-kind" asset, you make a "like-kind exchange." If you receive no cash or debt relief on the trade, you have no taxable income. This can be a great tax strategy.

> **EXAMPLE:** Jack trades in his computer system to a computer dealer. He gives the dealer the old system plus $5,000 cash for a new $10,000 system. He ends up with a new computer system and no taxable income. Moreover, he can deduct in one year the $5,000 he paid for the new computer system using Section 179.

Abandonment of Long-Term Assets

If you abandon long-term business property instead of selling it, you may deduct its adjusted basis as a business loss. Of course, if your adjusted basis in the property is zero, you get no deduction. You abandon property when you voluntarily and permanently give up possessing and using it with the intention of ending your ownership and without passing it on to anyone else. Loss from abandonment of business property is deductible as an ordinary loss, even if the property is a capital asset.

For more information on the tax implications of selling or otherwise disposing of business property, refer to IRS Publication 544, *Sales and Other Dispositions of Assets.*

Section 179 Deductions

If you learn only one section number in the tax code, it should be Section 179. This humble piece of the tax code is one of the greatest tax boons ever for small business owners, including professionals. Section 179 doesn't increase the total amount you can deduct, but it allows you to get your entire depreciation deduction in one year, rather than taking it a little at a time over the term of an asset's useful life—which can be up to 39 years. This is called first-year expensing or Section 179 expensing. (Expensing is an accounting term that means currently deducting a long-term asset.)

Property You Can Deduct

You qualify for the Section 179 deduction only if you buy long-term, tangible personal property that you use in your business more than 50% of the time. Let's look at these requirements in more detail.

Tangible Personal Property

Under Section 179, you can deduct the cost of tangible personal property (new or used) that you buy for your business, if the property will last more than one year. Examples of tangible personal property include computers, business equipment, and office furniture. Although it's not really tangible property, computer software can also be deducted under Section 179. (See "Computer Software," below, for more on deducting software.)

You can't use Section 179 to deduct the cost of:

- land
- permanent structures attached to land, including buildings and their structural components, fences, or paved parking areas
- inventory (see Chapter 13)
- intangible property, such as patents, copyrights, and trademarks, or
- property used outside the United States.

However, nonpermanent property attached to a nonresidential, commercial building is deductible. For example, refrigerators, testing equipment, and signs are all deductible under Section 179. Special rules apply to cars. (See Chapter 5 for more about deducting car expenses.)

Property That You Purchase

You can use Section 179 expensing only for property that you purchase—not for leased property or property you inherit or receive as a gift. You also can't use it for property that you buy from a relative or a corporation or an organization that you control. The property you purchase may be used or new.

Calculating Your Deduction

The total amount you can deduct under Section 179 annually will depend on:

- what you paid for the property
- how much you use the property for business
- how much Section 179 property you buy during the year, and
- your annual business income.

Cost of Property

The amount you can deduct for Section 179 property is initially based on the property's cost. The cost includes the amount you paid for the property, plus sales tax, delivery, and installation charges. It doesn't matter if you pay cash or finance the purchase with a credit card or bank loan. However, if you pay for property with both cash and a trade-in, the value of the trade-in is not deductible under Section 179. You must depreciate the amount of the trade-in.

> EXAMPLE: Stuart, a physician with his own practice, buys a $3,000 microscope. He pays $2,500 cash and is given a $500 trade-in for an older microscope that he owns. He may deduct $2,500 of the $3,000 purchase under Section 179; he must depreciate the remaining $500.

Percentage of Business Use

If you use eligible Section 179 property solely for business, you can deduct 100% of the cost (subject to the other limitations discussed below). However, if you use property for both business and personal purposes, you must reduce your deduction by the percentage of the time that you use the property for personal purposes.

> EXAMPLE: Max buys a $4,000 computer that he uses 75% for his consulting business and 25% for personal purposes. The year that he buys the computer, he may currently deduct 75% of its cost (or $3,000) under Section 179. The remaining $1,000 is not deductible as a business expense.

You must continue to use property that you deduct under Section 179 for business at least 50% of the time for as many years as it would take to depreciate the item under the normal depreciation rules. For example, computers have a five-year depreciation period. If you deduct a computer's cost under Section 179, you must use the computer at least 50% of the time for business for five years.

If you don't meet these rules, you'll have to report as income part of the deduction you took under Section 179 in the prior year. This is called recapture, and is discussed in more detail below.

Annual Deduction Limit

Section 179 is intended to help small businesses, thus there is a limit on how much you can expense each year. The limit has changed over the years (it was originally just $25,000), but has been pegged at $500,000 since 2010. Congress made the $500,000 limit permanent in 2016, subject to annual inflation adjustments.

The annual deduction limit applies to all of your businesses combined, not to each business you own and run.

You don't have to claim the full amount—it's up to you to decide how much to deduct under Section 179. Whatever amount you don't claim under Section 179 must be depreciated instead. (See below—depreciation is *not* optional.)

There is also a limit on the total amount of Section 179 property you can purchase each year. You must reduce your Section 179 deduction by one dollar for every dollar your annual purchases exceed the applicable limit. The limit is $2,030,000 for 2017 and is adjusted for inflation each year.

Year	Section 179 Deduction Limit	Property Value Limit
2017	$510,000	$2,030,000

If you purchase enough business property in one year to exceed the limit, you can divide the deduction among the items you purchase in any way you want, as long as the total deduction is not more than the Section 179 limit. It's usually best to apply Section 179 to property that has the longest useful life and, therefore, the longest depreciation period. This reduces the total time you will have to wait to get your deductions, which usually works to your financial benefit.

Business Profit Limitation

You can't use Section 179 to deduct more in one year than your net taxable business income for the year. In determining this amount, you subtract your business deductions from your business income. However, don't subtract your Section 179 deduction, the deduction for 50% of self-employment tax, or any net operating losses you are carrying back or forward.

If you have a net loss for the year, you get no Section 179 deduction for that year. If your net taxable income is less than the cost of the property you wish to deduct under Section 179, your deduction for the year is limited to the amount of your income. Any amount you cannot deduct in the current year is carried forward to the next year to be deducted then (or any other year in the future).

> **EXAMPLE:** Rich had $100,000 in net income this year from his optometric practice. However, he spent $150,000 buying equipment for his office. Even though the Section 179 maximum limit for the year is $500,000, Rich's deduction for the year is limited to $100,000. He must carry forward the remaining $50,000 to the following year and deduct it then (provided he has sufficient income).

If you're a married sole proprietor (or the owner of a one-person LLC taxed as a sole proprietorship) and file a joint tax return, you can include your spouse's salary and business income in the total business income as well. You can't count investment income—for example, interest you earn on your personal savings account—as business income. But you can include interest you earn on your business working capital—for example, interest you earn on your business bank account.

> **EXAMPLE:** James purchased $100,000 of equipment for his fledgling dental practice, but earned only $5,000. James's wife, however, earned $75,000 from her job as a college professor. Because James and his wife file a joint return, their Section 179 deduction is limited to $80,000 ($5,000 + $75,000 = $80,000). Thus, James may deduct $80,000 of his equipment purchases for that year under Section 179 and must deduct the remaining $20,000 in a future year.

If you're a partner in a partnership or an LLP, member of a multi-owner LLC, or shareholder in an S corporation, the Section 179 income limit applies both to the business entity and to each owner personally. The business determines its Section 179 deduction subject to the income limits. It then allocates the deduction among the partners or shareholders who each apply their own Section 179 income limit.

If your practice is organized as a C corporation, nothing is allocated to the shareholders. The corporation takes the Section 179 deduction on its own return, based on its own taxable income. This puts professionals who have C corporations in a bit of a quandary, because they ordinarily want their C corporations to have little or no taxable income for the year to avoid double taxation (see Chapter 15). If you have a C corporation and want to take a Section 179 deduction, you must make sure the corporation has sufficient taxable income at the end of the year to cover the amount of your desired deduction.

Date of Purchase

As long as you meet the requirements, you can deduct the cost of Section 179 property up to the limits discussed above, no matter when you place the property in service during the year (that is, when you buy the property and make it available for use in your ongoing business). This differs from regular depreciation rules, by which property bought later in the year may be subject to a smaller deduction for the first year. (See below for more on regular depreciation rules about placing property in service.) This is yet another advantage of the Section 179 deduction over regular depreciation.

Recapture Under Section 179

Recapture is a nasty tax trap an unwary business owner can easily get caught in. It requires you to give back part of a tax deduction that you took in a previous year. You may have to recapture part of a Section 179 tax deduction if, during the property's recovery period either of the following occurs:

- Your business use of the property drops below 51%.
- You give the property away.

The recovery period is the property's useful life as determined under IRS rules. The IRS has determined the useful life of all types of property that can be depreciated. The useful life of an asset is the time period over which you must depreciate the asset. For personal property that can be expensed under Section 179, the useful life ranges from three years for computer software to seven years for office furniture and business equipment. If you deduct property under Section 179, you must continue to use it in your business at least 51% of the time for its entire useful life—this is the IRS recovery period. For example, if you buy office furniture, you must use it over half of the time for business for at least seven years.

If your business use falls below 51% or you give the property away before the recovery period ends, you become subject to recapture. This means that you have to give back to the IRS all of the accelerated deductions you took under Section 179. You get to keep the amount you would have been entitled to under regular depreciation, but you must include the rest of your Section 179 deduction in your income for the year. If you're a sole proprietor, you'll have to include this income on your Schedule C and pay both income tax and self-employment tax on it.

Bonus Depreciation

In an ongoing effort to help the faltering economy, business owners have been allowed to claim first-year bonus depreciation for qualifying personal property. Bonus depreciation enables a business owner to deduct in a single year a substantial amount of a new long-term asset's cost. In recent years, the bonus depreciation amount has been 50%. Bonus depreciation expired at the end of 2014, but Congress retroactively extended it through 2019. However, the bonus depreciation percentage will be gradually phased down as follows:

- 50% for 2015 through 2017
- 40% in 2018, and
- 30% for 2019.

Using bonus depreciation, a taxpayer can deduct in one year 50% of the cost of an item that qualifies and is placed in service during 2015 through 2017. For example, if an item that costs $10,000 is placed in service in 2016, $5,000 (50% of the cost) may be deducted the first year through bonus deprecation, with the remaining $5,000 deducted using regular depreciation over several years. If the same item is purchased in 2018, only 40% of the cost can be deducted in the first year with bonus depreciation. If it is placed in service in 2019, only 30% can be deducted with bonus depreciation. Bonus depreciation will not be available in 2020 or later, unless it's extended by Congress.

However, many professionals won't need to use bonus depreciation because they'll be able to deduct 100% of an asset's cost in the first year using Section 179 expensing or the de minimis safe harbor. Nevertheless, bonus depreciation will still be useful where Section 179 and/or the de minimis safe harbor can't be used. For example, bonus depreciation can be used for an asset (other than listed property) that is used less than 50% of the time for business; this is not the case for Section 179.

Bonus depreciation is optional—you don't have to take it if you don't want to. But if you want to get the largest depreciation deduction you can, you will want to take advantage of this option whenever possible.

Property That Qualifies for Bonus Depreciation

Property qualifies for bonus depreciation only if all the following are true:
- It is new (if the newly purchased property contains used parts, it is still treated as new if the cost of the used parts is less than 20% of the total cost of the property).
- It has a useful life of 20 years or less (this includes all types of tangible personal business property and software you buy, but not real property—see above).
- You purchase it from someone who is unrelated to you (it can't be a gift or an inheritance).

In addition, if the asset is listed property, it must be used over 50% of the time for business to qualify for bonus depreciation. Listed property consists of automobiles and computers and certain other personal property—see "Listed Property," above. In contrast, you can use the Section 179 deduction and regular depreciation for both used and new personal property. And, you can use regular depreciation for any long-term business property, including listed property, without any restrictions on the percentage of business use.

Placed-in-Service Date

Bonus depreciation is only available for the year you place personal property in service in your business. Property is "placed in service" when it's ready and available for use in your business. As long as it is available for use, you don't have to actually use the property for business during the year to take depreciation.

Class-Wide Requirement

If you use bonus depreciation, you must use it for all assets that fall within the same class. Unlike Section 179 expensing, you may not pick and choose the assets you want to apply it to within a class. For example, if you buy a car and take bonus depreciation, you must take bonus depreciation for any other property you buy that year within the same class. Cars are five-year property, so you must take bonus depreciation that year for any other five-year property—for example, computers and office equipment. (See "Depreciation Period," below, for a list of the various classes of property.)

Calculating the Bonus Amount

You use bonus depreciation to figure out your depreciation deduction for the first year that you own an asset. You figure the deduction by multiplying the depreciable basis of the asset by the applicable bonus percentage. For property placed in service during 2012 through 2017, this calculation is easy because the bonus percentage is 50%.

The bonus percentage will be reduced to 40% in 2018 and 30% for 2019. Unless the law is changed again, there will be no bonus depreciation in 2020 or later.

If you want to claim the Section 179 deduction and 50% bonus depreciation for the same asset, you first use Section 179, then 50% bonus depreciation, and then regular depreciation, in that order. This can give you an enormous deduction.

> **EXAMPLE:** During 2017, Mark purchases and places in service $1 million worth of furnishings and equipment for his medical practice. Mark had $500,000 in net taxable income in 2017. First, he may take the maximum $500,000 Section 179 deduction for 2017—that is, he may currently deduct this entire amount from his business income. Next, he may take a 50% bonus depreciation deduction on the remaining $500,000 cost of the equipment— this amounts to a $250,000 deduction. He may then deduct the remaining $250,000 of the equipment's cost under the normal depreciation rules. Using the 200% double declining balance method, he gets $50,000 in regular depreciation (20% × $250,000 = $50,000). His total deduction for the year is $800,000: $500,000 Section 179 deduction + $250,000 bonus depreciation + $50,000 regular depreciation. The next year, he'll get a regular depreciation deduction of $80,000 (32% × $250,000= $80,000).

Opting Out of the Bonus

The bonus depreciation deduction is applied automatically to all taxpayers who qualify for it. However, the deduction is optional. You need not take it if you don't want to. You can elect not to take the deduction by attaching a note to your tax return. It may be advantageous to do this if you expect your income to go up substantially in future years, placing you in a higher tax bracket.

CAUTION
When you opt out, you do so for the entire class of assets. It's very important to understand that if you opt out of the bonus, you must do so for the entire class of assets, not just one asset within a class. This is the same rule that applies when you decide to take the bonus.

Deducting Inexpensive Property

Starting in 2014, new IRS regulations went into effect that include two new special deductions for business property that is relatively inexpensive. These regulations allow current deductions for:

- items that come within the de minimis safe harbor, and
- materials and supplies.

They are particularly helpful for smaller businesses that don't purchase a lot of expensive equipment or other property. Indeed, you may be able to currently deduct all the long-term property you buy for your business by taking advantage of these rules alone. Moreover, these rules allow you to remove the affected assets from your books and tax returns. This simplifies your tax and business records because you don't have the assets cluttering your books.

These deductions may be used in addition to, or in place of, the Section 179 deduction. However, these deductions are simpler and easier to use than Section 179 for most taxpayers. For one thing, they may be used even if your business earns no profit during the year. Moreover, unlike the Section 179 deduction or accelerated regular depreciation, the deductions taken for property under these methods are not subject to later recapture if the property is later used over 50% of the time for personal use. Recapture requires you to recognize as income the increased deductions you took under Section 179 or accelerated depreciation.

Property Costing $2,500 or Less: The De Minimis Safe Harbor

The most significant of these new deductions is the de minimis safe harbor (de minimis is Latin for minor or inconsequential). (IRS Reg. § 1.263(a)-1(f).) Most businesses can use the de minimis safe harbor to currently deduct the cost of personal property items that cost up to $2,500 apiece. This can result in a substantial deduction.

To use this deduction, you must file an annual election with your tax return—something that is easy to do. When you make this election, it applies to all expenses you incur that qualify for the de minimis safe harbor. You cannot pick and choose which items you want to include. You must also include items that would otherwise be deductible as materials and supplies.

The de minimis safe harbor can't be used to deduct the cost of land, inventory (items held for sale to customers), certain spare parts for machinery or other equipment, or amounts that you pay for property that you produce or acquire for resale.

You can use the de minimis safe harbor to deduct the cost of property you don't use 100% of the time for business. Your deduction is limited to the dollar amount of your business use percentage.

> EXAMPLE: Sheila purchases a $2,000 computer she uses 50% of the time for her accounting practice and 50% of the time for personal purposes. She may deduct $1,000 of the cost using the de minimis safe harbor.

However, to determine whether property qualifies for the de minimis safe harbor, you look at its total cost, without subtracting the personal use percentage.

> EXAMPLE: Assume that Sheila (from the above example) purchases a $3,000 computer she uses 50% of the time for business. She may not deduct the computer under the safe harbor because it cost more than $2,500.

What if you sell property you deducted using the de minimis safe harbor? You'll likely have taxable gain because your adjusted basis in the property will be zero. The entire amount of gain you realize from the sale is treated as ordinary income—that is, it is taxed at your normal individual tax rates, not lower capital gain rates. The gain is also subject to self-employment (Social Security and Medicare) tax.

> EXAMPLE: John used the de minimis safe harbor to fully deduct in one year the $1,000 camera he purchased for his real estate business. His adjusted basis in the camera after the sale is $0. He sells the camera for $500 one year later. He has a $500 taxable gain ($500 sale price − $0 adjusted basis = $500). He adds the $500 to his income on his Schedule C.

Maximum De Minimis Amount

Unless you have an applicable financial statement for your business (something relatively few professionals have), you may use the de minimis safe harbor only for property whose cost does not exceed $2,500 *per invoice*, or $2,500 *per item* as substantiated by the invoice. If the cost exceeds $2,500 per invoice (or per item), no part of the cost may be deducted by using the de minimis safe harbor.

If you have an applicable financial statement, then you may increase the per item or per invoice amount up to $5,000.

> **EXAMPLE:** Alice purchases the following items for her accounting practice from a local computer supply store:
> - a computer for $2,000
> - an office chair for $1,000, and
> - an office desk for $3,000.
>
> Alice's total bill is $6,000. However, she applies the de minimis safe harbor rule item by item as shown on the invoice. Each item is less than the $2,500 de minimis safe harbor limit except the desk. Thus, Alice may immediately deduct $3,000 of the total using the safe harbor. She can't use the safe harbor to deduct the $3,000 cost of the desk. Instead, she may deduct the desk in one year using Section 179 or depreciate it over five years.

Be sure to save all your receipts and invoices for property you deduct using the de minimis safe harbor.

Since the $2,500 de minimis limit is based on the cost of an item as shown on the invoice, you might be tempted to artificially break an item down into separate costs on the invoice, each of which is less than the limit. However, the IRS does not allow this. You cannot break into separate components property that you would normally buy as a single unit.

> **EXAMPLE:** Alice (from the example above) purchased an office desk for $3,000. She instructs the office supply store to separately bill her $250 for each of four desk drawers and $2,000 for the remainder of the desk. Since an office desk is normally purchased along with its drawers as a single unit, the IRS adds the cost of each component to determine that the actual cost is $3,000. Thus, the desk does not qualify for the de minimis safe harbor.

In determining whether the cost of an item exceeds the $2,500 (or $5,000) threshold, you must include all additional costs included on the same invoice with the property—for example, delivery and installation fees. If the additional costs on a single invoice apply to several items, you must divide the costs among them in a reasonable way. IRS regulations give you three options: (1) equal division for each item, (2) specific identification (for example, if the installation costs apply only to one item), or (3) weighted average based on the property's relative cost.

> EXAMPLE: Alexander pays $6,000 for three microscopes for his medical lab. They cost $2,000 each, and he also paid a single $750 fee for installation. He can treat the installation cost as $250 per microscope ($750 ÷ 3). This results in a total price of $2,250 for each microscope. Since this is less than the $2,500 de minimis limit, he can currently deduct the entire $6,750 cost using the de minimis safe harbor.

Do You Have an Applicable Financial Statement?

If you have an applicable financial statement for your business, you may increase your de minimis amount to $5,000 per item—twice the $2,500 limit for businesses without such statements. The most common type of applicable financial statement is a certified financial statement prepared by a CPA. These usually cost at least several thousand dollars, so few professionals with smaller practices have them. A financial statement (other than a tax return) filed with the SEC or another state or federal agency (not including the IRS) can also qualify—for example, a Form 10-K or an annual statement to shareholders. Only larger corporations or businesses that are publicly traded usually file such statements.

Qualifying for the Safe Harbor

To qualify for this de minimis expensing safe harbor, a taxpayer must:

- establish before the first day of the tax year (January 1 for calendar year taxpayers) an accounting procedure requiring it to expense amounts paid for property either (1) costing less than a certain dollar amount, and/or (2) with an economic useful life of 12 months or less, and
- actually treat such amounts as currently deductible expenses on its books and records.

If you have an "applicable financial statement" and wish to qualify to use the $5,000 de minimis limit, your accounting procedure must be in writing and signed before January 1 of the tax year. If you don't have such a statement and qualify only for the $2,500 limit, you do not need to put your procedure in writing (although you still may do so). But it should still be in place before January 1 of the tax year. Here is an example of a written procedure for a taxpayer without an applicable financial statement:

De Minimis Safe Harbor Procedure

Effective January 1, 2016, XYZ hereby adopts the following policy regarding certain expenditures: Amounts paid to acquire or produce tangible personal property will be expensed, and not capitalized, in the year of purchase if: (1) the property costs less than $2,500, or (2) the property has a useful life of 12 months or less.

Claiming the Safe Harbor

To take advantage of the de minimis safe harbor, you must file an election with your tax return each year, using the following format:

Section 1.263(a)-1(f) De Minimis Safe Harbor Election

Taxpayer's name:

Taxpayer's address:

Taxpayer's identification number:

The taxpayer is hereby making the de minimis safe harbor election under Section 1.263(a)-1(f).

Deducting Materials and Supplies

Another deduction that took effect in 2014 is for materials and supplies. Items that fall within the definition of materials and supplies in IRS regulations may be currently deducted. However, many small businesses won't need (or be able) to use this deduction because these items can usually be deducted using the de minimis safe harbor.

"Materials and supplies" are tangible property used or consumed in your business operations that fall within any of the following categories:

- any item of tangible personal property that cost $200 or less
- any item of personal property with an economic useful life of 12 months or less, and
- components acquired to maintain or repair a unit of tangible property—that is, spare parts.

The cost of such items may be deducted the year the item is used or consumed in your business—which may be later than the year purchased. To use this deduction, you are supposed to keep records of when such items are used or consumed in your business—something few small business owners do in practice. For this reason, this deduction may be useless for most small businesses. Fortunately, they can use the de minimis safe harbor discussed above instead to deduct materials and supplies.

Incidental Materials and Supplies

"Incidental" materials and supplies are personal property items that are carried on hand and for which no record of consumption is kept or for which beginning and ending inventories are not taken. In other words, these are inexpensive items not worth keeping track of. Examples include pens, paper, staplers, toner, and trash baskets. Costs of incidental materials and supplies are deductible the year in which they are paid for, not when the items are used or consumed in the business.

> EXAMPLE: John, a lawyer, purchases two packs of pens and three boxes of paper clips he plans to use for his law practice over the next two years. The cost was minimal and he does not keep inventory of each pen or paperclip. These are incidental compared to his business and deductible the year he paid for them.

Interaction With De Minimis Safe Harbor

If you elect to use the de minimis safe harbor discussed above, and any materials and supplies also qualify for the safe harbor, you must deduct the amounts paid for them under the safe harbor in the tax year in which the amounts are paid or incurred. (IRS Reg. § 1.263(a)-1(f)(3)(ii).) Thus, if you use the de minimis safe harbor, you can largely ignore the materials and supplies deduction. This is to your advantage since the de minimis safe harbor has a $2,500 limit for most businesses, as opposed to the $200 materials and supplies limit. Moreover, the de minimis safe harbor permits you to deduct the cost of items in the year they are purchased, instead of when they are actually used or consumed in your business.

One exception where the materials and supplies deduction could prove useful, even where a de minimis safe harbor election is made, is for components used to repair property. If the components cost more than $2,500, the de minimis safe harbor can't be used. But the materials and supplies deduction can be used, no matter how much the components cost. The deduction may be taken in the year when the components are actually used in the course of a repair or maintenance.

Regular Depreciation

The traditional method of getting back the money you spend on long-term business assets is to deduct the cost a little at a time over several years (exactly how long is determined by the IRS). This process is called depreciation.

Depreciation is a complicated subject. The IRS instruction booklet on the subject (Publication 946, *How to Depreciate Property*) is over 100 pages long. For a comprehensive discussion of depreciation, read Publication 946. In this section, we cover the depreciation basics that all business owners should know.

> CAUTION
>
> **Regular depreciation is not optional.** Unlike the Section 179 deduction or bonus depreciation, regular depreciation is not optional. You must take a depreciation deduction if you qualify for it. If you fail to take it, the IRS will treat you as if you had taken it. This means that you could be subject to depreciation recapture when you sell the asset—even if you never took a depreciation deduction. This would increase your taxable income by the amount of the deduction you failed to take. (See "Depreciation Recapture," below.) So if you don't expense a depreciable asset under Section 179, or claim bonus depreciation, be sure to take the proper depreciation deductions for it. If you realize later that you failed to take a depreciation deduction that you should have taken, you may file an amended tax return to claim any deductions that you should have taken in prior years.

When to Use Regular Depreciation

With Section 179 and bonus depreciation (if available), and the de minimis safe harbor and materials and supplies deductions, you might not need to use regular depreciation for the foreseeable future. However, you may need to use regular depreciation to write off the cost of long-term assets that don't qualify for Section 179 expensing or bonus depreciation. Also, under some circumstances, it may be better to use depreciation and draw out your deduction over several years instead of getting your deductions all at once under Section 179 and/or bonus depreciation.

When You Can't Use Section 179

There are many more limitations on using Section 179 than there are for regular depreciation. For example, you can't use Section 179 to deduct the cost of something that you use less than 50% of the time for business. There is no such minimum percentage business use for regular depreciation—you can use and deduct 1% of an item's cost if that's your business use. Other restrictions apply to Section 179 that don't apply to regular depreciation. Under Section 179, you can't deduct:

- personal property items that you convert to business use
- structures, such as a building or building component
- items financed with a trade-in (the value of the trade-in must be depreciated)
- intangible assets, such as patents, copyrights, trademarks, or business goodwill
- an item purchased from a relative
- property inherited or received as a gift, or
- personal property used inside rental property—for example, kitchen appliances, carpets, drapes, or blinds.

None of these limitations apply to regular depreciation.

In addition, your Section 179 deduction may not exceed your business income. If you're married and file a joint return, your spouse's income can be included. But if your business is making little or no money and you have little or no income from wages or your spouse, you may not be able to take a Section 179 deduction for the current year. In contrast, there is no income limitation on regular or bonus depreciation deductions. You can deduct regular or bonus depreciation from your business income; if this results in a net loss for a year, you can deduct the loss from income taxes you paid in prior years.

You will also have to use depreciation instead of Section 179 to the extent you exceed the Section 179 annual limit.

When You Can't Use Bonus Depreciation

There are also rules that limit the availability of bonus depreciation that don't apply to regular depreciation. With bonus depreciation, you can't deduct:

- used property, including property you convert to business use
- real property
- listed property used less than 51% of the time for business
- property received as a gift or an inheritance, or
- intangible assets, such as patents, copyrights, trademarks, or business goodwill.

None of these limitations apply to regular depreciation, so there may be instances when you can't use bonus depreciation but the property is still eligible for regular depreciation.

Depreciation Period

The depreciation period (also called the recovery period) is the time over which you must take your depreciation deductions for an asset. The tax code has assigned depreciation periods to all types of business assets, ranging from three to 39 years. These periods are somewhat arbitrary. However, property that can be expected to last a long time generally gets a longer recovery period than property that has a short life—for example, nonresidential real property has a 39-year recovery period, while software has only a three-year period. Most of the property that you buy for your practice will probably have a five- or seven-year depreciation period.

The major depreciation periods are listed below. These periods are also called recovery classes, and all property that comes within a period is said to belong to that class. For example, computers have a five-year depreciation period and thus fall within the five-year class, along with automobiles and office equipment.

First-Year Depreciation

The IRS has established certain rules (called conventions) that govern how many months of depreciation you can take for the first year that you own an asset.

Depreciation Periods	
Depreciation Period	**Type of Property**
3 years	Computer software
	Tractor units for over-the-road use
	Any racehorse over two years old when placed in service
	Any other horse over 12 years old when placed in service
5 years	Automobiles, taxis, buses, and trucks
	Computers and peripheral equipment
	Office machinery (such as typewriters, calculators, and copiers)
	Any property used in research and experimentation
	Breeding cattle and dairy cattle
	Appliances, carpets, furniture, and so on used in a residential rental real estate activity
7 years	Office furniture and fixtures (such as desks, files, and safes)
	Agricultural machinery and equipment
	Any property that does not have a class life and has not been designated by law as being in any other class
10 years	Vessels, barges, tugs, and similar water transportation equipment
	Any single-purpose agricultural or horticultural structure
	Any tree or vine bearing fruits or nuts
15 years	Improvements made directly to land or added to it (such as shrubbery, fences, roads, and bridges)
	Any retail motor fuels outlet, such as a convenience store at a gas station
	Interior improvements to leased nonresidential property and certain restaurant property placed in service between October 22, 2004 and December 31, 2009
20 years	Farm buildings (other than single-purpose agricultural or horticultural structures)
27.5 years	Residential rental property—for example, an apartment building
39 years	Nonresidential real property, such as a home office, office building, store, or warehouse

Half-Year Convention

The basic rule is that, no matter what month and day of the year an asset you purchase becomes available for use in your business, you treat it as being placed in service on July 1—the midpoint of the year. This means that you get one-half year of depreciation for the first year that you own an asset.

Midquarter Convention

You are not allowed to use the half-year convention if more than 40% of the long-term personal property that you buy during the year is placed in service during the last three months of the year. The 40% figure is determined by adding together the basis of all the depreciable property you bought during the year and comparing that with the basis of all of the property you bought during the fourth quarter only.

If you exceed the 40% ceiling, you must use the midquarter convention. You group all the property that you purchased during the year by the quarter it was bought and treat it as being placed in service at the midpoint of that quarter. (A quarter is a three-month period: The first quarter is January through March; the second quarter is April through June; the third quarter is July through September; and the fourth quarter is October through December.)

As a general rule, it's best to avoid having to use the midquarter convention. To do this, you need to buy more than 60% of your total depreciable assets before September 30 of the year. Assets you currently deduct using Section 179 do not count toward the 40% limitation, so you can avoid the midquarter convention by using Section 179 to deduct most or all of your purchases in the last three months of the year.

Depreciation Methods

There are several ways to calculate depreciation. However, most tangible property is depreciated using the Modified Accelerated Cost Recovery System, or MACRS. A slightly different system, called the Alternative Depreciation System or ADS, applies to certain listed property (see below), property used outside the United States, and certain farm property and imported property.

You can ordinarily use three different methods to calculate the depreciation deduction under MACRS: straight-line or one of two accelerated depreciation methods. Once you choose your method, you're stuck with it for the entire life of the asset.

In addition, you must use the same method for all property of the same class that you purchase during the year. For example, if you use the straight-line method to depreciate a computer, you must use that method to depreciate all other property in the same class as computers. Computers fall within the five-year class, so you must use the straight-line method for all other five-year property you buy during the year, such as office equipment.

Straight-Line Method

The straight-line method requires you to deduct an equal amount each year over the useful life of an asset. However, if the half-year convention applies, you deduct only a half-year's worth of depreciation in the first year. You make up for this by adding an extra one-half year of depreciation at the end. You can use the straight-line method to depreciate any type of depreciable property.

Accelerated Depreciation Methods

There is nothing wrong with straight-line depreciation, but the tax law provides an alternative that most businesses prefer: accelerated depreciation. As the name implies, this method provides faster depreciation than the straight-line method. It does not increase your total depreciation deduction, but it permits you to take larger deductions in the first few years after you buy an asset. You make up for this by taking smaller deductions in later years.

The fastest and most commonly used form of accelerated depreciation is the double declining balance method. This is a confusing name, but all it means is that you get double the deduction that you would get for the first full year under the straight-line method. You then get less in later years. This method may be used to depreciate all property within the three-, five-, seven-, and ten-year classes, excluding farm property. This covers virtually all the tangible personal property you buy for your business.

Depreciation Tables

Figuring out your annual depreciation deduction might seem to require some complicated math, but actually it's not that difficult. Of course, if you use a tax professional to do your taxes, he or she will do the math for you. Tax preparation software can also do this. However, if you want to do it yourself, you can use depreciation tables prepared by the IRS. These tables factor in the depreciation convention and method. They are all available in IRS Publication 946, *How to Depreciate Property*. Alternatively, you can use one of the many online depreciation calculators.

How to Deduct Listed Property

The IRS imposes special rules on listed property—items that can easily be used for personal as well as business purposes. (See "Listed Property," above, for a discussion of listed property.) If you use listed property for business more than 50% of the time, you may deduct its cost just like any other long-term business property (under Section 179 or bonus or regular depreciation rules).

However, if you use listed property 50% or less of the time for business, you may not deduct the cost under Section 179 or use bonus depreciation or accelerated depreciation. Instead, you must use the slowest method: straight-line depreciation. In addition, you are not allowed to use the normal depreciation periods allowed under the MACRS depreciation system. Instead, you must use the depreciation periods provided for by the Alternative Depreciation System (ADS for short). These are generally longer than the ordinary MACRS periods. However, you may still depreciate cars, trucks, and computers over five years. The main ADS depreciation periods for listed property are provided in the following chart.

If you start out using accelerated depreciation and in a later year your business use drops to 50% or less, you have to switch to the straight-line method and ADS period for that year and subsequent years. In addition, you are subject to depreciation recapture for the prior years—that is, you must calculate how much more depreciation you got in the prior years by using accelerated depreciation and count that amount as ordinary taxable income for the current year. This will, of course, increase your tax bill for the year.

ADS Depreciation Periods	
Property	**Depreciation Period**
Cars and light trucks	5 years
Computers and peripheral equipment	5 years
Communication equipment	10 years
Personal property with no class life	12 years

Computer Software

Most professionals buy computer software; some also create it themselves. The tax law favors the latter group.

Software You Buy

The software you buy comes in two basic types for tax purposes: software that comes already installed on a computer that you buy and software you purchase separately and install yourself (often called off-the-shelf software).

Software that comes with a computer you buy and is included in the price—for example, your operating system—is depreciated as part of the computer, unless you're billed separately for the software.

Any off-the-shelf computer software that is (1) not custom designed, and (2) available to the general public is qualified for Section 179 expensing in the year that you put the software into service. Alternatively, off-the-shelf software may be depreciated over three years using the straight-line method. You can also use bonus depreciation for off-the-shelf software.

If you acquire software that is not off-the-shelf software by buying another business or its assets, the rules discussed above don't apply. This software must be depreciated over 15 years using the straight-line method; this type of depreciation is called amortization. (IRC § 197.)

Software You Create

If, instead of buying off-the-shelf software, you create it yourself, you can currently deduct the cost under Section 174 of the Internal Revenue Code. This section allows deductions for research and experimentation expenses incurred in developing an invention or a patent, process, prototype, formula, technique, or similar product.

You may currently deduct the costs under Section 174 whether the software is developed for your own use or to sell or license to others. (Rev. Proc. 2000-50.)

Real Property

Land cannot be depreciated because it never wears out. However, this doesn't mean you don't get a tax deduction for land. When you sell it, you may deduct the cost of the land from the sale price to determine your taxable gain, if any. The cost of clearing, grading, landscaping, or demolishing buildings on land is not depreciable. It is added to the tax basis of the land—that is, to its cost—and subtracted from the money you get when you sell the land.

Unlike land, buildings do wear out over time and therefore may be depreciated. This means that when you buy property with buildings on it, you must separate out the cost of the buildings from the total cost of the property to calculate your depreciation.

As you might expect, the depreciation periods for buildings are quite long (after all, buildings usually last a long time). The depreciation period for nonresidential buildings placed in service after May 12, 1993 is 39 years. You must use the straight-line method to depreciate real property. This means you'll be able to deduct only a small fraction of its value each year—1/39th of its value each year if the 39-year period applies.

Home Office Depreciation

If you have an office or other workplace you use solely for business in your home, you are entitled to depreciate the business portion of the home. For example, if you use 10% of your home for business, you may depreciate 10% of its cost (excluding the cost of the land). In the event your home has gone down in value since you bought it, you must use its fair market value on the date you began using your home office as your tax basis. You depreciate a home office over 39 years—the term used for nonresidential property. A home office is nonresidential property because you don't live in it.

Intangible Assets

Long-term assets do not consist only of tangible things like office equipment and buildings. Intangible assets can also be deductible long-term assets. Intangible assets are things you can't see or touch. They include business goodwill, covenants not to compete, and intellectual property—patents, copyrights, trade secrets, and trademarks.

Buying Assets of an Existing Practice

Professionals who purchase the assets of an existing practice ordinarily buy intangible property along with tangible property such as office equipment. This intangible property may consist of:

- business goodwill
- going concern value
- covenants not to compete
- business books and records, including patient or client files
- the value of having an existing workforce in place
- customer-based intangibles, such as the practice's existing client base
- patents, copyrights, trademarks, trade names, know-how, designs, and processes
- licenses, permits, and similar rights granted by government agencies, and
- supplier-based intangibles, such as a favorable arrangement with a supplier that will continue after the acquisition. (IRC § 197.)

You can deduct the cost of these intangible assets in equal amounts over 15 years. This process is called amortization. It is similar to straight-line depreciation. You deduct an equal amount of the cost of the asset each year over its useful life.

> **EXAMPLE:** Anita purchases all the assets of DDS, Inc., an incorporated dental practice wholly owned by Ralph, for $200,000. The purchase includes a small building and all of Ralph's dental equipment. All the tangible assets are worth $180,000. The remaining $20,000 of the purchase price is allocated to goodwill. Anita may amortize the $20,000 over 15 years—she deducts $1,333 per year.

However, you may amortize intangible assets only when you individually purchase the assets of an existing practice. You get no amortization if you acquire the assets of an incorporated practice by purchasing its stock; likewise if you purchase a partnership, or an LLP or LLC rather than its assets. Corporate stock and LLC, LLP, or partnership interests are not considered to be amortizable intangible assets.

> **EXAMPLE:** Assume that Anita purchases 100% of the stock of DDS, Inc., for $200,000. She has control over all of DDS's assets, but gets no amortization deduction for goodwill or any other of its intangible assets.

Self-Created Intangible Assets

You may not amortize any of the intangible assets listed above if you created them yourself. For example, you can't amortize goodwill you create yourself by conducting your practice. It is not deductible at all.

However, if you create an invention or a trademark, trade name, or copyrighted work of authorship like a book or film yourself, you may currently deduct the cost. Any costs that you can't currently deduct may be amortized as described above.

SEE AN EXPERT

Amortization can be tricky, particularly determining how much intangible assets are worth. This is a complex area of taxation. Consult with a knowledgeable tax pro if you need to amortize intangible assets.

Depreciation Recapture

To currently deduct long-term property under Section 179 or depreciate listed property using bonus or accelerated depreciation, you must use the property for your business at least 51% of the time. If your business use falls under 51%, you'll have to give back part of the Section 179 bonus or accelerated depreciation deductions you received. This is called recapture because the IRS is getting back—recapturing—part of your deduction.

Recapture is required for listed property (personal use property) when your business use falls below 51% and for any property for which you took a Section 179 deduction. It is not required for nonlisted property for which you took no Section 179 deduction. For example, it is not required for a building or office equipment the business use of which falls below 51%.

Tax Reporting and Record Keeping for Section 179 and Depreciation

Depreciation and Section 179 deductions are reported on IRS Form 4562, *Depreciation and Amortization*. If you have more than one business for which you're claiming depreciation, you must use a separate Form 4562 for each business. You need to file Form 4562 only for the first year a deduction is claimed.

If you're a sole proprietor (or the owner of a one-person LLC taxed as a sole proprietorship), you carry over the amount of your depreciation and Section 179 deductions to your Schedule C and subtract them from your gross business income along with your other business expenses.

Multi-member LLCs, LLPs, and partnerships report their depreciation deductions on IRS Form 1065. These deductions are subtracted from the entity's income, along with all other deductions. The resulting profits or losses are passed through to the owners' individual returns. S corporations use Form 1065S, but the principle is the same. If a Section 179 deduction is taken by an entity taxed as a partnership or an S corporation, it must be separately stated on the Schedule K-1 forms given to each owner.

C corporations take all of their deductions, including depreciation, on their own tax returns, IRS Form 1120.

You need to keep accurate records for each asset you depreciate or expense under Section 179, showing:

- a description of the asset
- when and how you purchased the property
- the date it was placed in service
- its original cost
- the percentage of time you use it for business
- whether and how much you deducted under Section 179
- the amount of depreciation you took for the asset in prior years, if any
- its depreciable basis
- the depreciation method used
- the length of the depreciation period, and
- the amount of depreciation you deducted for the year.

If you have an accountant or a bookkeeper, he or she should prepare these records for you.

If you do your taxes yourself, you can use tax preparation software to create a worksheet containing this information. You can also use an accounting program such as *QuickBooks* to keep track of your depreciating assets. (Simple checkbook programs like *Quicken* are not designed to keep track of depreciation.) You may also use a spreadsheet program to create your own depreciation worksheet. Spreadsheet templates are available for this purpose. Of course, you can also do the job by hand. The instructions to IRS Form 4562 contain a worksheet you can use.

For listed property, you'll also have to keep records showing how much of its use is for business and how much is personal. (See Chapter 18.) You should also keep proof of the amount you paid for the asset—receipts, canceled checks, and purchase documents. You need not file these records with your tax return, but you must have them available to back up your deductions if you're audited.

Leasing Long-Term Assets

When you're acquiring a long-term asset for your practice, you should consider whether it makes more sense to lease the item than to purchase it. Almost everything a professional needs can be leased—computers, office furniture, equipment. And leasing can be an attractive alternative to buying. However, it's important to understand the tax consequences of leasing when making your decision.

Leasing Versus Purchasing

So which is better, leasing or buying? It depends. Leasing equipment can be a better option for professionals who have limited capital or who need equipment that must be upgraded every few years. Purchasing equipment can be a better option for professionals with ample capital or who need equipment that has a long usable life. Each professional's situation is different and the decision to buy or lease must be made on a case-by-case basis.

Before deciding whether to purchase or lease an expensive item, it's a good idea to determine the total actual costs of each option. This depends on many factors, including:

- the cost of the lease
- the purchase price for the item
- the item's useful life
- the interest rate on a loan to purchase the item
- the item's residual value—how much it will be worth at the end of the lease term
- whether you will purchase the item at the end of the lease and how much this will cost
- how much it would cost to dispose of the item
- your income tax bracket
- whether the item qualifies for one-year Section 179 expensing or must be depreciated, and
- if the item must be depreciated, the length of the depreciation period.

There are several lease-versus-buy calculators on the Internet that you can use to compare the cost of leasing versus buying, including www. lease-vs-buy.com and www.chooseleasing.org.

Commercial software and computer spreadsheets can also be used for this purpose.

Start-Up Expenses

Every professional knows that it costs money to get a new practice up and running or to buy an existing practice. What many professionals don't know is that these costs (called start-up expenses) are subject to special tax rules. This chapter explains what types of expenditures are start-up expenses and how you can deduct these costs as quickly as possible.

What Are Start-Up Expenses?

To have business deductions, you must actually be running a business. This commonsense rule can lead to problems if you want to start or buy a new practice. The money you spend to get your practice up and running is not a business operating expense because your business hasn't yet begun.

Instead, business start-up expenses are capital expenses because you incur them to acquire an asset (a business) that will benefit you for more than one year. Normally, you can't deduct these types of capital expenses until you sell or otherwise dispose of the business. However, a special tax rule allows you to deduct up to $5,000 in start-up expenses the first year you are in business, and then deduct the remainder in equal amounts over the next 15 years. (IRC § 195.) Without this special rule for business start-up expenses, these costs (capital expenses) would not be deductible until you sold or otherwise disposed of your practice.

Once your practice begins, the same expenses that were start-up expenses before it began become currently deductible business operating expenses. For example, rent you pay for office space *after* your practice starts is a currently deductible operating expense, but rent you pay *before* your practice begins is a start-up expense.

> EXAMPLE: Diana graduates from law school, passes the bar exam, and decides to open up her own law office. Before opening for business in June, Diana incurs various expenses, including travel expenses to obtain office space, office rent and utilities, lease expenses for office furniture and computer equipment, and advertising expenses. She spends $20,000 of her life savings to get her law practice up and running. These are all start-up expenses, so she can deduct up to $5,000 the first year she is in business and the remainder in equal amounts over the next 15 years. (IRC § 195.)

Starting a New Practice

Most of the money you spend investigating whether, where, and how to start a new practice, as well as the cost of actually creating it, are deductible business start-up expenses. The tax law is much more generous with deductions for start-up costs if you are creating a new practice than if you are buying an existing practice.

Common Start-Up Expenses

Here are some common types of deductible start-up expenses:
- the cost of investigating what it will take to create a successful practice, including market research
- advertising costs, including advertising for your practice's opening
- costs for employee training before the practice begins
- travel expenses related to finding a suitable business location
- expenses related to obtaining financing, suppliers, and clients
- business licenses, permits, and other fees
- fees paid to lawyers, accountants, consultants, and others for professional services, and
- operating expenses incurred before the practice begins, such as rent, telephone, utilities, office supplies, and repairs.

Costs That Are Not Start-Up Expenses

There are some costs related to opening a business that are not considered start-up expenses. Many of these costs are still deductible, but different rules and restrictions apply to the way they are deducted.

Only Business Operating Expenses Qualify

You can deduct as start-up expenses only those costs that would be currently deductible as business operating expenses after your practice begins. This means the expenses must be ordinary, necessary, directly related to the business, and reasonable in amount. (See Chapter 3 for a discussion of business operating expenses.) For example, you can't deduct the cost of pleasure travel or entertainment *unrelated* to your practice. These expenses would not be deductible as operating expenses by an ongoing business, so you can't deduct them as start-up expenses either. (In fact, you can't deduct them at all.)

Inventory

Some professionals—for example, optometrists, veterinarians, and pharmacists—incur substantial costs for inventory before they start their practice. An optometrist starting a new practice would have to buy an inventory of eyeglass frames and lenses to provide to patients. The cost of purchasing this inventory is not treated as a start-up expense. Instead, you deduct inventory costs as you sell the inventory. (See Chapter 12 for more on deducting inventory costs.)

Long-Term Assets

Long-term assets are things you purchase for your practice that will last for more than one year, such as computers, office equipment, cars, and machinery. Long-term assets you buy before your practice begins are not considered part of your start-up costs. Instead, you treat these purchases like any other long-term asset you buy *after* your practice begins—you must either depreciate the item over several years or deduct the cost in one year under IRS Section 179. (Chapter 9 explains how to deduct long-term assets.) However, you can't take depreciation or Section 179 deductions until after your business begins.

Research and Development Costs

The tax law includes a special category for research and development expenses. These are costs a business incurs to discover something new (in the laboratory or experimental sense), such as a new invention, formula, prototype, or process. They include laboratory and computer supplies, salaries, rent, utilities, other overhead expenses, and equipment rental, but not the purchase of long-term assets. Research and development costs are currently deductible under Section 174 of the Internal Revenue Code, even if you incur them before the business begins operations.

Taxes and Interest

Any tax and interest that you pay before your practice begins is not a start-up expense. Instead, these costs are currently deductible as business operating expenses once your business begins. There are a few exceptions to this rule. Sales tax you pay for long-term assets for your practice is added to the cost of the asset for purposes of depreciation or Section 179 deduction. (See Chapter 9.) And money you borrow to buy an interest in an S corporation, a partnership, or an LLC must be allocated among the company's assets. Interest on money you borrow to buy stock in a C corporation is treated as investment interest and may be currently deducted as a personal itemized deduction. (See Chapter 13.)

Organizational Costs

Costs you incur to form a partnership, limited liability company, or corporation are not part of your start-up costs. However, they are deductible in the same amounts as start-up expenses under a separate tax rule.

You cannot deduct education expenses you incur to qualify for a new business or profession. For example, courts have held that IRS agents could not deduct the cost of going to law school, because a law degree would qualify them for a new business—being a lawyer. (*Jeffrey L. Weiler*, 54 T.C. 398 (1970).) (See Chapter 13.)

You also can't deduct fees you must pay to become accredited to initially practice a profession. For example, you may not deduct:

- bar exam fees and other expenses paid to obtain admission to the bar
- medical and dental license fees paid to get initial licensing, or
- accounting certificate fees paid for the initial right to practice accounting.

However, after you begin practicing your profession, you may currently deduct your annual licensing fees as an operating expense—for example, lawyers may deduct their annual bar association dues.

Buying an Existing Practice

Different rules apply if you buy an existing practice rather than create a new one. If you are buying a practice, you can deduct as start-up expenses only the costs you incur to decide *whether* to purchase a practice and *which* practice you should buy.

You don't have to make an offer, sign a letter of intent, or enter into a binding legal agreement to purchase an existing practice for your expenses to cease being start-up expenses. You just have to make up your mind to purchase a specific practice and focus on acquiring it. (Rev. Rul. 1999-23.)

> **EXAMPLE:** Sean, a dentist who works as an employee for a successful dental corporation, wants to purchase his own existing dental practice. He hires Duane, a professional practice broker, to help him. Duane evaluates several dental practices for sale, including the Acme DentalWorks. Sean decides he would like to buy Acme and hires accountant Al to conduct an in-depth review of its books and records to determine a fair acquisition price. Sean then enters into an acquisition agreement with Acme to purchase all its assets. The fees Sean paid to Duane are start-up expenses because they were paid to help Sean determine whether to purchase an existing business and which business to buy. The fees Sean paid to Al are not start-up expenses because they were incurred to help Sean purchase a specific existing business—the Acme DentalWorks.

The money you pay to actually purchase an existing practice is neither a start-up expense nor a currently deductible business operating expense. Instead, it is a capital expense. If you purchase an incorporated practice by buying its stock, or buy a professional LLC, LLP, or partnership by purchasing the LLC or partnership interests, the cost becomes part of the tax basis of your stock or LLC or partnership interest. If and when you sell your stock or LLC or partnership interest, you will be able to deduct this amount from any profit you make on the sale before taxes are assessed. If, instead of buying the legal entity that owns a practice, you simply purchase its individual assets, you may depreciate the cost of tangible assets and amortize the cost of any intangible assets you purchase. (See Chapter 9.)

Expanding an Existing Practice

What if you already have an existing practice and decide to expand it? The cost of expanding an existing practice is considered a business operating expense, not a start-up expense. As long as these costs are ordinary and necessary, they are currently deductible.

> EXAMPLE: Sam, a highly successful sole practitioner dentist, decides to expand his practice. He rents larger office space in a new location and hires three new employees. The costs of renting and moving to the new office and training the new employees are currently deductible as ordinary and necessary operating expenses.

However, this rule applies only when the expansion involves a business that is the same as—or similar to—the existing business. The costs of expanding into a new business are start-up costs, not operating expenses.

> EXAMPLE: Assume that Sam, an avid golfer, decides to start a business to manufacture and sell a new type of golf putter he has invented. This business is unrelated to his dental practice. Therefore, the ordinary and necessary expenses he incurs before the business begins are start-up costs.

In addition, even though you perform the same services, you are not expanding an existing business when you create a new business entity for your practice.

> EXAMPLE: Art and Nicole, associates at a large law firm, decide to go out on their own and start their own law practice. They form an LLP, with themselves as the partners. Although Art and Nicole are performing the same legal services as they were when they were associates, the new law firm is a new business for tax purposes, not an expansion of an existing business. Thus, Art and Nicole's start-up costs would not be currently deductible operating expenses.

When Does a Professional Practice Begin?

The date when your practice begins for tax purposes marks an important turning point. Operating expenses you incur once your practice starts are currently deductible, while expenses you incur before this crucial date may have to be deducted over many years.

The general rule is that a new business begins for tax purposes when it starts to function as a going concern and performs the activities for which it was organized. (*Richmond Television Corp. v. U.S.*, 345 F.2d 901 (4th Cir. 1965).) The IRS says that a venture becomes a going concern when it acquires all of the assets necessary to perform its intended functions and puts those assets to work. In other words, your practice begins when you start doing business, whether or not you are actually earning any money.

Applying this rule, a professional practice begins when you first offer your services to the public. No one has to hire you; you just have to be available for hire by clients or patients. For example, a dentist's practice begins when he or she opens a dental office and is ready to perform dental work on patients.

If you purchase an existing practice, your practice begins when the purchase is completed—that is, when you take over ownership.

How to Deduct Start-Up Expenses

You can deduct $5,000 in start-up expenses the first year you're in business. Any expenses you have in excess of the first-year limit you'll have to deduct in equal amounts over the first 180 months (15 years) you're in business. This process is called amortization. One hundred and eighty months is the minimum amortization period; you can choose a longer period if you wish (almost no one does).

If you have more than $50,000 in start-up expenses, you are not entitled to the full first-year deduction. You must reduce your deduction by the amount that your start-up expenditures exceed the $50,000 annual threshold amount. For example, if you have $53,000 in start-up expenses, you may deduct only $2,000 the first year, instead of $5,000. If you have $55,000 or more in start-up expenses, you get no current deduction for start-up expenses. Instead, the whole amount must be deducted over 180 months.

In the past, you had to attach a separate written statement to your return electing to claim start-up expenses as a current deduction. However, this is no longer required. Instead, you are automatically deemed to have made the election for the year in which your business began. All you need do is list your start-up costs as "Other expenses" on your Schedule C (or another appropriate return if you are not a sole proprietor or a one-person LLC taxed as a sole proprietorship). You need not specifically identify the deducted amounts as start-up expenditures for the election to be effective.

However, if you have more than $5,000 in start-up expenses, you must amortize (deduct) the excess over 180 months. To do so, you must complete and attach IRS Form 4562 to your return for the first tax year you are in business.

If you don't want to currently deduct your first year of start-up expenses, you may choose to forgo the deemed election by clearly electing to capitalize your start-up on your federal income tax return for the tax year in which your business began. Your tax return must be timely filed (including any extensions). This election is irrevocable and your start-up costs become part of the tax basis of your business.

Who Gets Start-Up Deductions

If, like many professionals, you're a sole proprietor (or have a one-person LLC taxed as a sole proprietorship), you'll deduct your start-up expenses on your Schedule C along with your other business expenses. It makes no practical difference if you use personal funds or money from a separate business account for start-up expenses.

Things are different if you have a corporation, a partnership, an LLP, or an LLC. Deductions for start-up expenses belong to the business entity, not to you personally. If you pay for them out of your personal funds, you should seek reimbursement from the entity. (See Chapter 16 for a detailed discussion.)

Keep Good Expense Records

Whether you intend to start a new practice or buy an existing one, you should keep careful track of every expense you incur before the business begins. Obviously, you should keep receipts and canceled checks. You should also keep evidence that will help show that the money went to investigate a new business—for example, correspondence and emails with accountants, attorneys, business brokers, and consultants; marketing or financial reports; and copies of advertisements. You will need these records to calculate your deductions and to prove your expenses to the IRS if you face an audit.

If Your Practice Doesn't Last 15 Years

Not all professional practices last for 15 years. If your start-up expenses exceeded the $5,000 first-year limit, you don't lose the value of your deductions if you sell or close your practice before you have had a chance to deduct all of your start-up expenses. You can deduct any leftover start-up expenses as ordinary business losses. (IRC § 195(b)(2).) This means that you may be able to deduct them from any income you have that year, deduct them in future years, or deduct them from previous years' taxes.

If you sell your practice or its assets, your leftover start-up costs will be added to your tax basis in the business. This is just as good as getting a tax deduction. If you sell your practice at a profit, the remaining start-up costs will be subtracted from your profits before taxes are assessed, which reduces your taxable gain. If you sell at a loss, the start-up costs will be added to the money you lost—because this shortfall is deductible, a larger loss means lower taxes.

Organizational Expenses

Many professionals form business entities, such as corporations, partnerships, LLPs, or limited liability companies. (See Chapter 2 for a discussion of different possible business structures.) The costs of forming an entity to run your practice are deductible. These organizational expenses are not considered start-up expenses, although they are deducted in much the same way.

If you form a corporation, you can deduct the cost of creating the corporation, including legal fees for drafting articles of incorporation, bylaws, minutes of organizational meetings and other organizational documents, and accounting fees for setting up the corporation and its books. You can also deduct state incorporation fees and other filing fees. However, you may not deduct the cost of transferring assets to the corporation or fees associated with issuing stock or securities—for example, commissions and printing costs. These are capital expenses.

If you form a partnership or an LLC with two or more members, you may deduct the cost of negotiating and drafting the partnership or LLC agreement, accounting services to organize the partnership, and LLC filing fees.

Organizational expenses are deducted in the same way as start-up costs. You may deduct the first $5,000 the first year you are in business, and any excess over the first 180 months. Again, your first-year deduction is reduced by the amount by which your organizational expenditures exceed $50,000. You must file IRS Form 4562, *Depreciation and Amortization,* with your tax return.

CAUTION

If you form a single-member LLC, don't spend more than $5,000 in organizational expenses. Because single-member LLCs are considered "disregarded entities" for tax purposes, the IRS doesn't allow these entities to deduct organizational expenses over $5,000. Instead any expenses over that amount must be capitalized, which means they would not be deductible until the LLC is dissolved. (Treasury Regs. Secs. 1.263(a)-5(d)(1) and (3).) So, if you're forming a single-member LLC, it's best to avoid spending over $5,000 in organizational expenses, which generally should not pose a problem.

Medical Expenses

Obtaining affordable health care insurance is one of the greatest challenges facing all small business owners, including professionals. Affordable coverage has been particularly difficult to obtain for those with preexisting medical conditions.

This chapter explains how the Affordable Care Act (Obamacare) affects small business owners, and the array of tax deductions and strategies available to them to help lower their health care costs.

> CAUTION
> **Check the Nolo update webpage for changes to the tax, health care, and other laws.** There have been proposed changes to health care, tax, and other laws that could affect information covered here. If there are any significant changes due to laws enacted after the publication of this book, we will post updates online at **www.nolo.com/back-of-book/DEPO.html**. You can check this page to make sure you have the most current information.

The Affordable Care Act (Obamacare)

The Patient Protection and Affordable Care Act enacted by Congress in 2010 (commonly referred to as Obamacare) took effect in 2014. Obamacare affects all businesses, no matter how large or small. However, it is particularly significant for self-employed professionals—particularly those who have had trouble obtaining affordable health insurance.

Obamacare includes the following five changes to our health care system:

- Every person is required to have at least minimal health insurance coverage or pay a tax penalty.
- Employers with a certain minimum number of employees are required to provide health insurance to their employees or pay penalties (the "employer mandate").
- Health insurers cannot deny coverage due to preexisting conditions or base insurance rates on health status.
- Self-employed people and small businesses can purchase health insurance through state health insurance exchanges.
- Moderate- and low-income individuals may qualify for tax credits to help pay for their health insurance.

RESOURCE

For more information on the all aspects of Obamacare, see www.healthcare.gov.

Health Insurance Mandate

One of the most significant changes created by Obamacare is the health insurance mandate: the requirement that, subject to certain exceptions, all Americans have at least minimal comprehensive health insurance coverage or pay a penalty to the IRS. Before 2014, there was no federal law requiring individuals to have any health coverage. The health insurance mandate applies to self-employed professionals as well as everybody else. This is true whether you're a sole proprietor, a partner in a partnership or limited liability company, or an employee of your own professional corporation.

If you're covered by any of the following, you're considered covered and don't have to pay a penalty:

- any plan you obtain through your state health exchange
- any individual insurance plan you obtain from any source that meets Obamacare's health insurance requirements
- any plan you had before March 2010 that was grandfathered in without meeting all of the Obamacare requirements
- any employer plan (including COBRA), with or without grandfathered status (including retiree plans), or
- Medicare.

Exemptions From the Mandate

Several groups of people are exempt from the mandate. The most significant exemptions are based on income: Anyone who would have to pay over 8% of his or her household income to obtain the minimal coverage required by law is exempt. (To determine your out-of-pocket costs, you must subtract the amount of any premium credits you qualify for from the total premiums.)

Tax Penalty for Noncompliance

If you're not exempt from the health insurance mandate you must pay a fee if you, your spouse, or your dependents don't have health insurance. This fee is officially called the individual shared responsibility payment (but is sometimes called the penalty, fine, or individual mandate). This is the only punishment for those who flout the mandate. There are no criminal or other penalties for noncompliance.

The exact amount of the penalty is based on household income and is prorated based on the number of months during the year that you're uninsured. However, you will not be subject to the penalty if you're uninsured for less than three months in a given year.

For 2017, the penalty is the higher of $695 per person ($347.50 per child) or 2.5% of household income (household income only includes the portion of income above the yearly tax filing threshold—$10,350 for individuals, $20,700 for couples filing jointly in 2017). The penalty cannot exceed the average cost for a bronze level health plan available through the Marketplace.

For more details on calculating the penalty, visit the IRS Individual Shared Responsibility Provision – Reporting and Calculating the Payment webpage at www.irs.gov/affordable-care-act/individuals-and-families/aca-individual-shared-responsibility-provision-calculating-the-payment.

The penalty tax is paid annually on IRS Form 1040.

The penalty is enforced by the IRS and is assessed as a federal tax liability that you're supposed to pay when you file your tax return. However, the only power the IRS has to collect the penalty from people who don't pay it is to withhold it from their tax refunds, if any. The IRS cannot file a lien on your property or levy against your assets to collect the penalty; it is not even allowed to charge interest on the unpaid balance of the penalty.

The Employer Mandate

Starting January 1, 2016, businesses with at least 50 full-time employees (or a combination of full-time and part-time employees that's "equivalent" to at least 100 full-time employees) had to provide at least 95% of their employees and their families with "minimum essential health care coverage," or pay a tax penalty. Employers who provide no coverage at all must pay a penalty to the IRS equal to $2,000 per employee minus 30 employees. The penalty is smaller for employers who provide coverage that doesn't meet the minimum standards. Employees can be required to help contribute toward their coverage, but the amount of any employee contribution is capped at 9.5% of household income.

For detailed guidance on how to determine whether your business has more than 50 full-time employees for Obamacare purposes, visit the IRS ACA Information Center for Applicable Large Employers (ALEs) at www.irs.gov/affordable-care-act/employers/aca-information-center-for-applicable-large-employers-ales.

Smaller employers—those with fewer than 50 full-time equivalent employees—are not subject to the pay-or-play rules. However, if they do elect to provide their employees with health coverage, they may qualify for tax credits. (See "Tax Credits for Employee Health Insurance," below.) Moreover, smaller employers will be able to purchase coverage through state small business health insurance exchanges (also called "SHOP exchanges").

Obamacare Health Insurance Rules

To help everyone obtain coverage, Obamacare imposed some revolutionary reforms on all health insurers and the coverage they provide.

No preexisting condition exclusions. First, health insurers are not allowed to use your health status to deny you coverage. This means you are able to purchase health insurance regardless of any current or past health conditions. This requirement only applies during health insurers' open-enrollment periods.

Insurance premium rates. Insurers may vary their premiums based on the following factors only: your age (older people may be charged up to 300% more than the young), tobacco use, geography, and the number of family members covered. They may not charge you more based on your health status.

Minimal comprehensive coverage. All health insurers must offer comprehensive health insurance that provides at least the following ten essential health benefits:

- ambulatory ("walk-in") patient services
- emergency services
- hospitalization
- maternity/newborn care
- mental health and substance use disorder services (including behavioral health treatment)
- prescription drugs
- rehab and habilitative services/devices
- lab services
- preventive/wellness services and chronic disease management, and
- pediatric services (including oral and vision care).

No rescission. Your insurer can't cancel your insurance if you get sick.

No dollar caps. Health insurers cannot impose lifetime or annual dollar limits on their coverage. This means that no matter how much your health care costs, your insurer must pay for it all once you've paid your total annual out-of-pocket limit.

State Health Insurance Exchanges

Online health insurance exchanges (also called marketplaces) have been established to help individuals and small businesses obtain health coverage. These exchanges are not health insurance companies. Rather, they are a competitive marketplace set up by the government through which private insurers offer insurance to the public. Twenty-three states have established their own online health care exchanges that they run themselves. The other states use the federal government's insurance exchange at www.healthcare.gov. The states and federal government have also established call centers for those who prefer to obtain information from a person over the phone.

You aren't required to obtain your health insurance through your state's exchange. You can obtain it on your own or through an insurance broker. You may have more choices if you shop outside your state's exchange, but you'll probably have to pay more. Moreover, you must obtain your insurance through a state exchange to qualify for health insurance premium credits.

The health insurance plans offered though state exchanges are standardized to enable consumers to better compare their costs. The four levels of coverage available—each of which covers a specified percentage of an individual enrollee's covered benefits—are:

- bronze, which covers 60% of covered benefits
- silver, which covers 70% of covered benefits
- gold, which covers 80% of covered benefits, and
- platinum, which covers 90% of covered benefits.

The law also requires that plans cap the maximum annual out-of-pocket costs for enrollees, based on the out-of-pocket limits in high-deductible plans that are eligible to be paired with Health Savings Accounts. These limits for 2017 are $6,550 for individuals and $13,100 for families.

Thus, for example, a single person with a silver plan that covers 70% of expenses will pay 30% of covered expenses out of his or her own pocket through some combination of deductibles, co-pays, and coinsurance, up to a maximum of no more than $6,550 per year.

In addition, people under 30 and some people with limited incomes are able to buy catastrophic health plans. These are low-cost plans with large deductibles and are intended to protect you from very high medical costs in case you have a serious medical problem.

Open Enrollment Periods

Under the Obamacare rules, unless you have a qualifying life event as described below, individual nongroup coverage for yourself and your dependents can be obtained only if you apply during the annual open enrollment period. This is so whether you obtain coverage from your state health insurance exchange or directly from a private health insurer. The open enrollment period for 2017 closed on January 31, 2017. The open enrollment period for 2018 coverage is November 1, 2017 to December 15, 2017.

Qualifying Life Events

After the open enrollment period ends, individual nongroup health insurance coverage will be available for purchase only for individuals who have a qualifying life event during the year. These include:

- losing your existing health insurance coverage—for example, because you quit your job, were laid off, or your work hours were reduced below the level required for you to qualify for employer-provided coverage
- getting married, divorced, or legally separated
- giving birth to or adopting a child
- losing your coverage because you moved to another state or a part of the same state outside of your health plan service area
- losing your eligibility to receive coverage as someone else's dependent—for example, you turn 26 and are no longer eligible for coverage through your parents' plan
- being timely enrolled in coverage through your state exchange, and your income increases or decreases enough to change your eligibility for subsidies, or
- becoming a U.S. citizen.

Once a qualifying life event occurs, you have 60 days to obtain individual coverage, either through your state health insurance exchange or private insurers. This period is called your special enrollment opportunity.

Note carefully that the following are not qualifying life events:

- getting sick
- getting pregnant
- losing your coverage because you didn't pay your premiums, or
- voluntarily quitting your existing health coverage.

Thus, for example, you can't go without coverage past the open enrollment deadline and then decide you want to enroll because you get sick (or get pregnant; but after you have a child you can obtain coverage).

Health Insurance Premium Assistance Credits

Health insurance is available through the state exchanges to everyone who can't get affordable coverage elsewhere.

To help moderate- and low-income people afford this coverage, a premium assistance credit will be provided for those who purchase health insurance from a state exchange. The purpose of the credits is to ensure that moderate- and lower-income people don't have to spend more than a specified percentage of their household income on health insurance. You'll be eligible for premium credits if you meet the following requirements:

- Your household income is between 100% and 400% of the federal poverty level (FPL).
- You are not eligible for other affordable coverage.
- You file a joint tax return if you're married.

Based on the 2017 FPL, the credit would be available for individuals with household incomes below $48,240 and families of four with incomes below $98,400. Not very many professionals earn such small incomes.

The Personal Deduction for Medical Expenses

All taxpayers—whether or not they own businesses—are entitled to personal income tax deductions for medical and dental expenses for themselves and their dependents. Eligible expenses include both health insurance premiums and out-of-pocket expenses not covered by insurance. However, there are two significant limitations on the deduction, which make it virtually useless (unusable) for most taxpayers.

In order to take the personal deduction, you must comply with both of the following requirements:

- You must itemize your deductions on IRS Schedule A. (You can itemize deductions only if all of your itemized deductions exceed the standard deduction for the year—$12,700 for joint returns and $6,350 for single returns in 2017.)
- If you're under age 65, you can deduct only the amount of your medical and dental expenses that is more than 10% of your adjusted

gross income (AGI). (Your AGI is your net business income and other taxable income, minus deductions for retirement contributions and one-half of your self-employment taxes, plus a few other items (as shown at the bottom of your Form 1040).)

EXAMPLE: Al is a self-employed accountant whose adjusted gross income for 2017 is $100,000. He pays $1,000 per month for health insurance for himself and his wife. He spends another $2,200 in out-of-pocket medical and dental expenses for the year. Al may deduct his medical expenses using the personal deduction only if all of his itemized deductions exceed the $12,600 standard deduction for the year. If they do exceed the standard deduction, his personal medical expense deduction is limited to the amount he paid that's more than $10,000 (10% × $100,000 = $10,000). Because he paid a total of $14,200 in medical expenses for the year, his personal deduction is limited to $4,200 ($14,200 − $10,000).

As you can see, unless your medical expenses are substantial, the 10% limitation eats up most or all of your personal deduction. The more money you make, the less you can deduct. For this reason, professionals need to look elsewhere for meaningful medical expense deductions.

Self-Employed Health Insurance Deduction

There is another health expense deduction that is more useful to professionals than the personal deduction: the self-employment health insurance income tax deduction. It allows self-employed people to deduct health insurance premiums (including dental and long-term care coverage) for themselves, their spouses, and their dependents. Self-employed people who have Medicare coverage may deduct their Medicare premiums as part of the self-employed health insurance deduction—this includes all Medicare parts (not just Part B).

In addition, this insurance can cover their children up to age 26, whether or not they are dependents. For these purposes, a child includes a son, daughter, stepchild, adopted child, or eligible foster child.

Self-Employment Tax Primer

Self-employment taxes consist of a 12.4% Social Security tax on income up to an annual ceiling. In 2017, the annual Social Security ceiling was $127,200. Medicare taxes are not subject to any income ceiling and are levied at a 2.9% rate up to an annual ceiling ($200,000 for single taxpayers or $250,000 for married filing jointly), and a 3.8% tax on amounts over those ceilings. This combines to a total 15.3% tax on employment or self-employment income up to the Social Security tax ceiling. If you earn more than the ceiling, being able to deduct your health insurance costs from your self-employment income will not give you a very significant tax savings, because you would have had to pay only a 2.9% or 3.8% tax on that income.

Professionals who are sole proprietors, partners in partnerships, LLC members, or S corporation shareholders who own more than 2% of the company stock can use this deduction. Basically, any business owner, other than a shareholder-employee of a regular C corporation, can take this deduction. It's important to understand, however, that this is not a business deduction. It is a special personal deduction for the self-employed. The deduction applies to your federal, state, and local income taxes, but not to self-employment taxes (Social Security and Medicare taxes).

> EXAMPLE: Kim is a sole proprietor lawyer who pays $10,000 each year for health insurance for herself, her husband, and her three children. Her practice earned a $100,000 profit for the year. She may deduct her $10,000 annual health insurance expense from her gross income for federal and state income tax purposes. Her combined federal and state income tax rate is 35%, so she saves $3,500 in income taxes (35% × $10,000 = $3,500). She may not deduct her premiums from her income when she figures her self-employment taxes—in other words, she must pay the 15.3% self-employment tax on her full $100,000 business profit.

You get the deduction whether you purchase your health insurance policy as an individual or have your practice obtain it. If your practice obtains health insurance for you, it will add the amount of the premiums to your compensation (see "Deducting Health Insurance as an Employee Fringe Benefit," below).

Business Income Limitation

There is a significant limitation on the health insurance deduction for the self-employed: You may deduct only as much as you earn from your practice. If your practice earns no money or incurs a loss, you get no deduction. Thus, for example, if Kim from the above example earned only $3,000 in profit from her practice, her self-employed health insurance deduction would be limited to that amount; she wouldn't be able to deduct the remaining $7,000 in premiums she paid for the year.

If your practice is organized as an S corporation, your deduction is limited to the amount of wages you are paid by your corporation.

If you have more than one business, you cannot combine the income from all your businesses for purposes of the income limit. You may only use the income from a single business you designate to be the health insurance plan sponsor.

Designating Your Plan Sponsor

If you purchase your health insurance plan in the name of one of your businesses, that business will be the sponsor. However, the IRS says you may purchase your health coverage in your own name and still get the self-employed health insurance deduction. (IRC Chief Counsel Memo 200524001.) This may be advantageous, because it allows you to pick which of your businesses will be the sponsor at the start of each year. Obviously, you should pick the business you think will earn the most money that year.

Moreover, if you have more than one business, you can have one purchase medical insurance and the other purchase dental insurance and deduct 100% of the premiums for each policy subject to the income limits discussed above. This will be helpful if no single business earns enough income for you to deduct both policies through it.

> **EXAMPLE:** Robert is a sole proprietor medical doctor who has a sideline business running a medical lab. He purchases a medical insurance policy for himself and his family with his medical practice as the sponsor. He also purchases a dental insurance plan with his lab business as the sponsor. He may deduct 100% of the premiums for each policy, subject to the income limits.

No Other Health Insurance Coverage

You may not take the self-employed health insurance deduction if you are eligible to participate in a health insurance plan maintained by your employer or your spouse's employer. This rule applies separately to plans that provide long-term care insurance and those that do not. Thus, for example, if your spouse has employer-provided health insurance that does not include long-term care, you may purchase your own long-term care policy and deduct the premiums.

Tax Reporting

Because the self-employed health insurance deduction is a personal deduction, you take this deduction directly on your Form 1040 (it does not go on your Schedule C if you're a sole proprietor). If you itemize your deductions and do not claim 100% of your self-employed health insurance costs on your Form 1040, you may include the rest with all other medical expenses on Schedule A, subject to the 10% limit (until 2017, the threshold is 7.5% for taxpayers over age 65). You would have to do this, for example, if your health insurance premiums exceeded your business income.

Caution: IRS Restrictions on Reimbursing Employee Health Insurance Costs

For many years, small employers who did not want to deal with the hassle and expense of purchasing companywide group health insurance coverage for their employees had another way to indirectly cover the cost for their employees. Employers could have employees purchase their own individual health insurance coverage and then they would reimburse them for all or part of the cost, or they could pay the premiums directly on their behalf. These payments were considered a tax-free employee fringe benefit.

Starting July 1, 2015, a new rule went into effect that put an end to this practice. Employers are no longer allowed to tell their employees to obtain their own individual coverage and then reimburse them for the cost, even if the payments are included in the employees' taxable income. Employers who violate this rule will be subject to a fine of $100 per day per employee—up to $36,500 per employee per year. (IRS Notice 2015-17.)

The IRS, Department of Labor, and Department of Health and Human Services now want all employers to provide their employees with group health insurance either through the Obamacare SHOP exchanges (see health-care.gov for details) or directly through health insurance companies. In their view, individual policies employees obtain themselves do not fully comply with Obamacare's requirements. The only other alternative for small employers is to choose not to provide health coverage at all. Employers with fewer than 50 full-time equivalent employees are not required by Obamacare to provide any health care insurance for their employees; it is purely voluntary.

There are some important exceptions to this nonreimbursement rule. First, it does not apply if a business has only one employee, which can include your spouse. Reimbursement for a sole employee's individual policy—which can cover the single employee's entire family—is still permitted. Nor does the rule apply if you operate your business as an S corporation and the corporation treats its health insurance payment or reimbursement as taxable compensation to you, the owner. In this event, if you otherwise qualify, you may claim the self-employed personal income tax deduction for health insurance. This rule only applies to 2% or more shareholders in an S corporation, not S corporation employees. Moreover, the IRS may change the rule.

> ## Caution: IRS Restrictions on Reimbursing Employee Health Insurance Costs (continued)
>
> Employers with fewer than 50 full-time employees may establish a special type of health reimbursement arrangement called a Qualified Small Employer Health Reimbursement Arrangement (QSEHRA) for employees who obtain their own health coverage. However, there are numerous restrictions on such QSWHRAs (see "HRAs for Businesses With Multiple Employees" below).
>
> If you have multiple employees and want to help them pay for health insurance without obtaining group coverage for them, you can always increase their wages which will, of course, help them purchase their own coverage. But you cannot condition the raise on your employees actually obtaining health coverage or even tell them that the reason for the raise is to help cover health insurance. And the increase in pay will be fully taxable—it won't qualify as a tax-free fringe benefit.

Deducting Health Insurance as an Employee Fringe Benefit

You can deduct health insurance costs as a currently deductible business expense if your business pays them on behalf of an employee. The benefit to treating these costs as a business expense is that you can deduct them from your business income for tax purposes. The premiums are an employee fringe benefit and are not taxable income for the employee. Unfortunately, if (like many professionals) you are a sole proprietor, a partner in a partnership, or an LLC member or S corporation shareholder with more than 2% of the company stock, you can't deduct these costs as a business expense because you cannot be an employee of your own business for these purposes.

Deducting Health Insurance Costs Paid on Behalf of Employees

For 2016 and later, all businesses with 50 or more full-time equivalent employees are required to provide health insurance to their full-time employees or pay a penalty to the IRS. In addition, the tax code encourages businesses to provide health insurance by allowing the insurance costs paid for employees, their spouses, and dependents to be deducted as a business expense. The premiums are an employee fringe benefit and are not taxable income for the employee.

> **EXAMPLE:** Mona, a sole proprietor optometrist, hires Milt to work as an employee in her practice. She pays $400 per month to provide Milt with health insurance. The payments are a business expense that she can deduct from her business income. Milt need not count the value of the insurance as income or pay any tax on it. Mona deducts her $4,800 annual payments for Milt's insurance from her business income for both income tax and self-employment tax purposes.

If, like most professionals, you don't have 50 or more employees, you have great flexibility on how you provide health insurance benefits to your employees. For example, you can:

- contribute to a group health insurance policy to cover your employees
- contribute to group health insurance and also offer your employees an FSA (flexible spending arrangement) in which employees set aside a portion of their pretax earnings to pay for health expenses not covered by insurance; you the employer may make FSA contributions as well, or
- not buy group health insurance and instead contribute to the Health Savings Accounts (HSAs) for eligible employees (see "Health Savings Accounts" below).

If you have multiple employees and want to contribute to their health insurance, you must obtain group health insurance coverage for them. Under Obamacare rules that took effect in 2014, you cannot have each employee purchase his or her own policy and reimburse all or part of the cost. When you obtain group coverage, you don't have to pay all of the cost—your employees can be required to contribute as well. However, you should expect to pay at least 50% of the cost of your employees' premiums.

Unlike the case with most employee fringe benefits, health insurance can be provided on a discriminatory basis, as long as you don't discriminate based on health factors, such as an employee's medical history. (IRC § 9802.) Thus, you can give some employees better coverage than others, provided the selection criteria have nothing to do with health factors. For example, you could provide key employees with better health coverage than less vital employees. However, starting in 2020, a 40% excise tax is scheduled to be imposed on "Cadillac" health plans offered by employers to their employees. These are plans whose value exceeds a threshold amount. For employee self-only coverage, the threshold will be $10,200 plus an adjustment for inflation in the cost of health care. For family coverage, the threshold will be $27,500 plus inflation adjustments. The 40% tax will be imposed on the amount the employee's coverage exceeds the limits.

Sole Proprietors, LLCs, S Corporations, Partnerships, and LLPs

If (like the majority of professionals) you are a sole proprietor, a partner in a partnership, or an LLC member, LLP partner, or S corporation shareholder with over 2% of the company stock, you cannot be an employee of your own practice for health insurance purposes. If your partnership, LLC, LLP, or S corporation buys health insurance on your behalf, it may deduct the cost as a business expense, but it must also add the amount to your taxable income.

If your practice is organized as a partnership, an LLC, or an LLP, the premiums are ordinarily treated as a guaranteed payment. The practice lists the payment on the Schedule K-1 it provides the IRS and you showing your income from the practice. You'll then have to pay income and self-employment tax on the amount.

You can still take the self-employed health insurance tax deduction discussed above in "Self-Employed Health Insurance Deduction," which will effectively wipe out the extra income tax you had to pay. But this is a personal deduction, not a business deduction, and thus does not reduce your business income for self-employment tax purposes.

> **EXAMPLE:** Jim is a co-owner of a five-lawyer law firm organized as an LLC. The firm spends $10,000 for health insurance for Jim. It treats the money as a guaranteed payment and lists it as income to Jim on the K-1 form it provides the IRS. The LLC gets to deduct the payment as a business expense. Although Jim must pay tax on the $10,000, he may deduct the $10,000 from his income tax as a personal deduction using the self-employed health insurance deduction. The net result is that Jim pays self-employment tax only on the $10,000. The same result would have been achieved if Jim had purchased his health insurance himself.

Partnerships, LLCs, and LLPs can avoid having to report health insurance payments as income if they don't take a tax deduction for them. This will have the same tax result and make things simpler.

If your practice is an S corporation, the insurance costs are added to your employee compensation and are deducted as such by the corporation. However, you only have to pay income taxes on that amount, not employment taxes or unemployment tax. Again, if you qualify, you can take the self-employed health insurance deduction and wipe out the extra income tax you had to pay. To qualify for the deduction, your medical insurance must be either: (1) established by your S corporation, in its own name, and paid for with its funds, or (2) purchased in your own name, and your S corporation either directly pays for the health insurance, or reimburses you for it, and includes the premium payments as wages in your IRS Form W-2, *Wage and Tax Statement*. (IRS Notice 2008-1.) You cannot qualify for the deduction if your S corporation neither pays for the insurance directly with its own funds nor reimburses you for your payments.

C Corporations

If your practice is organized as a C corporation, you ordinarily will work as its employee and will be entitled to the full menu of tax-free employee fringe benefits, including health insurance. This means the corporation can purchase health insurance for you, deduct the cost as a business expense, and not have to include the cost in your employee compensation. Your health insurance is completely tax free.

If you want to convert your health insurance premiums to a tax-free fringe benefit and you don't have a C corporation, you must form one to run your practice and work as its employee. You can do this even if you're running a one-person practice.

However, because your health insurance is 100% deductible from your income taxes if you use the self-employed health insurance tax deduction, it may not be worthwhile to incorporate just to save on Social Security and Medicare taxes. This is particularly true if your employee income would substantially exceed the Social Security tax ceiling—$127,200 in 2017—with the result that you'd only save having to pay the 2.9% or 3.8% Medicare tax.

On the other hand, it may be worthwhile to convert to a C corporation if you want to use an HRA. (See "Adopting a Health Reimbursement Arrangement," below.)

Employing Your Spouse

There's another way to make your health insurance costs a completely tax-free employee fringe benefit: Hire your spouse to work in your practice as an employee and provide him or her with health insurance. The insurance should be purchased in the name of the spouse/employee, not in the employer's name. The policy can cover your spouse, you, your children, and other dependents as well. Moreover, this insurance can cover your children up to age 26, whether or not they are your dependents. You (or your practice if it is a business entity) can deduct the cost of the health insurance as a business expense, but your spouse will not have to pay any tax on it (income tax, Social Security, or Medicare tax).

EXAMPLE: Joe is a self-employed consultant. He hires his wife, Martha, to work as his employee assistant. He pays her $25,000 per year and provides her with a health insurance policy covering both of them and their two children. The annual policy premiums are $5,000. Joe may deduct the $5,000 as a business expense for his consulting practice, listing it as an expense on his Schedule C. He gets to deduct the $5,000 not only from his $80,000 income for income tax purposes, but also from his self-employment income.

If you do this and you're self-employed, do *not* take the health insurance deduction for self-employed people discussed in "Self-Employed Health Insurance Deduction," above.

There are a couple of catches to this deduction. First, this method ordinarily doesn't work if you have an S corporation because your spouse is deemed to be a shareholder of the corporation along with you and can't also be a corporate employee. In addition, your spouse must be a bona fide employee. In other words, he or she must do real work in your business, you must pay applicable payroll taxes, and you must otherwise treat your spouse like any other employee. (See Chapter 14 for a detailed discussion.)

You'll probably want to pay your spouse as low a salary as possible, because both of you will have to pay Social Security and Medicare taxes on that salary (but not on employee benefits like health insurance and medical expense reimbursements). You should, however, regularly pay your spouse at least some cash wages, or the IRS could claim your spouse is not a real employee. You can make the cash wages a relatively small part of your spouse's total compensation—wages plus fringe benefits like your HRA.

No matter how you pay your spouse, the total compensation must be reasonable—that is, you can't pay more than your spouse's services are worth. For example, you can't pay your spouse at a rate of $100 per hour for simple clerical work. Total compensation means the sum of the salary, plus all fringe benefits, including health insurance and medical expense reimbursements.

Tax Credits for Employee Health Insurance

If your practice has employees and provides them with health insurance coverage, you may qualify for the Small Business Health Care Tax Credit. The tax credit is available to eligible employers for two consecutive tax years.

This credit is equal to 50% of the premiums small employers pay for their employees' health insurance. For example, if your nonprofit paid $20,000 for employee health insurance in 2017, you'd be entitled to a whopping $10,000 tax refund.

To qualify for the credit, you must:

- have no more than 25 full-time equivalent employees
- pay your employees average annual full-time wages of less than $52,000
- pay at least 50% of the annual premiums for your employees' health insurance, and
- purchase your employees' health insurance through a Small Business Health Options Program (SHOP) Marketplace (these are health insurance exchanges specifically designed for employers with 50 or fewer full-time employees; see www.healthcare.gov/ small-businesses/employers)

If you have questions about the Small Business Health Care Tax Credit, refer to the IRS's website at www.irs.gov/affordable-care-act/employers/ small-business-health-care-tax-credit-and-the-shop-marketplace.

Adopting a Health Reimbursement Arrangement

Health insurance usually doesn't cover all your medical expenses. For example, it doesn't cover deductibles or copayments—that is, amounts you must pay yourself before your insurance coverage kicks in. Many costs aren't covered at all, including fertility treatment and optometric care. As a result, the average American family of four pays about $3,500 a year in out-of-pocket health-related expenses. One way to deduct these expenses is to establish an HRA.

A health reimbursement arrangement (HRA) is an arrangement under which an employer reimburses its employees for health or dental expenses. These plans are usually self funded—that is, the employer pays the expenses out of its own pocket, not through insurance.

Why would an employer do this? One good reason is that the reimbursements are tax-deductible business expenses for the employer. Also, the employee doesn't have to include the reimbursements as taxable income (as long as the employee has not taken a deduction for these amounts as a personal medical expense).

There are two different types of HRAs:

- spouse-only HRAs for businesses with one employee-spouse, and
- Qualified Small Employer Health Reimbursement Arrangements (QSEHRAs) for businesses with multiple employees.

Spousal Health Reimbursement Accounts

Obamacare imposes severe restrictions on the ability of employers to use HRAs. Businesses with more than one employee may establish HRAs only if they comply with the requirements for Qualified Small Employer Health Reimbursement Arrangements (QSEHRAs) discussed below. However, Obamacare does not apply to HRAs established by businesses with only one employee. Thus, if you're married, you can hire your spouse as the sole employee of your business and provide him or her with an HRA that is not subject to the restrictions on QSEHRAs. However, this only works if your spouse is your only employee. The plan may cover not only your spouse, but also you, your children, and other dependents. This allows your business to reimburse your and your family's out-of-pocket medical expenses and deduct the amounts as a business expense. And you need not include the reimbursements in your own taxable income. The IRS has ruled that this is perfectly legal. (Tax Advice Memo 9409006.)

EXAMPLE: Jennifer has her own public relations firm. She hires her husband Paul to work as her part-time employee assistant. She establishes an HRA covering Paul, herself, and their young child. Paul spends $12,000 on medical expenses. Jennifer reimburses Paul for the $12,000 as provided by their plan. Jennifer may deduct the $12,000 from her business income for the year, meaning she pays neither income nor self-employment tax on that amount. Paul need not include the $12,000 in his income—it's tax free to him. The deduction saves Jennifer and Paul $4,000 in taxes for the year.

CAUTION

Your spouse must be a legitimate employee. Your spouse must be a legitimate employee for your HRA to pass muster with the IRS. You can't simply hire your spouse on paper—he or she must do real work in your business. If you can't prove your wife or husband is a legitimate employee, the IRS will disallow your deductions. The IRS will be particularly suspicious if your spouse is your only employee.

Make sure to comply with all the legal requirements for hiring an employee, including providing workers' compensation insurance (required in many states), paying any state unemployment insurance premiums, and paying and withholding income tax. If this is too much trouble or too expensive, forget about establishing an HRA.

Conversely, you also need to make sure that you and your spouse do not end up being partners (co-owners) in the business. Your spouse cannot be your partner and your employee in the same business. You must own the business and your spouse must work under your direction and control. Factors that indicate that your spouse is your partner include joint ownership of business assets, joint sharing of profits, and joint control over business operations.

Again, the HRA deduction is available only to your employees, not to you (the business owner). The only way you can qualify as an employee is if your business is a C corporation. (See "Deducting Health Insurance as an Employee Fringe Benefit," above.) However, if you don't have a spouse to employ, you could employ your child and provide him or her with an HRA. But the plan may not cover you or any other family members.

What Expenses May Be Reimbursed?

One of the great things about HRAs is that they can be used to reimburse employees for a wide variety of health-related expenses. Indeed, deductible medical expenses include any expense for the diagnosis, cure, mitigation, treatment, or prevention of disease, or any expense paid to affect the structure or function of the human body. (IRS Reg. § 1.213.1(e).)

This includes, of course, premiums in health and accident insurance, and health insurance deductibles and co-payments. But it also includes expenses for acupuncture, chiropractors, eyeglasses and contact lenses, dental treatment, laser eye surgery, psychiatric care, and treatment for learning disabilities. It includes prescription medications, but not over-the-counter or nonprescription medications unless you have a prescription. You can draft your plan to include only those expenses you wish to reimburse. Presumably, though, you'd want to include as many expenses as possible if the plan covers only your spouse, yourself, and your family.

How to Establish a Spousal HRA

If a spousal HRA sounds attractive to you, you should act to establish one as early in the year as possible because it applies only to medical expenses incurred after the date the plan is adopted. (Rev. Rul. 2002-58.) Forget about using an HRA to reimburse your spouse or yourself for expenses you have already incurred. If you do, the reimbursement must be added to your spouse's income for tax purposes and you must pay employment tax on it.

A written HRA must be drawn up and adopted by your practice. If your practice is incorporated, the plan should be adopted by a corporate resolution approved by the corporation's board of directors. You can find a form for this purpose in *The Corporate Records Handbook: Meetings, Minutes & Resolutions*, by Anthony Mancuso (Nolo).

Sample Spousal HRA

A sample spousal HRA is provided below.

Health Reimbursement Arrangement

[_Your business name_] ("Employer") and [_employee's name_] ("Employee") enter into this Health Reimbursement Arrangement ("HRA") under which Employer agrees to reimburse Employee for medical expenses incurred by Employee and Employee's spouse and dependents, subject to the conditions and limitations set forth below.

1. Uninsured Expenses
Employer will reimburse eligible Employee and Employee's spouse and dependents only for medical expenses that are not covered by health or accident insurance.

2. Medical Expenses Defined
Medical expenses are those expenses defined by Internal Revenue Code Sec. 213(d).

3. Eligible Employee
This plan is a one-employee plan that does not include group health insurance. All full- and part-time employees of Employer may participate in this plan, but should the plan cover more than one eligible employee, it will be amended to purchase qualified Affordable Care Act "group health coverage" as a plan component.

4. Dependent Defined
Dependent is defined by IRC Sec. 152. It includes any member of an eligible Employee's family for whom the Employee and his or her spouse provide more than half of the financial support.

5. Submission of Claims
To obtain reimbursement under this HRA, Employee shall submit to Employer, at least annually, all bills for medical care, including those for accident or health insurance. Such bills and other claims for reimbursement shall be verified by Employer prior to reimbursement. Employer, in its sole discretion, may terminate Employee's right to reimbursement if the Employee fails to comply.

6. Payments

At its option, Employer may pay the medical expenses directly to the medical provider or by purchasing insurance that pays Employee's expenses. Such a direct payment or provision of such insurance shall relieve Employer of all further liability for the expense.

7. Effective Date; Plan Year

This HRA shall take effect on [_date_] and operates on a calendar year basis thereafter. The HRA year is the same as the tax year of Employer. HRA records shall be kept on a calendar year basis.

8. Benefits Not Taxable

Employer intends that the benefits under this HRA shall qualify under IRC Sec. 105 so as to be excludable from the gross income of the Employees covered by the HRA.

9. Termination

Employer may terminate this HRA at any time. Medical expenses incurred prior to the date of termination shall be reimbursed by Employer. Employer is under no obligation to provide advance notice of termination.

_____   _____

Employer's Signature   Date

_____   _____

Employee's Signature   Date

HRAs for Businesses With Multiple Employees

If your business has more than one employee, you may not establish a spousal HRA. However, starting in 2017, Obamacare's rules were amended to enable small businesses with multiple employees to establish Qualified Small Employer Health Reimbursement Arrangements (QSEHRAs). Unfortunately, there are far more restrictions on these plans than on spousal HRAs. QSEHRAs are intended for smaller businesses that don't provide their employees with group health insurance and whose employees obtain coverage. With a QSEHRA an eligible small business can reimburse an employee's individually purchased health insurance and other deductible medical costs up to $4,950 per year for an individual and up to $10,000 for a family. The cost of the QSEHRA benefit must be entirely covered by the employer.

Which Employers May Offer QSEHRAs?

QSEHRAs may be offered only by employers with fewer than 50 full-time (or full-time equivalent) employees during the prior year and who do not offer a group health plan to any of their employees.

Which Employees May be Covered by QSEHRAs?

Only employees who obtain their own health insurance that meets the minimum requirements of Obamacare (called minimum essential coverage) may benefit from a QSEHRA. Reimbursements paid to an employee without such coverage must be included in the employee's taxable income. Minimum essential coverage includes all individually purchased private insurance, government insurance such as Medicare, and the employee's or spouse's job-based insurance. The employees should provide their employer with proof that they have such coverage.

All eligible employees must be covered by the QSEHRA. This includes all employees except those who:

- have not completed 90 days of service
- are under age 25
- are part-time or seasonal employees

- are covered by a collective bargaining agreement if health benefits were the subject of good-faith bargaining, or
- are nonresident aliens with no earned income from sources within the United States.

Thus, QSEHRA benefits cannot be offered to only a select group, such as to only a company's owner and top level employees.

A QSEHRA plan may be used only for employees. It may not be used by sole proprietors, partners in partnerships, members of limited liability companies (LLCs), or those who own more than 2% of an S corporation. Such individuals do not qualify as employees for QSEHRA purposes.

How to Establish a QSEHRA

The employer begins a QSEHRA by giving all of its eligible employees written notice of the plan, which can also serve as the document establishing the plan. The notice must be given 90 days before the beginning of a plan year. The notice must:

- list the amount of the employee's permitted benefit for the year
- require the employee to provide information about the QSEHRA to any health insurance exchange to which the employee applies for advance payment of premium assistance tax credits to help pay for health insurance, and
- contain a warning that, if the employee is not covered under minimum essential coverage for any month, the employee may have to pay tax on any plan reimbursements.

An employer that fails to provide the required notice may be subject to a $50 per-employee, per-failure penalty, up to a $2,500 calendar year maximum for all such failures.

Health Savings Accounts

Another tax-advantaged method of buying health insurance has been available since 2004: health savings accounts (HSAs). Although HSAs can save you taxes, they are not for everybody.

What Are Health Savings Accounts?

The HSA concept is very simple: Instead of relying on health insurance to pay small or routine medical expenses, you pay them yourself. To help you do this, you establish a health savings account with a health insurance company, a bank, or another financial institution. Contributions to the account are tax deductible, and you don't have to pay tax on the interest or other money you earn on the money in your account. You can withdraw the money in your HSA to pay almost any kind of health-related expense, and you don't have to pay any tax on these withdrawals.

In case you or a family member gets really sick, you must also obtain a health insurance policy with a high deductible—in 2017, at least $1,300 for individuals, and $2,600 for families. The money in your HSA can be used to pay this large deductible and any co-payments you're required to make.

Using an HSA can save you money in two ways:

- You'll get a tax deduction for the money you deposit in your account.
- The premiums for your high-deductible health insurance policy should be lower than those for traditional comprehensive coverage policies or HMO coverage.

Establishing an HSA

You may individually establish an HSA for yourself and your family and pay for your health insurance with personal funds. Alternatively, if your practice is a corporation, an LLC, a partnership, or an LLP, you can have it establish an HSA for you and make contributions to your HSA on your behalf with business funds. In either event, the rules discussed below apply.

To participate in the HSA program, you need two things:

- a high-deductible health plan that qualifies under the HSA rules, and
- an HSA.

HSA-Qualified Plans

You can't have an HSA if you're covered by health insurance other than a high-deductible HSA plan—for example, if your spouse has family coverage for you from his or her job. So you may have to change your existing coverage. However, you may get your own HSA if you are not covered by your spouse's health insurance. In addition, people eligible to receive Medicare may not participate in the HSA program.

You need to obtain a bare-bones health plan that meets the HSA criteria (is "HSA qualified"). You may obtain coverage from a health maintenance organization, a preferred provider organization, or another traditional plan. The key feature of an HSA-qualified health plan is that it has a relatively high annual deductible (the amount you must pay out of your own pocket before your insurance kicks in). In 2017, the minimum annual deductible for individuals was $1,300 and $2,600 for families.

You can have a higher deductible if you wish, but there is an annual ceiling on the total amount you can have for your deductible plus other out-of-pocket expenses you're required to pay before your health plan provides coverage. (Such out-of-pocket expenses include co-payments, but do not include health insurance premiums.) For example, in 2016 the annual ceiling for an individual HSA plan was $6,550. This means that your annual deductible and other out-of-pocket expenses you're required to pay before your insurance kicks in cannot exceed that amount. Thus, if your annual deductible is $3,000, your other annual out-of-pocket expenses would have to be limited to $3,550. In 2017, the maximum limits were $6,550 for individuals and $13,100 for families. These numbers are adjusted for inflation each year (see the chart below).

In addition, your health insurance plan must be HSA qualified. To become qualified, the insurer must agree to participate in the HSA program and give the roster of enrolled participants to the IRS. If your insurer fails to report to the IRS that you are enrolled in an HSA-qualified insurance plan, the IRS will not permit you to deduct your HSA contributions.

An HSA-qualified health insurance policy should be clearly labeled as such on the cover page or declaration page of the policy. It might be possible to convert a high-deductible health insurance policy you already have to an HSA-qualified health insurance policy; ask your health insurer for details.

You can obtain an HSA-qualifying health plan from health insurers that participate in the program. You can also contact your current health insurer.

The premiums you pay for an HSA-qualified health plan are deductible to the same extent as any other health insurance premiums. This means that if you're a sole proprietor, you may deduct your entire premium from your federal income tax as a special personal deduction. (See "The Personal Deduction for Medical Expenses," above.)

HSA Account

Once you have an HSA-qualified health insurance policy, you may open your HSA account. An HSA must be established with a trustee. The HSA trustee keeps track of your deposits and withdrawals, produces annual statements, and reports your HSA deposits to the IRS.

Health insurers can administer both the health plan and the HSA. However, you don't have to have your HSA administered by your insurer. You can establish an HSA with banks, insurance companies, mutual funds, or other financial institutions offering HSA products.

Whoever administers your account will usually give you a checkbook or debit card to use to withdraw funds from the account. You can also make withdrawals by mail or in person.

Making Contributions to Your HSA

When you have your HSA-qualified health plan and HSA account, you can start making contributions to your account. There is no minimum amount you are required to contribute each year; you may contribute nothing if you wish.

If your practice is a corporation, a partnership, or an LLC or LLP, you don't have to make all the contributions to your HSA from your personal funds. All or part of your annual contribution can be paid for by your practice from its funds. But, as described in the following section, this changes how the contributions are deducted.

There are maximum limits on how much may be contributed to an HSA each year:

- If you have individual coverage, the maximum annual contribution is $3,400.
- If you have family coverage, the maximum annual contribution is $6,750.

These figures are for 2017. They are adjusted for inflation each year.

Taxpayers who have HSAs may make a one-time tax-free rollover of funds from their individual retirement accounts (IRAs) to their HSAs. The rollover amount is limited to the maximum HSA contribution for the year (minus any HSA contributions you've already made for the year).

Catch-Up Contributions

Optional tax-free catch-up contributions can be made to HSAs for individuals who are 55 to 65 years old. This rule is intended to compensate for the fact that older folks won't have as many years to fund their accounts as younger taxpayers. If you're in this age group, it's wise to make these contributions if you can afford them so your HSA account will have enough money to pay for future health expenses.

HSA Annual Minimums and Maximums for 2017		
	Self Only	Family
Maximum contribution	$3,400	$6,750
Catch-up contribution (55 and over)	$1,000	$1,000
Minimum deductible	$1,300	$2,600
Maximum out-of-pocket payments	$6,550	$13,100

Where to Invest HSA Contributions

HSA contributions may be invested just like IRA contributions. You can invest in almost anything: money market accounts, bank certificates of deposit, stocks, bonds, mutual funds, Treasury bills, and notes. However, you can't invest in collectibles such as art, antiques, postage stamps, or other personal property. Most HSA funds are invested in money market accounts and in certificates of deposit.

Deducting HSA Contributions

The amounts contributed each year to HSA accounts, up to the annual limit, are deductible from federal income taxes.

Individual Contributions

You can deduct HSA contributions made with your personal funds as a personal deduction on the first page of your IRS Form 1040. You deduct the amount from your gross income, just like a business deduction. This means you get the full deduction whether or not you itemize your personal deductions.

> **EXAMPLE:** In 2017, Martin, an actuary, establishes an HSA for himself and his family with a $2,600 deductible. He contributes the maximum amount to his account—$6,750. Because he is in the 25% federal income tax bracket, this saves him $1,688 in federal income tax for 2017.

Contributions by Your Practice

If your practice is a partnership or an LLP or LLC and it makes an HSA contribution for you as a distribution of partnership or LLC funds, that amount is reported as a cash distribution to you on your Schedule K-1 (Form 1065). You may take a personal deduction for the HSA contribution on your tax return (IRS Form 1040) and the contribution is not subject to income or self-employment taxes.

However, the tax result is very different if the contribution is made as a guaranteed payment to the partner or LLC member. A guaranteed payment is like a salary paid to a partner or an LLC member for services performed for the partnership or LLC. The amount of a guaranteed payment is determined without reference to the partnership's or LLC's income. The partnership or LLC deducts the guaranteed payment on its return and lists it as a guaranteed payment to you on your Schedule K-1 (Form 1065). You must pay income and self-employment tax on the amount. You may take a personal income tax deduction on your Form 1040 for the HSA contribution.

Contributions by an S corporation to a shareholder-employee's HSA are treated as wages subject to income tax, but they normally are not subject to employment taxes. The shareholder can deduct the contribution on his or her personal tax return (IRS Form 1040) as an HSA contribution.

If you've formed a C corporation and work as its employee, your corporation can make a contribution to your HSA and deduct the amount as employee compensation. The contribution is not taxable to you. However, if you have other employees, similar contributions must be made to their HSAs. You may also make contributions from your own funds. (See "Making Contributions to Your HSA," above.)

Withdrawing HSA Funds

If you or a family member needs health care, you can withdraw money from your HSA to pay your deductible or any other medical expenses. You pay no federal tax on HSA withdrawals used to pay qualified medical expenses. However, you cannot deduct qualified medical expenses as an itemized deduction on Schedule A (Form 1040) that are equal to the tax-free distribution from your HSA. Qualified medical expenses are broadly defined to include many types of expenses ordinarily not covered by health insurance—for example, dental or optometric care. This is one of the great advantages of the HSA program over traditional health insurance.

No Approval Required

HSA participants need not obtain advance approval from their HSA trustee (whether their insurer or someone else) that an expense is a qualified medical expense before they withdraw funds from their accounts. You make that determination yourself. However, your HSA trustee will report any distribution to you and the IRS on Form 1099-SA, *Distributions From an HSA, Archer MSA, or Medicare Advantage MSA.* You should keep records of your medical expenses to show that your withdrawals were for qualified medical expenses and are therefore excludable from your gross income.

However, you may not use HSA funds to purchase nonprescription medications.

Tax-Free Withdrawals

If you withdraw funds from your HSA to use for something other than qualified medical expenses, you must pay the regular income tax on the withdrawal plus a 20% penalty. For example, if you were in the 25% federal income tax bracket, you'd have to pay a 45% tax on your nonqualified withdrawals.

Once you reach the age of 65 or become disabled, you can withdraw your HSA funds for any reason without penalty. If you use the money for nonmedical expenses, you will have to pay regular income tax on the withdrawals. When you die, the money in your HSA account is transferred to the beneficiary you've named for the account. The transfer is tax free if the beneficiary is your surviving spouse. Other transfers are taxable.

If you elect to leave the HSA program, you can continue to keep your HSA account and withdraw money from it tax free for health care expenses. However, you won't be able to make any additional contributions to the account.

What HSA Funds Can Be Used For

Health insurance ordinarily may not be purchased with HSA funds. However, there are three exceptions to this general rule. HSA funds can be used to pay for:

- a health plan during any period of continuation coverage required under any federal law—for example, when you are terminated from your job and purchase continuing health insurance coverage from your employer's health insurer, which the insurer is legally required to make available to you under COBRA
- long-term health care insurance, or
- health insurance premiums you pay while you are receiving unemployment compensation.

You can use HSA funds to pay for a broad array of medical expenses, including many that ordinarily are not covered by health insurance. This includes all your standard physician, dental, eye care, and mental health costs, as well as alcoholism and fertility treatment, nursing home expenses, and many other health-related costs.

For a complete list of what is and is not covered, refer to IRS Publication 502, *Medical and Dental Expenses*. Copies may be obtained from the IRS website at www.irs.gov or by calling 800-TAX-FORM.

Are HSAs a Good Deal?

Should you get an HSA? It depends. HSAs appear to be a very good deal if you're young or in good health and don't go to the doctor often or take many expensive medications. You can purchase a health plan with a high deductible, pay lower premiums, and have the security of knowing you can dip into your HSA if you get sick and have to pay the deductible or other uncovered medical expenses.

If you don't tap into the money, it will keep accumulating free of taxes. You also get the benefit of deducting your HSA contributions from your income taxes. And you can use your HSA funds to pay for many health-related expenses that aren't covered by traditional health insurance.

If you enjoy good health while you have your HSA and don't have to make many withdrawals, you may end up with a substantial amount in your account that you can withdraw without penalty for any purpose once you turn 65. Unlike all other existing tax-advantaged savings or retirement accounts, HSAs provide a tax break when funds are deposited and when they are withdrawn. No other account provides both a "front end" and "back end" tax break. With IRAs, for example, you must pay tax either when you deposit or when you withdraw your money. This feature can make your HSA an extremely lucrative tax shelter—a kind of super IRA.

On the other hand, HSAs are not for everybody. You could be better off with traditional comprehensive health insurance if you or a member of your family has substantial medical expenses. When you're in this situation, you'll likely end up spending all or most of your HSA contributions each year and earn little or no interest on your account (but you'll still get a deduction for your contributions). Of course, whether traditional health insurance is better than an HSA depends on its cost, including the deductibles and co-payments you must make.

In addition, the cost of an HSA-qualified health insurance plan may be too great to make the program cost-effective for you. However, if your choice is an HSA or nothing, get an HSA.

HSAs for Employees

Employers may provide HSAs to their employees. If you have employees, this may be an attractive option for you because it could cost less than providing your employees with traditional health insurance.

Any business, no matter how small, may participate in the HSA program. The employer purchases an HSA-qualified health plan for its employees, and they establish their own individual HSA accounts. The employer may pay all or part of its employees' insurance premiums and make contributions to their HSA accounts. Employees may also make their own contributions to their individual accounts. The combined annual contributions of the employer and employee may not exceed the limits listed in "Establishing an HSA," above.

HSAs are portable when an employee changes employers. Contributions and earnings belong to the account holder, not the employer. Employers are required to report amounts contributed to an HSA on the employee's Form W-2.

Health insurance payments and HSA contributions made by businesses on behalf of their employees are currently deductible business expenses. The employees do not have to report employer contributions to their HSA accounts as income. Employers deduct them on the "Employee benefit programs" line of their business income tax return.

Are You an Employee?

A professional in private practice is an employee for HSA purposes only if the practice is legally organized as a C corporation (or it is a partnership, or an LLP or LLC that has elected to be taxed as a C corporation). You are not an employee for these purposes if your practice is an S corporation, LLC or LLP, or a partnership.

Your C corporation employer may establish an HSA on your behalf and deduct its contributions on its own tax return. The contributions are not taxable to you, but you get no personal deduction for them. You do get a deduction, however, if you make contributions to your HSA account from your personal funds.

Hiring Your Spouse

If you're a sole proprietor or have formed any business entity other than an S corporation, you may hire your spouse as your employee and have your business pay for an HSA-qualified family health plan for your spouse, you, and your children and other dependents. Moreover, your HSA-qualified health plan can cover your children up to age 26, whether or not they are your dependents. But, you can't pay for your child's health insurance with withdrawals from your HSA account after the child reaches 24 years of age. Your spouse can then establish an HSA in his or her own name, which your business may fully fund each year. The money your business spends for your spouse's health insurance premiums and to fund the HSA is a fully deductible business expense. This allows you to reduce both your income and self-employment taxes. (See "Self-Employed Health Insurance Deduction," above.)

Nondiscrimination Rules

If your practice is a C corporation and you have employees other than yourself, your spouse, or other family members, you'll need to comply with nondiscrimination rules—that is, you'll have to make comparable HSA contributions for all employees with HSA-qualified health coverage during the year. Contributions are considered comparable if they are either of the same amount or the same percentage of the deductible under the plan. The rule is applied separately to employees who work fewer than 30 hours per week. Employers who do not comply with these rules are subject to a 35% excise tax.

Tax Reporting for HSAs

You must report to the IRS each year how much you deposit to and withdraw from your HSA. You make the report using IRS Form 8889, *Health Savings Accounts.* You'll also be required to keep a record of the name and address of each person or company whom you pay with funds from your HSA.

Inventory

Many professionals must carry inventories even though their primary businesses provide professional services. This chapter provides an overview of how to determine which of your purchases, if any, constitute inventory, how to value your inventory, and how to calculate your deduction for inventory costs.

SKIP AHEAD

If you only provide services to clients or customers, you don't need to worry about inventories. You can skip ahead to the next chapter.

What Is Inventory?

Inventory is made up of merchandise—the goods and products that a business keeps on hand to sell to customers in the ordinary course of business. It includes almost any tangible personal property that a business offers for sale. It does not include real estate or intangible personal property, like patents or copyrights. It makes no difference whether a business manufactures the goods itself or buys finished goods to resell to customers. Merchandise includes not only finished products, but also unfinished work in progress, as well as the raw materials and supplies that will become part of the finished merchandise. (IRS Reg. § 1.471-1.)

> **EXAMPLE:** Gloria, a sole proprietor optometrist, provides her patients with eye exams. In addition to providing this service, she also sells eyeglasses and contact lenses to her patients. The eyeglasses and lenses are inventory. This is so whether she purchases finished lenses from a commercial supplier or grinds her own lenses. (G.C.M. 37699; 1978 IRS GCM LEXIS 378.)

Separately billing patients or clients for an item tends to show it is merchandise. (For example, Gloria, like most optometrists, gives her patients separate bills for eyeglasses and for her optometric services.) However, this factor is not determinative in and of itself.

Long-term assets that you purchase to use in your business—for example, equipment, office furniture, and vehicles—are not a part of your inventory. These items are deductible capital expenses that you may depreciate over several years or, in many cases, deduct in a single year under Section 179. (See Chapter 9 for more on deducting long-term assets.)

> **EXAMPLE:** Gloria, from the example above, buys a new computer to help keep track of her patient records. The computer is not part of Gloria's inventory because she bought it to use in her practice, not to resell to patients. Because it will last for more than one year, it's a long-term asset, which she must either depreciate or expense under Section 179.

Only things to which you hold title—that is, things you own— constitute merchandise that must be inventoried. This includes items you haven't yet received or paid for, as long as you own them. For example, an item you buy with a credit card counts as inventory, even if you haven't paid the bill yet. However, if you buy merchandise that is sent C.O.D., you acquire ownership only after the goods are delivered and paid for.

Supplies Are Not Inventory

Supplies are materials and property consumed or used up during the production of merchandise or provision of services. These include:

- parts and other components acquired to maintain, repair, or improve business property
- fuel, lubricants, water, or similar items that are reasonably expected to be consumed in 12 months or less
- property that has an economic useful life of 12 months or less, and
- property with an acquisition or production cost of $100 or less. (IRS Reg. § 1.162-3T(c)(1).)

Good examples are rubber gloves and disposable syringes used by doctors and nurses to provide medical services. These items do not physically become part of merchandise a business sells so they are not included in the inventory.

Unless they are incidental supplies, the cost of the supplies must be deducted *in the year in which they are used or consumed*, which is not necessarily the year when you purchase them. This means that you must keep track of how much material you use each year.

The same item can constitute supplies for one business and inventory for another. It all depends on whether the item is furnished to the patient or client or consumed in performing a service. For example, the paper and ink used to prepare blueprints are inventory in the hands of a paper and ink manufacturer, but supplies in the hands of an architect.

With professionals, it is not always as clear when a product is merchandise and when it should be classified as supplies. For example, are drugs a doctor provides to a patient merchandise or supplies consumed while performing medical services? In one case, the tax court held that drugs were supplies, not merchandise, because they were an "indispensable and inseparable part" of the rendering of medical services to patients. The case involved a medical corporation treating cancer patients with chemotherapy drugs. The drugs were expensive and billed separately to Medicare. In reaching its conclusion, the court noted that the drugs could be obtained only by cancer patients undergoing treatment, and that the doctors kept only a small amount on hand and did not maintain a formal written record of the supply. (*Osteopathic Medical Oncology and Hematology, PC v. Comm'r*, 113 T.C. 26.)

On the other hand, the IRS ruled that crowns, bridges, and dentures used by a dentist were merchandise, even though they were sold only to patients who obtained dental services from the dentist. (LTR 9848001.) Similarly, the IRS said that artificial limbs and orthopedic braces were merchandise, not supplies used to perform a service, even though the company that manufactured and sold them performed considerable services fitting the braces to handicapped patients and instructing them in their use. (Rev. Rul. 73-485.)

SEE AN EXPERT

The standards are far from clear in this area. If you are unsure whether you sell merchandise to your patients or clients, talk to a tax professional for advice on dealing with inventory.

Incidental Supplies

There is an important exception to the rule that the cost of materials and supplies may be deducted only as they are used or consumed. You may deduct the entire cost of supplies that are *incidental* to your business in the year when you purchase them. Supplies are incidental if the following are true:

- You do not keep a record of when you use the supplies.
- You do not take a physical inventory of the supplies at the beginning and end of the tax year.
- Deducting the cost of supplies in the year you purchase them does not distort your taxable income. (IRS Reg. § 1.162-3T(a)(2).)

If you treat the cost of supplies on hand as an asset for financial reporting purposes, they are not incidental (you do *not* keep a record of when you use the supplies).

Do You Have to Carry an Inventory?

A business is said to maintain or carry an inventory when it must include unsold inventory items as assets on its books, to be deducted only when the items are sold or become worthless. If you are required to carry an inventory, you may currently deduct only the value of the inventory you sell during the year, not your entire inventory.

> **EXAMPLE:** Gloria purchased $20,000 worth of eyeglasses to sell to her patients last year. However, she sold only $10,000 worth of them during the year. If Gloria is required to carry an inventory, she'll be able to deduct only the cost of the eyeglasses she sold. The $10,000 worth of unsold eyeglasses is inventory, which she must include as a business asset on her books. She will have to wait until she sells the glasses (or they become worthless) to deduct their cost.

A business—even one that provides professional services—is required to carry an inventory if the production or sale of merchandise is an income-producing factor for the business—that is, it accounts for a substantial portion of the business's revenues. When do sales become substantial enough to be considered an income-producing factor?

There's no exact figure, but many tax experts believe that a business that derives 8% or less of its total gross revenue from the sale or production of merchandise need not maintain an inventory. A business that makes at least 15% of its money from selling or producing merchandise should maintain an inventory, and a business that earns 9% to 14% of its money from merchandise is in a gray area.

Thus, for example, the IRS held that a veterinarian had to maintain inventories because the sale of drugs, pet foods, and livestock antibiotic food additives constituted approximately 50% of his gross receipts each year. (IRS Private Letter Ruling 9218008.) However, even though a dentist's crowns, bridges, and dentures were merchandise, the IRS ruled he didn't have to carry an inventory because he didn't earn enough money from those items. (IRS Private Letter Ruling 9848001.)

Deducting Inventory Costs

If you are required to carry an inventory, you may deduct only the cost of the goods you sold during the year (or the cost of goods that became worthless). To do this, you must calculate the cost (to you) of the merchandise you sold during the year. You then deduct this amount from your gross income.

Computing the Cost of Goods Sold

To figure out the cost of goods sold, start with the cost of any inventory on hand at the beginning of your tax year. Add the cost of inventory that you purchased or manufactured during the year. Subtract the cost of any merchandise you withdrew for personal use. The sum of all this is the cost of all goods available for sale during the tax year. Subtract from this amount the value of your inventory at the end of your tax year. (See "Determining the Value of Inventory," below, for information on how to calculate this value.) The cost of all goods sold during the year (and therefore, the amount you can deduct for inventory expenses on your taxes) is the remainder. This can be stated by the following equation:

	Inventory at beginning of year
Plus:	Purchases or additions during the year
Minus:	Goods withdrawn from sale for personal use
Equals:	Cost of goods available for sale
Minus:	Inventory at end of year
Equals:	Cost of goods sold

EXAMPLE: Gloria, the optometrist from the above examples, had $50,000 in inventory at the beginning of the year and purchased another $20,000 of inventory during the year. She removed $500 of inventory for her own personal use. The value of the inventory she had left at the end of the year is $29,000. She would calculate her cost of goods sold as follows:

Inventory at beginning of year	$ 50,000
Purchases or additions during the year	+ 20,000
Goods withdrawn from sale for personal use	– 500
Cost of goods available for sale	= 69,500
Inventory at end of year	– 29,000
Cost of goods sold	= $ 40,500

Note that all of these costs are based on what Gloria paid for her inventory, not what she sold it for (which was substantially greater).

Determining the Value of Inventory

To use the equation in "Computing the Cost of Goods Sold," above, you must be able to calculate the value of the inventory you have left at the end of the year. There is no single way to do this: Standard methods for tracking inventory vary according to the type and size of business involved. As long as your inventory methods are consistent from year to year, the IRS doesn't care which method you use.

RESOURCE

Need more information on how to value your inventory? This section provides only a small overview of a large subject. For more information on valuing inventory, refer to:

- *The Accounting Game*, by Darrell Mullis and Judith Orloff (Sourcebooks, Inc.)
- *Small Time Operator*, by Bernard B. Kamoroff (Taylor Trade Publishing)
- IRS Publication 334, *Tax Guide for Small Businesses* (Chapter 7), and
- IRS Publication 538, *Accounting Periods and Methods*.

Until recently, the IRS required all businesses that sold or manufactured goods to make a physical inventory of the merchandise they owned—that is, to actually count it. This process, often called taking inventory, is usually done at the end of the year, although it doesn't have to be. Nor is it necessary to count every single item in stock. Businesses can make a physical inventory of a portion of their total merchandise, then extrapolate their total inventory from the sample.

The IRS no longer requires small businesses to take physical inventories. (Small businesses are those that earn less than $1 million in gross receipts per year, and service businesses that earn up to $10 million per year.) But even small businesses must keep track of how much inventory they buy and sell to determine their cost of goods sold for the year. With modern inventory software, it is possible for a business to keep a continuous record of the goods on hand during the year. Keep copies of your invoices and receipts to prove to the IRS that you correctly accounted for your inventory, in case you are audited.

IRS Reporting

You must report the cost of goods sold on your tax return. If you're a sole proprietor or owner of a one-person limited liability company (LLC), the amount goes directly on your Schedule C. Part III of Schedule C tracks the cost of goods equation provided in "Deducting Inventory Costs," above. Multi-member LLCs and partnerships report their cost of goods sold on Schedule A of IRS Form 1065, *U.S. Return of Partnership Income*. S corporations report cost of goods sold on

Schedule A of Form 1120-S, *U.S. Income Tax Return for an S Corporation.* C corporations report this information on Schedule A of Form 1120, *U.S. Corporation Income Tax Return.*

Technically speaking, the cost of goods sold is not a business expense. Rather, it is subtracted from a business's gross income to determine its gross profit for the year. Business expenses are then subtracted from the gross profit to determine the business's taxable net profit, as shown by the following formula:

	Gross income
Minus:	Cost of goods sold
Equals:	Gross profit
Minus:	Deductible business expenses
Equals:	Net profit

As a practical matter, this is a distinction without a difference—both the cost of goods sold and business expenses are subtracted from your business income to calculate your taxable profit. However, you cannot deduct the cost of goods sold to determine your gross profit and then deduct it again as a business expense—this would result in a double deduction.

> **EXAMPLE:** Gloria subtracts her $29,000 cost of goods sold from her gross income (all the money she earned from her optometry practice) to determine her gross profit. She earned $250,000 in total income for the year and had $100,000 in business expenses, including rent and employee salaries. She calculates her net profit as follows:
>
> | Gross income | | $ 250,000 |
> |--------------------|---|-----------|
> | Cost of goods sold | – | 29,000 |
> | Gross profit | = | 221,000 |
> | Business expenses | – | 100,000 |
> | Net profit | = | $ 121,000 |
>
> Gloria has to pay tax only on her $121,000 in net profit.

Obviously, the larger the cost of goods sold, the smaller your taxable income will be and the less tax you'll have to pay.

More Deductions

This chapter looks at some of the most common deductible business expenses that professionals incur. You can deduct these costs as business operating expenses as long as they are ordinary, necessary, and reasonable in amount and meet the additional requirements discussed below.

Advertising

Almost any type of business-related advertising is a currently deductible business operating expense. You can deduct advertising undertaken to help obtain new clients, establish goodwill for your practice, or just to get your practice known. Advertising includes expenses for:

- business cards
- brochures
- client newsletters
- advertisements in the local yellow pages
- newspaper and magazine advertisements
- professional publication advertisements
- radio and television advertisements
- advertisements on the Internet
- fees you pay to advertising and public relations agencies
- billboards, and
- signs.

However, advertising to influence government legislation is never deductible. And help-wanted ads you place to recruit workers are not advertising costs, but you can deduct them as ordinary and necessary business operating expenses.

Goodwill Advertising

If it relates to business you reasonably expect to gain in the future, you can usually deduct the cost of institutional or goodwill advertising meant to keep your name before the public. Examples of goodwill advertising include:

- advertisements that encourage people to contribute to charities, such as the Red Cross or similar causes
- sponsoring a little league baseball team, bowling team, or golf tournament
- giving away product samples, and
- holding contests and giving away prizes.

However, you can't deduct time and labor that you give away as an advertising expense, even though doing so promotes goodwill. You must actually spend money to have an advertising expense. For example, a lawyer who does pro bono work for indigent clients to advertise his law practice may not deduct the cost of his services as an advertising expense.

Giveaway Items

Giveaway items that you use to publicize your practice (such as pens, coffee cups, T-shirts, refrigerator magnets, calendars, tote bags, and key chains) are deductible. However, you are not allowed to deduct more than $25 in business gifts to any one person each year. (See "Gifts," below.) This limitation applies to advertising giveaway items unless they:

- cost $4 or less
- have your name clearly and permanently imprinted on them, and
- are one of a number of identical items you distribute widely.

EXAMPLE 1: David, a dentist, orders 1,000 toothbrushes with his name and office address printed on them and gives them to his patients. Each toothbrush costs $1. The toothbrushes do not count toward the $25 gift limit. David may deduct the entire $1,000 expense for the toothbrushes.

EXAMPLE 2: The Abel and Baker law firm buys a $200 fountain pen and gives it to its most valuable client as a Christmas gift. The pen is a business gift to an individual, so Abel and Baker can deduct only $25 of the cost.

Signs, display racks, and other promotional materials that you give away to other businesses to use on their premises do not count as gifts.

Website Development and Maintenance

The costs of developing and maintaining a website for a business vary widely. Your website design can be relatively inexpensive if you use a standard template you purchase from a template company. However, the cost will be much higher if you want to create a custom design.

Many businesses currently deduct all website development and ongoing maintenance expenses as advertising expenses. However, some tax experts believe that the cost of initially setting up a website is a capital expense, not a currently deductible business operating expense, because the website is a long-term asset that benefits the business for more than one year. Under normal tax rules, capital expenses must be deducted over several years. Three years is the most common deduction period used for websites, since this is the same period as for software. However, even if website development costs are capital expenses, they may be currently deducted in a single year under Section 179, which allows businesses to deduct a substantial amount of capital expenses in a single year (see Chapter 9).

Most tax experts agree that ongoing website hosting, maintenance, and updating costs are currently deductible operating expenses. Money you spend to get people to view your website, such as SEO (search engine optimization) campaigns, is a currently deductible advertising expense.

Permanent Signs

Signs that have a useful life of less than one year—for example, paper or cardboard signs—are currently deductible as business operating expenses. However, a permanent metal or plastic sign that has a useful life of more than one year is a long-term business asset, which you cannot currently deduct as a business operating expense. Instead, you must either depreciate the cost over several years or deduct it in one year under Section 179. (See Chapter 9 for more on deducting long-term assets.)

Business Bad Debts

Business bad debts are those that arise from your business activities, such as those when you:

- lend money for a business purpose
- sell inventory on credit, or
- guarantee business-related loans.

Strict requirements must be met to deduct a business debt.

Three Requirements for Deduction

The following three requirements must be satisfied to deduct a business bad debt as a business operating expense:

- You must have a bona fide business debt.
- The debt must be wholly or partly worthless.
- You must have suffered an economic loss from the debt.

Most debts owed to professionals do not satisfy all these requirements, thus they cannot be deducted. If the requirements are satisfied, however, you can currently deduct business bad debts as business operating expenses when they become wholly or partly worthless.

A Bona Fide Business Debt

A bona fide debt exists when someone has a legal obligation to pay you a sum of money—for example, you provide your services on credit. A bona fide debt also exists if there is written evidence to support it—for example, a signed promissory note or another writing stating the amount of the debt, when it is due, and the interest rate (if any). An oral promise to pay may also be legally enforceable, but would be looked upon with suspicion by the IRS.

A business debt is a debt that is created or acquired in the course of your practice or becomes worthless as part of your practice. Your primary motive for incurring the debt must be business related. Debts taken on for personal or investment purposes are not business debts. (Remember, investing is not a business.)

EXAMPLE 1: Mark, an attorney, lends $10,000 to his brother-in-law, Scott, to invest in his bird diaper invention. Mark will get 25% of the profits if the invention proves successful. This is an investment, not a business debt.

EXAMPLE 2: Mark lends $10,000 to one of his best business clients to help keep the client's business running. Because the main reason for the loan was business related (to keep his client in business so he will continue as a client), the debt is a business debt.

A Worthless Debt

A debt must be wholly or partly worthless to be deductible. A debt becomes worthless when there is no longer any chance that the amount owed will be paid back to you. You don't have to wait until a debt is due to determine that it is worthless, and you don't have to go to court to try to collect it. You just have to be able to show that you have taken reasonable steps to try to collect the debt or that collection efforts would be futile. For example:

- You've made repeated collection efforts that have proven unsuccessful.
- The debtor has filed for bankruptcy or has already been through bankruptcy and has had all or part of the debt discharged (forgiven) by the bankruptcy court.
- You've learned that the debtor has gone out of business, gone broke, died, or disappeared.

Keep all documentation that shows a debt is worthless, such as copies of unpaid invoices, collection letters you've sent the debtor, logs of collection calls you've made, bankruptcy notices, and credit reports.

You must deduct the entire amount of a bad debt in the year it becomes totally worthless. If only part of a business debt becomes worthless—for example, you received a partial payment before the debt became uncollectible—you can deduct the unpaid portion that year, or you can wait until the following year to deduct it. For example, if you think you might get paid more the next year, you can wait and see what your final bad debt amount is before you deduct it.

An Economic Loss

You are not automatically entitled to deduct a debt because the obligation has become worthless. To get a deduction, you must have suffered an economic loss. According to the IRS, you have a loss only when you:

- have already reported as business income the amount you were supposed to be paid
- paid out cash, or
- made credit sales of inventory that were not paid for.

This requirement makes it impossible for professionals to deduct most of their business debts.

Applying the Rules

Let's apply the rules to the various types of debts professionals are commonly owed.

Nonpaying Clients or Patients

Unfortunately, if, like most professionals, you're a cash basis taxpayer, you can't claim a bad debt deduction if a client fails to pay you. As a cash basis taxpayer, you don't report income until you actually receive it. As a result, you don't have an economic loss (in the eyes of the IRS) when a client fails to pay.

> EXAMPLE: Bill, a self-employed consultant, works 50 hours for a client and bills the client $2,500. The client never pays. Bill is a cash basis taxpayer, so he doesn't report the $2,500 as income because he never received it. As far as the IRS is concerned, Bill has no economic loss and cannot deduct the $2,500 the client failed to pay.

The IRS strictly enforces this rule (harsh as it may seem). Absent the rule, the IRS fears that businesses will inflate the value of their services in order to get larger deductions.

Accrual basis taxpayers, on the other hand, report sales as income in the year the sales are made—not the year payment is received. These taxpayers can take a bad debt deduction if a client fails to pay for services rendered, because they have already reported the money due as income. Therefore, accrual taxpayers have an economic loss when their services are not paid for.

> **EXAMPLE:** Acme Consulting Co. bills a client $10,000 for consulting services it performed during the year. Because Acme is an accrual basis taxpayer, it characterizes the $10,000 as income on its books and includes this amount in its gross income in the year in which it billed for the services, even though Acme hasn't actually received payment. The client later files for bankruptcy, and the debt becomes worthless. Acme may take a business bad debt deduction to wipe out the $10,000 in income it previously charged on its books.

There's no point in trying to switch from cash basis to the accrual method to deduct bad debts. The accrual method doesn't result in lower taxes—the bad debt deduction merely wipes out a sale that was previously reported as income.

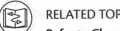 RELATED TOPIC
Refer to Chapter 18 for a detailed discussion of the cash basis and accrual accounting methods.

Credit Sales of Inventory

Most deductible business bad debts result from credit sales of inventory by professionals to their patients. If you sell merchandise on credit to a patient or customer and are not paid, you get a deduction whether you are an accrual or cash basis taxpayer. You deduct the cost of the inventory at the end of the year to determine the cost of goods sold for the year. (See Chapter 12 for more about deducting inventory.)

Business Loan Guarantees

If you guarantee a debt that becomes worthless, it qualifies as a business bad debt only if you:
- made the guarantee in the course of your business
- have a legal duty to pay the debt
- made the guarantee before the debt became worthless, and

- received reasonable consideration (compensation) for the guarantee—you meet this requirement if the guarantee is for a good-faith business purpose or according to normal business practices.

EXAMPLE: The Acme Medical Corporation is the owner of a subsidiary corporation called the Reliable Medical Lab, Inc. Reliable needed to borrow money to expand its operation, but had poor credit. To help it obtain the money, Acme guaranteed a $100,000 loan for Reliable. Reliable later filed for bankruptcy and defaulted on the loan. Acme had to make full payment to the bank. It can take a business bad debt deduction because its guarantee was made for a good-faith business purpose—its desire to help the lab expand.

Loans or Guarantees to Your Corporation

If your practice is incorporated, you cannot take a bad debt deduction for a loan to your corporation if the loan is actually a contribution to capital—that is, part of your investment in the practice. You must be careful to treat a loan to your corporation in the same way that you treat a loan made to a business in which you have no ownership interest. You should have a signed promissory note from your corporation setting forth:

- the loan amount
- the interest rate—which should be a reasonable rate
- the due date, and
- a repayment schedule.

When you are a principal shareholder in a small corporation, you'll often be asked to personally guarantee corporate loans and other extensions of credit. Creditors do this because they want to be able to go after your personal assets if they can't collect from your corporation. If you end up having to make good on your guarantee and can't get repaid from your corporation, you will have a bad debt. You can deduct this bad debt as a business debt if your dominant motive for making the loan or guarantee was to protect your employment status and ensure your continuing receipt of a salary. If your primary motive was to protect your investment in the corporation, the debt is a personal debt. The IRS is more likely to think you are protecting your investment if you receive little or no salary from the corporation or your salary is not a major source of your overall income.

EXAMPLE: Andre, a chiropractor, is employed by, and the sole shareholder of, ABC Chiropractic, Inc. The corporation pays Andre a $75,000 annual salary, which is his sole source of income. ABC applies for a $50,000 bank loan. Before approving the loan, the bank requires Andre to personally guarantee payment of the loan. ABC defaults on the loan and Andre has to make full payment to the bank from his personal funds. Andre is entitled to a business bad debt deduction because his primary motive for guaranteeing the loan was to protect his job with his corporation, not to protect his investment in the corporation.

Personal Debts

The fact that a debt doesn't arise from your business doesn't mean it's not deductible. However, unlike business bad debts, personal bad debts are deductible only if they become wholly worthless. A deductible nonbusiness bad debt is classified as a short-term capital loss for tax purposes. As such, it is subject to the limitations on taking short-term capital losses: You can deduct such a loss against any short- or long-term capital gains you have for the year from the sale of capital assets (such as real estate and stocks). Any remaining amount of your loss is deductible only up to $3,000 per year against your other ordinary income. Nondeductible losses may be carried over to be deducted in future years.

Client Costs Advanced by Attorneys

Lawyers often pay for various costs themselves while they are working on cases with the expectation that they will later be reimbursed by the clients. Such advances are particularly common by personal injury lawyers who take cases on a contingency fee basis, and who expect to obtain reimbursement from any recovery that is made when the cases are settled or court awards obtained. Advances typically include attorney travel expenses, medical record costs, costs of reports, witness fees, deposition costs, filing fees, investigation costs, costs of photographs, laboratory test fees, and process server fees.

You might think attorneys could deduct these costs as business operating expenses, but you'd be wrong. Client costs advanced by attorneys are not deductible because they are viewed as loans made by attorneys to their clients. Loans are not deductible business expenses because they are made on the condition that they be repaid by the borrower. (*Canelo v. Comm'r*, 53 T.C. 217 (1969).)

Because advances are loans, they are deductible only if they become uncollectible. Then the bad debt rules discussed above apply. If an advance is repaid, it is not taxable income for the law firm.

There is one exception that allows attorneys to deduct client costs: when an attorney enters into a gross fee contingency agreement with a client. Under such a fee agreement, the attorney pays all the litigation costs and does not obtain reimbursement from any recovery made for the client. Because the attorney has no expectation of having the advanced costs repaid by the client, they are not loans. They may be deducted as a business operating expense in the year they are incurred. (*Boccardo v. Comm'r*, 56 F.3d 1016 (9th Cir. 1995).)

Casualty Losses

Casualty losses are damage to property caused by fire, theft, vandalism, earthquake, storm, floods, terrorism, or some other "sudden, unexpected or unusual event." There must be some external force involved for a loss to be a casualty loss. Thus, you get no deduction if you simply lose or misplace property or it breaks or wears out over time.

You may take a deduction for casualty losses to business property if, and only to the extent that, the loss is not covered by insurance. Thus, if the loss is fully covered, you'll get no deduction.

Amount of Deduction

How much you may deduct depends on whether the property involved was stolen or completely destroyed, or only partially destroyed. However, you must always reduce your casualty losses by the amount of any insurance proceeds you actually receive or reasonably expect to receive.

If more than one item was stolen or wholly or partly destroyed, you must figure your deduction separately for each and then add them all together.

Total Loss

If the property is stolen or completely destroyed, your deduction is figured as follows:

$$
\begin{aligned}
&\text{Adjusted basis} \\
-\ &\text{Salvage value} \\
-\ &\underline{\text{Insurance proceeds}} \\
=\ &\underline{\text{Casualty loss} }
\end{aligned}
$$

Your adjusted basis is the property's original cost, plus the value of any improvements, minus any deductions you took for depreciation or Section 179 expensing (see Chapter 9). Obviously, if an item is stolen, there will be no salvage value.

> **EXAMPLE:** Sean's business computer is stolen from his apartment by a burglar. The computer cost $2,000. Sean has taken no tax deductions for it because he purchased it only two months ago, so his adjusted basis is $2,000. Sean is a renter and has no insurance covering the loss. Sean's casualty loss is $2,000. ($2,000 Adjusted basis – $0 Salvage value – $0 Insurance proceeds = $2,000.)

Partial Loss

If the property is only partly destroyed, your casualty loss deduction is the lesser of the decrease in the property's fair market value or its adjusted basis, reduced by any insurance you receive or expect to receive.

> **EXAMPLE:** Assume that Sean's computer (from the example above) is partly destroyed due to a small fire in his home. Its fair market value in its partly damaged state is $500. Since he spent $2,000 for it, the decrease in its fair market value is $1,500. The computer's adjusted basis is $2,000. He received no insurance proceeds. Thus, his casualty loss is $1,500.

Special Rules for Losses Related to Federally Declared Disasters

The cost of repairing damaged property is not part of a casualty loss. Neither is the cost of cleaning up after a casualty. Instead, these expenses are deductible in addition to any deductible casualty loss you have. You have to depreciate over several years the cost to clean up hazardous waste on business property, or any repairs to property or equipment that make the property better than it was before it was repaired.

Inventory

You don't have to treat damage to or loss of inventory as a casualty loss. Instead, you may deduct it as part of the cost of your goods sold. (See Chapter 12 for a detailed discussion of inventory.) However, if you do this, you must include any insurance proceeds you receive for the inventory loss in your practice's gross income for the year.

Charitable Contributions

Tax deductions can be taken for charitable contributions to qualified organizations. To become a qualified organization, most organizations, other than churches and governments, must apply to the IRS. You can ask any organization whether it is a qualified organization, and most will be able to tell you. You can check the tax status of a nonprofit by using the IRS online Exempt Organizations Select Check Tool (www.irs.gov/Charities-&-Non-Profits/Exempt-Organizations-Select-Check).

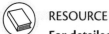

RESOURCE

For detailed guidance on tax deductions for charitable contributions, refer to *Every Nonprofit's Tax Guide,* by Stephen Fishman (Nolo).

Contributions of Money

If you are a sole proprietor, a partner in a partnership, or an LLC member or S corporation shareholder, the IRS treats any charitable contributions of money your practice makes as personal contributions by you and any co-owners. As such, the contributions are not business expenses—you can deduct them only as personal charitable contributions. You may deduct these contributions only if you itemize deductions on your personal tax return; they are subject to certain income limitations. See IRS Publication 526, *Charitable Contributions*.

Charitable contributions are treated very differently for C corporations. C corporations can deduct charitable contributions as a business expense on their own corporate tax returns.

Contributions of Property

If you contribute business property to a qualified charitable organization, you may deduct its fair market value on the date of the contribution.

> **EXAMPLE:** Barry, a sole proprietor engineer, wants to buy a new computer and get rid of his old one. He decides to donate the old computer to a local charity. By looking at sales data for similar computers on eBay, he determines that the computer's fair market value is $1,000. He may deduct this amount as an itemized deduction on Schedule A of his tax return. He may not deduct it as a business expense on Schedule C.

The rules differ somewhat if the property you contribute is inventory (merchandise you sell to patients or customers; see Chapter 12). You may deduct the smaller of:

- its fair market value on the day you contributed it, or
- its tax basis.

A C corporation can claim a larger than normal deduction by donating certain types of inventory or other property to a public charity or operating foundation. This includes:

- property used for the care of the ill, needy, or infants, and
- computer equipment no more than three years old donated to an educational organization.

C corporations that make such donations may add 50% of the difference between the property's tax basis (cost) and fair market value (up to twice the basis) to the deduction amount. This makes these contributions particularly attractive for C corporations.

You must remove the amount of your deduction from your opening inventory. It is not part of the cost of goods sold.

There are several organizations that specialize in facilitating charitable donations of unsold inventory by corporations, including the National Association for Exchange of Industrial Resources (NAEIR) at www.naeir.org.

Contributions of Services

If you contribute your personal services to a charity, you get no deduction for the value of your time or services. However, you may take a personal deduction for your out-of-pocket expenses, such as travel expenses. To be deductible, such expenses must be:

- unreimbursed
- directly connected with the charitable services
- expenses you had only because of the services you gave, and
- not personal, living, or family expenses.

For example, you can deduct unreimbursed out-of-pocket expenses, such as the cost of gas and oil, that are directly related to the use of your car in giving services to a charitable organization. If you do not want to bother keeping track of your actual expenses, you can use a standard mileage rate of 14 cents per mile (charitable rate) to figure your contribution.

> EXAMPLE: Dr. Smith, a radiologist, volunteers ten hours of his time every week to a nonprofit hospital in his community. He may deduct the cost of his gas and parking, but not the value of his time or medical services.

Clothing

You can only deduct the cost of clothing that:
- is essential for your practice
- is not suitable for ordinary street wear, and
- you don't wear outside of business.

Thus, for example, a doctor may deduct the cost of scrubs or lab coats, because they are not suitable for street wear. But an attorney may not deduct the cost of a business suit because it is suitable for ordinary street wear. Likewise a doctor can't deduct the cost of comfortable shoes he wears with his scrubs because the shoes can be worn on the street.

If your clothing is deductible, you may also deduct the cost of dry cleaning and other care.

Disabled Access Tax Credit

The Americans with Disabilities Act (ADA) prohibits private employers with 15 or more employees from discriminating against people with disabilities in the full and equal enjoyment of goods, services, and facilities offered by any "place of public accommodation." Professionals' offices are included in the definition of public accommodation.

The tax law provides a tax credit to help small businesses defray the costs of complying with the ADA. Among other things, the credit may be used help offset amounts paid to acquire or modify equipment or devices for the disabled. The credit may be used by any business with either:
- $1 million or less in gross receipts for the preceding tax year, or
- 30 or fewer full-time employees during the preceding tax year.

Use of Credit by Health Care Providers

The disabled access credit can be used by health care professionals who purchase or modify equipment to satisfy the ADA's prohibition on discrimination against the disabled. For example, the credit may be used when a health care provider purchases equipment to allow him or her to treat disabled patients who couldn't be treated previously.

EXAMPLE: Dr. David Hubbard, a Nevada optometrist, was unable to treat deaf or wheelchair-bound patients because he used a manual refractor that required that they sit in an examination chair and answer questions while viewing an eye chart. Deaf people couldn't hear the questions and wheelchair-bound people couldn't fit behind the refractor. To eliminate this problem, Dr. Hubbard purchased an automatic refractor/keratometer for $18,000. This instrument enabled him to measure patients' vision without using eye charts. Dr. Hubbard took the maximum $5,000 disabled tax credit for his purchase. The IRS claimed that Dr. Hubbard was not entitled to the credit because he used the refractor for all his patients, not just the disabled. The tax court disagreed; it held that Dr. Hubbard was entitled to the credit because it enabled him to treat disabled patients he couldn't treat previously. (*Hubbard v. Comm'r*, T.C. Memo 2003-245.)

Amount of Credit

The disabled tax credit is a tax credit, not a tax deduction. Tax credits are better than tax deductions because, instead of just reducing your taxable income, they reduce the amount of tax you have to pay dollar for dollar. The amount of the credit is equal to 50% of eligible access expenditures of at least $250 but not more than $10,000 for a tax year. Thus, the maximum credit is $5,000. A business may take the credit each year that it makes an eligible access expenditure. To claim the credit, you must file IRS Form 8826, *Disabled Access Credit*.

License Fees, Dues, and Subscriptions

License fees and other dues you pay to a professional, business, or civic organization are deductible business expenses, as long as the organization's main purpose is not to provide entertainment facilities to members. This includes dues paid to:

- bar associations, medical associations, and other professional organizations
- trade associations, local chambers of commerce, real estate boards, business leagues, and

- civic or public service organizations, such as a Rotary or Lions club.

You may also deduct dues to join professional societies, even if such membership is not required to practice your profession. For example, an architect could deduct the dues to be a member of the American Institute of Architects.

You get no deduction for dues you pay to belong to other types of social, business, or recreational clubs—for example, country clubs or athletic clubs. (See Chapter 4.) For this reason, it's best not to use the word dues on your tax return, because the IRS may question the expense. Use other words to describe the deduction—for example, if you're deducting membership dues for a trade organization, list the expense as professional association membership fees.

You may deduct subscriptions to professional, technical, and trade journals as a business expense.

Education Expenses

You can deduct your expenses for business-related education—for example, a continuing professional education course or seminar. You can also deduct the cost of attending a convention or professional meeting as an education expense. To qualify for an education deduction, you must be able to show that the education:

- maintains or improves skills required in your profession, or
- is required by law or regulation to maintain your professional status.

EXAMPLE 1: Sue is an attorney. Every year, she is required by law to attend 12 hours of continuing education to keep her status as an active member of the state bar. The legal seminars she attends to satisfy this requirement are deductible education expenses.

EXAMPLE 2: Jerry, a general practitioner doctor, takes a two-week course reviewing new developments in several specialized fields of medicine. The cost is a deductible education expense because the course maintains or improves Jerry's skills as a doctor.

Deductible education expenses include tuition, fees, books, and other learning materials. They also include transportation and travel (see below). You may also deduct expenses you pay to educate or train your employees.

Lifetime Learning Credit

Instead of taking a tax deduction for your business-related education expenses, you may qualify for the lifetime learning credit. A tax credit is a dollar-for-dollar reduction in your tax liability, so it's even better than a tax deduction.

The lifetime learning credit can by used to help pay for any undergraduate or graduate level education, including nondegree education to acquire or improve job skills (for example a continuing education course). If you qualify, your credit equals 20% of the first $10,000 of postsecondary tuition and fees you pay during the year, for a maximum credit of $2,000 per tax return. However, the credit is phased out and then eliminated at certain income levels: It begins to go down if your modified adjusted gross income is over $55,000 ($111,000 for a joint return) and you cannot claim the credit at all if your MAGI is over $65,000 ($131,000 for a joint return). These are the limits for 2017. The limits are adjusted for inflation each year.

You can take this credit not only for yourself, but for a dependent child (or children) for whom you claim a tax exemption, or your spouse as well (if you file jointly). And it can be taken any number of times. However, you can't take the credit if you've already deducted the education cost as a business expense.

Entering a New Profession

You cannot currently deduct education expenses you incur to qualify for a *new* profession. For example, courts have held that IRS agents could not deduct the cost of going to law school, because a law degree would qualify them for a new profession—being a lawyer. (*Jeffrey L. Weiler*, 54 T.C. 398 (1970).) On the other hand, a practicing dentist was allowed to deduct the cost of being educated in orthodontia, because becoming an orthodontist did not constitute the practice of a new business or profession for a dentist. (Rev. Rul. 74-78.)

Minimum Educational Requirements

You cannot deduct the cost required to meet the minimum or basic level educational requirements for a profession. Thus, for example, you can't deduct the expense of going to law school, medical school, or dental school.

Traveling for Education

Local transportation expenses paid to get to and from a deductible educational activity are deductible. This includes transportation between either your home or business and the educational activity. Travel between home and an educational activity does not constitute nondeductible commuting. If you drive, you may deduct your actual expenses or use the standard mileage rate. (See Chapter 5 for more on deducting car expenses.)

There's no law that says you must take your education courses as close to home as possible. You may travel outside your geographic area for education, even if the same or a similar educational activity is available near your home or place of business. Companies and groups that sponsor educational events are well aware of this rule and take advantage of it by offering courses and seminars at resorts and other enjoyable vacation spots such as Hawaii and California. Deductible travel expenses may include airfare or other transportation, lodging, and meals. However, if you don't spend the majority of your time on educational activities, your deduction will be greatly limited. (See Chapter 6 for more about travel expenses.)

You cannot claim travel itself as an education deduction. You must travel to some sort of educational activity. For example, an architect could not deduct the cost of a trip to Paris because he studied the local architecture while he was there—but he could deduct a trip to Paris to attend a seminar on French architecture.

Gifts

If you give someone a gift for business purposes, your business expense deduction is limited to $25 per person per year. Any amount over the $25 limit is not deductible. If this amount seems awfully low, that's because it was established in 1954!

> **EXAMPLE:** Lisa, a marketing consultant, gives a $200 Christmas gift to her best client. She may deduct $25 of the cost.

A gift to a member of a customer's family is treated as a gift to the customer, unless you have a legitimate nonbusiness connection to the family member. If you and your spouse both give gifts, you are treated as one taxpayer—it doesn't matter if you work together or have separate businesses.

The $25 limit applies only to gifts to individuals. It doesn't apply if you give a gift to an entire company, unless the gift is intended for a particular person or group of people within the company. Such company-wide gifts are deductible in any amount, as long as they are reasonable.

> **EXAMPLE:** The Acme Company is one of accountant Bob's best clients. Just before Christmas, he drops off a $100 cheese basket at the company's reception area for all of Acme's employees. He also delivers an identical basket to Acme's president. The first basket left in the reception area is a company-wide gift, not subject to the $25 limit. The basket for Acme's president is a personal gift and therefore is subject to the limit.

Insurance for Your Practice

You can deduct the premiums you pay for any insurance you buy for your practice as business operating expenses. This includes:

- medical insurance for your employees (see Chapter 11)
- fire, theft, and flood insurance for business property
- credit insurance that covers losses from business debts
- liability insurance
- professional malpractice insurance—for example, medical or legal malpractice insurance

- workers' compensation insurance you are required by state law to provide your employees (if you are an employee of an S corporation, the corporation can deduct workers' comp payments made on your behalf, but they must be included in your employee wages)
- business interruption insurance
- life insurance covering a corporation's officers and directors if you are not a direct beneficiary under the policy, and
- unemployment insurance contributions (either as insurance costs or business taxes, depending on how they are characterized by your state's laws).

Homeowners' Insurance for Your Home Office

If you have a home office and qualify for the home office deduction, you may deduct the home office percentage of your homeowners' or renters' insurance premiums. For example, if your home office takes up 20% of your home, you may deduct 20% of the premiums. You can deduct 100% of any special coverage that you add to your homeowners' or renters' policy for your home office and/or business property. For example, if you add an endorsement to your policy to cover business property, you can deduct 100% of the cost.

Car Insurance

If you use the actual expense method to deduct your car expenses, you can deduct the cost of insurance that covers liability, damages, and other losses for vehicles used in your practice as a business expense. If you use a vehicle only for business, you can deduct 100% of your insurance costs. If you operate a vehicle for both business and personal use, you can deduct only the part of the insurance premiums that applies to the business use of your vehicle. For example, if you use a car 60% for business and 40% for personal reasons, you can deduct 60% of your insurance costs. (See Chapter 5.)

If you use the standard mileage rate to deduct your car expenses, you get no separate deduction for insurance. Your insurance costs are included in the standard rate. (See Chapter 5.)

Interest on Business Loans

Interest you pay on business loans is usually a currently deductible business expense. It makes no difference whether you pay the interest on a bank loan, personal loan, credit card, line of credit, car loan, or real estate mortgage. Nor does it matter whether the collateral you used to get the loan was business or personal property. If you use the money for business purposes, the interest you pay to get that money is a deductible business expense. It's how you use the money that counts, not how you get it. Borrowed money is used for business when you buy something with the money that's deductible as a business expense.

> **EXAMPLE:** Dr. Smith borrows $50,000 from the bank to buy new medical equipment. He pays 6% interest on the loan. His annual interest expense is deductible as a business expense because the loan is a business loan.

Your deduction begins only when you spend the borrowed funds for business purposes. You get no business deduction for interest you pay on money that you keep in the bank. Money in the bank is considered an investment—at best, you might be able to deduct the interest you pay on the money as an investment expense.

Home Offices

If you are a homeowner and take the home office deduction, you can deduct the home office percentage of your home mortgage interest as a business expense. (See Chapter 7 for a detailed discussion of the home office deduction.)

Car Loans

If you use your car for business, you can deduct the interest that you pay on your car loan as an interest expense. You can take this deduction whether you deduct your car expenses using the actual expense method or the standard mileage rate, because the standard mileage rate does not include interest on a car loan.

If you use your car only for business, you can deduct all of the interest you pay. If you use it for both business and personal reasons, you can deduct the business percentage of the interest. For example, if you use your car 60% of the time for your practice, you can deduct 60% of the interest you pay on your car loan.

There is one important exception to this rule: Employees may not deduct car loan interest, even if they use their cars for business.

Loans to Buy a Practice

If you borrow money to buy an interest in an S corporation, a partnership, or an LLC, it's wise to seek an accountant's help to figure out how to deduct the interest on your loan. It must be allocated among the company's assets and, depending on what assets the business owns, the interest might be deductible as a business expense or an investment expense, which is more limited.

Interest on money you borrow to buy stock in a C corporation is always treated as investment interest. This is true even if the corporation is small (also called closely held) and its stock is not publicly traded.

Loans From Relatives and Friends

If you borrow money from a relative or friend and use it for business purposes, you may deduct the interest you pay on the loan as a business expense. However, the IRS is very suspicious of loans between family members and friends. You need to carefully document these transactions. Treat the loan like any other business loan: Sign a promissory note, pay a reasonable rate of interest, and follow a repayment schedule. Keep your canceled loan payment checks to prove you really paid the interest.

Interest You Can't Deduct

You can't deduct interest:
- on loans used for personal purposes
- on debts you or your practice don't owe
- on overdue taxes (only C corporations can deduct this interest)

- that you pay with funds borrowed from the original lender through a second loan (but you can deduct the interest once you start making payments on the new loan)
- that you prepay if you're a cash basis taxpayer (but you may deduct it the next year)
- on money borrowed to pay taxes or fund retirement plans, or
- on loans of more than $50,000 that are borrowed on a life insurance policy on yourself or another owner or employee of your business.

Points and other loan origination fees that you pay to get a mortgage on business property are not deductible business expenses. You must add these costs to the cost of the building and deduct them over time using depreciation.

Keeping Track of Borrowed Money

When you borrow money for your practice, you should not deposit it in a personal bank account. Deposit it in a separate account for your practice.

If you deposit a business loan in a personal account, you'll have to be able to prove that the money was actually spent on business. Complex IRS allocation rules may have to be followed.

However, if you buy something for your practice within 30 days of borrowing money, the IRS presumes that the payment was made from those loan proceeds (up to the amount of the loan proceeds). This is true regardless of the method or bank account you use to pay the business expense. If you receive the loan proceeds in cash, you can treat the payment as made on the date you receive the cash instead of the date you actually make the payment.

Legal and Professional Services

You can deduct fees that you pay to attorneys, accountants, consultants, and other professionals as business expenses if the fees are paid for work related to your practice.

> EXAMPLE: Ira, a doctor, hires attorney Jake to represent him in a malpractice suit. The legal fees Ira pays Jake are a deductible business expense.

Legal and professional fees that you pay for personal purposes generally are not deductible. For example, you can't deduct the legal fees you incur if you get divorced or you sue someone for a traffic accident injury. Nor are the fees that you pay to write your will deductible, even if the will covers business property that you own.

Buying Long-Term Property

If you pay legal or other fees in the course of buying long-term business property, you must add the amount of the fee to the tax basis (cost) of the property. You may deduct this cost over several years through depreciation or deduct it in one year under Section 179. (See Chapter 9 for more on depreciation.)

Starting a Practice

Legal and accounting fees that you pay to start your practice are deductible only as business start-up expenses. You can deduct $5,000 of start-up expenses the first year you're in business and any amounts over $5,000 over 180 months. The same holds true for incorporation fees or fees that you pay to form a partnership or an LLC. (See Chapter 10 for more on start-up expenses.)

Accounting Fees

You can deduct any accounting fees that you pay for your practice as a deductible business expense—for example, fees you pay an accountant to set up or keep your tax return, or give you tax advice for your practice.

Sole proprietor professionals may deduct the cost of having an accountant or another tax professional complete the business portion of their tax returns—Schedule C and other business tax forms—but they cannot deduct the time the preparer spends on the personal part of their returns. If you are a sole proprietor and pay a tax professional to complete your Form 1040 income tax return, make sure that you get an itemized bill showing the portion of the tax preparation fee allocated to preparing your Schedule C (and any other business tax forms attached to your Form 1040).

Taxes

Most taxes that you pay in the course of your practice are deductible.

Income Taxes

Federal income taxes that you pay on your business income are not deductible. However, a corporation or partnership can deduct state or local income taxes it pays. Individuals may deduct state and local income taxes only as an itemized deduction on Schedule A, Form 1040. This is a personal, not a business, deduction. However, an individual can deduct state tax on gross business income as a business expense. Of course, you can't deduct state taxes from your income for state income tax purposes.

Self-Employment Taxes

If you are a sole proprietor, a partner in a partnership, or an LLC member, you may deduct one-half of your self-employment taxes from your total net business income. This deduction reduces the amount of income on which you must pay personal income tax. It's an adjustment to gross income, not a business deduction. You don't list it on your Schedule C; instead, you take it on Page One of your Form 1040.

This deduction is intended to help ease the tax burden on the self-employed.

Employment Taxes

If you have employees, you must pay half of their Social Security and Medicare taxes from your own funds and withhold the other half from their pay. Employment taxes consist of a 12.4% Social Security tax on income up to an annual ceiling. In 2017, the annual Social Security ceiling was $127,200. Medicare taxes are not subject to any income ceiling and are levied at a 2.9% rate up to an annual threshold—$200,000 for single taxpayers and $250,000 for married couples filing jointly; all income above the threshold is taxed at a 3.8% rate. This combines to a total 15.3% tax on employment income up to the Social Security tax ceiling. You may deduct half of this amount as a business expense. You should treat the taxes you withhold from your employees' pay as wages paid to your employees on your tax return.

> **EXAMPLE:** You pay your employee $20,000 a year. However, after you withhold employment taxes, your employee receives $18,470. You also pay an additional $1,530 in employment taxes from your own funds. You should deduct the full $20,000 salary as employee wages and deduct the $1,530 as employment taxes paid.

Sales Taxes

Some states impose sales taxes on various types of services. You may not deduct state and local sales taxes on your goods and services that you are required to collect from a client or patient and turn over to your state or local government. Do not include these taxes in gross receipts or sales.

However, you may deduct sales taxes that you pay when you purchase goods or services for your practice. The amount of the tax is added to the cost of the goods or services for purposes of your deduction for the item.

> **EXAMPLE:** Jean, a sole proprietor lawyer, buys a $200 briefcase to use for her practice. She had to pay $15 in state and local sales taxes on the purchase. She may take a $215 deduction for the briefcase. She claims the deduction on her Schedule C as a purchase of supplies.

If you buy a long-term business asset, the sales taxes must be added to its basis (cost) for purposes of depreciation or expensing under IRC Section 179.

> **EXAMPLE:** Jean buys a $2,000 computer for her law office. She pays $150 in state and local sales tax. The computer has a useful life of more than one year and is therefore a long-term business asset for tax purposes. She can't currently deduct the cost as a business operating expense. Instead, Jean must depreciate the cost over several years or expense the cost (deduct the full cost in one year) under Section 179. The total cost to be depreciated or expensed is $2,150.

Real Property Taxes

You can deduct your current year's state and local property taxes on business real property as business expenses.

Home Offices

If you are a homeowner and take the home office deduction, you may deduct the home office percentage of your property taxes. However, as a homeowner, you are entitled to deduct all of your mortgage interest and property taxes, regardless of whether you have a home office. Taking the home office deduction won't increase your income tax deductions for your property taxes, but it will allow you to deduct them from your income for the purpose of calculating your self-employment taxes.

Charges for Services

Water bills, sewer charges, and other service charges assessed against your business property are not real estate taxes, but they are deductible as business expenses. If you have a home office, you can deduct your home office percentage of these items.

However, real estate taxes imposed to fund specific local benefits, such as streets, sewer lines, and water mains, are not deductible as business expenses. Because these benefits increase the value of your property, you should add what you pay for them to the tax basis (cost for tax purposes) of your property.

Buying and Selling Real Estate

When real estate is sold, the real estate taxes must be divided between the buyer and seller according to how many days of the tax year each held ownership of the property. You'll usually find information on this in the settlement statement you receive at the property closing.

Other Taxes

Other deductible taxes include:

- excise taxes—for example, Hawaii imposes a general excise tax on businesses that ranges from 0.5% to 4% of gross receipts
- state unemployment compensation taxes or state disability contributions
- corporate franchise taxes
- occupational taxes charged at a flat rate by your city or county for the privilege of doing business, and
- state and local taxes on personal property—for example, equipment that you use in your practice.

Hiring Employees and Independent Contractors

This chapter is about the host of tax rules that apply to professionals who hire other people to help them, whether as employees or independent contractors. These rules apply whether you hire strangers, friends, or family members.

If you are an employee of your own practice, however, different rules apply that are not covered in this chapter. This is usually the situation if you have incorporated your practice (or chosen corporate tax treatment for an unincorporated practice). Chapter 15 covers the rules for when professionals are employees of their own businesses.

Employees Versus Independent Contractors

As far as the IRS is concerned, there are only two types of people you can hire to help in your practice: employees and independent contractors. It's very important to understand the difference between the two because the tax rules are very different for each. If you hire an employee, you become subject to a wide array of state and federal tax requirements. You must withhold taxes from your employee's pay, and you must pay other taxes yourself. You must also comply with complex and burdensome bookkeeping and reporting requirements. If you hire an independent contractor, none of these requirements apply. Tax deductions for businesses that hire employees and independent contractors differ as well.

Independent contractors (ICs) go by a variety of names: self-employed, freelancers, free agents, consultants, entrepreneurs, or business owners. What they all have in common is that they are people who are in business for themselves. Employees work for someone else's business.

Initially, it's up to you to determine whether any person you hire is an employee or an IC. However, your decision about how to classify a worker is subject to review by various government agencies, including:

- the IRS
- your state's tax department
- your state's unemployment compensation insurance agency, and
- your state's workers' compensation insurance agency.

These agencies are mostly interested in whether you have classified workers as independent contractors when you should have classified them as employees. The reason is that you must pay money to each of these agencies for employees, but not for independent contractors. The more workers who are classified as employees, the more money flows into the agencies' coffers. In the case of taxing agencies, employers must withhold tax from employees' paychecks and hand it over to the government; ICs pay their own taxes, which means the government must wait longer to get its money and faces the possibility that ICs won't declare their income or will otherwise cheat on their taxes. An agency that determines that you misclassified an employee as an IC may impose back taxes, fines, and penalties.

Scrutinizing agencies use various tests to determine whether a worker is an IC or an employee. The determining factor is usually whether you have the right to control the worker. If you have the right to direct and control the way a worker performs—both as to the final results and the details of when, where, and how the work is done—then the worker is your employee. On the other hand, if your control is limited to accepting or rejecting the final results the worker achieves, then that person is an IC.

An employer may not always exercise its right of control. For example, if an employee is experienced and well trained, the employer may not feel the need to closely supervise him or her. But the employer still maintains the right to do so at any time.

> **EXAMPLE:** Mary, a lawyer in solo practice, hires Barry as her legal secretary. When Barry starts work, Mary closely supervises how he does his job. Virtually every aspect of Barry's behavior on the job is under Mary's control, including what time he arrives at and leaves work, when he takes his lunch break, and the sequence of tasks he must perform. If Barry proves to be an able and conscientious worker, Mary may choose not to look over his shoulder very often. But she has the right to do so at any time. Barry is an employee.

In contrast, a worker is an independent contractor if the hiring firm does not have the right to control the IC on the job. Because the worker is an independent businessperson not solely dependent on you (the hiring party) for a living, your control is limited to accepting or rejecting the final results the IC achieves.

EXAMPLE: Mary files a lawsuit and needs to serve the complaint on a hard-to-find defendant. She hires Jackie, a process server, to track down the defendant and serve him. Mary is just one of Jackie's many clients. Mary does not tell Jackie how to find the defendant or otherwise supervise her in any way. If Jackie is successful in serving the paper, Mary will pay her the agreed-upon fee. If Mary doesn't like the results Jackie achieves, she can refuse to pay her. Mary has no other control over Jackie. Jackie is an independent contractor.

The difficulty in applying the right-of-control test is determining whether you have the right to control a worker you hire. Government auditors can't look into your mind to see if you are controlling a worker. They rely instead on indirect or circumstantial evidence indicating control or lack of it—for example, whether you provide a worker with equipment, where the work is performed, how the worker is paid, and whether you can fire the worker. The following chart shows the primary factors used by the IRS and most other government agencies to determine if you have the right to control a worker.

CAUTION

Part-time workers and temps can be employees. Don't assume that a person you hire to work part time or for a short period automatically qualifies as an IC. People who work for you only temporarily or part time are your employees if you have the right to control the way they work.

RESOURCE

For a detailed discussion of the practical and legal issues hiring firms face when hiring ICs, see *Working With Independent Contractors*, by Stephen Fishman (Nolo).

IRS Test for Worker Status		
	Workers will more likely be considered ICs if:	**Workers will more likely be considered employees if:**
Behavioral Control	• you do not give them instructions • you do not provide them with training	• you give them instructions they must follow about how to do the work • you give them detailed training
Financial Control	• they have a significant investment in equipment and facilities • they pay business or travel expenses themselves • they make their services available to the public • they are paid by the job • they have opportunity for profit or loss	• you provide them with equipment and facilities free of charge • you reimburse their business or travel expenses • they make no effort to market their services to the public • you pay them by the hour or other unit of time • they have no opportunity for profit or loss—for example, because they're paid by the hour and have all expenses reimbursed
Relationship Between You and the Worker	• they don't receive employee benefits, such as health insurance • they sign a client agreement with the hiring firm • they can't quit or be fired at will • they perform services that are not part of your regular business activities	• they receive employee benefits • they have no written client agreement • they can quit at any time without incurring any liability to you • they can be fired at any time • they perform services that are part of your core business

Tax Deductions for Employee Pay and Benefits

Hiring employees costs you money, but you may deduct most or all of what you pay them as a business expense. Thus, for example, if you pay an employee $50,000 per year in salary and benefits, you'll ordinarily get a $50,000 tax deduction. You should factor this into your calculations whenever you're thinking about hiring an employee or deciding how much to pay him or her.

Employee Pay

Employee pay may be in the form of salary, bonuses, vacation allowances, sick pay (as long as it's not covered by insurance), or fringe benefits. For tax deduction purposes, it doesn't really matter how you measure or make the payments. Ordinarily, amounts you pay employees to work in your practice will be business operating expenses. These expenses are currently deductible as long as they are:

- ordinary and necessary
- reasonable in amount
- paid for services actually performed, and
- actually paid or incurred in the year the deduction is claimed (as shown by your payroll records).

An employee's services are ordinary and necessary if they are common, accepted, helpful, and appropriate for your business; they don't have to be indispensable. An employee's pay is reasonable if the amount is in the range of what other businesses would pay for similar services. These requirements usually won't pose a problem when you hire an employee to perform any legitimate business function.

> **EXAMPLE:** Ken, an architect, hires Kim to work as his personal assistant and pays her $5,000 per month—a typical salary for this kind of work. Ken can deduct Kim's $5,000 monthly salary as a business operating expense. If Kim works a full year, Ken will get a $60,000 deduction.

Payments to employees for personal services are not deductible as business expenses.

> **EXAMPLE:** Ken hires Samantha to work as a live-in nanny for his three children. Samantha is Ken's employee, but her services are personal, not related to his business. Thus, Ken may not deduct her pay as a business expense.

Special rules apply if you hire family members to work in your business. (See "Employing Your Family," below.)

Payroll Taxes

Whenever you hire an employee, you become an unpaid tax collector for the government. You are required to withhold and pay both federal and state taxes for the worker. These taxes are called payroll taxes or employment taxes. Federal payroll taxes consist of:

- Social Security and Medicare taxes—also known as FICA
- unemployment taxes—also known as FUTA, and
- federal income taxes—also known as FITW.

You must periodically pay FICA, FUTA, and FITW to the IRS, either electronically or by making federal tax deposits at specified banks which then transmit the money to the IRS. You are entitled to deduct as a business expense payroll taxes that you pay yourself. You get no deductions for taxes you withhold from employees' pay.

Every year, employers must file IRS Form W-2, *Wage and Tax Statement*, for each of their workers. The form shows the IRS how much the worker was paid and how much tax was withheld.

RESOURCE

IRS Publication 15, Circular E, *Employer's Tax Guide,* **provides detailed information on these requirements.** You can a get free copy by calling the IRS at 800-TAX-FORM, by calling or visiting your local IRS office, or by downloading it from the IRS website at www.irs.gov.

Employer's FICA Contributions

FICA is an acronym for Federal Income Contributions Act, the law requiring employers and employees to pay Social Security and Medicare taxes. Employment taxes consist of a 12.4% Social Security tax on income up to an annual ceiling. In 2017, the annual Social Security ceiling was $127,200. Medicare taxes are not subject to any income ceiling and are levied at a 2.9% rate up to an annual threshold—$200,000 for single taxpayers and $250,000 for married couples filing jointly; all income above these thresholds is taxed at a 3.8% rate. This combines to a total 15.3% tax on employment income up to the Social Security tax ceiling. You are entitled to deduct as a business expense the portion of the tax that you pay yourself.

The ceiling for the Social Security tax changes annually. You can find out what the Social Security tax ceiling is for the current year from IRS Publication 15, Circular E, *Employer's Tax Guide*; the amount is printed right on the first page.

FUTA

FUTA is an acronym for the Federal Unemployment Tax Act, the law that establishes federal unemployment taxes. Most employers must pay both state and federal unemployment taxes. Even if you're exempt from the state tax, you may still have to pay the federal tax. Employers alone are responsible for FUTA—you may not collect or deduct it from employees' wages.

You must pay FUTA taxes if either of the following is true:

- You pay $1,500 or more to employees during any calendar quarter— that is, any three-month period beginning with January, April, July, or October.
- You had one or more employees for at least some part of a day in any 20 or more different weeks during the year. The weeks don't have to be consecutive, nor does it have to be the same employee each week.

The FUTA tax rate is 6%. In practice, you rarely pay this much. You are given a credit of 5.4% if you pay the applicable state unemployment tax in full and on time. This means that the actual FUTA tax rate is usually 0.6%. The FUTA tax is assessed on the first $7,000 of an employee's annual wages. The FUTA tax, then, is usually $42 per year per employee.

FITW

FITW is an acronym for federal income tax withholding. You must calculate and withhold federal income taxes from your employees' paychecks. Employees are solely responsible for paying federal income taxes. Your only responsibility is to withhold the funds and remit them to the government. You get no deductions for FITW.

State Payroll Taxes

Employers in every state are required to pay and withhold state payroll taxes. These taxes include:

- state unemployment compensation taxes in all states
- state income tax withholding in most states, and
- state disability taxes in a few states.

Employers in every state are required to contribute to a state unemployment insurance fund. Employees make no contributions, except in Alaska, New Jersey, Pennsylvania, and Rhode Island, where employers must withhold small employee contributions from employees' paychecks. The employer contributions are a deductible business expense.

If your payroll is very small—below $1,500 per calendar quarter—you probably won't have to pay unemployment compensation taxes. In most states, you must pay state unemployment taxes for employees if you're paying federal FUTA taxes. However, some states have more strict requirements. Contact your state labor department for the exact rules and payroll amounts.

All states except Alaska, Florida, Nevada, South Dakota, Texas, Washington, and Wyoming have income taxation. If your state has income taxes, you must withhold the applicable tax from your employees' paychecks and pay it to the state taxing authority. Each state has its own income tax withholding forms and procedures. Contact your state tax department for information. Of course, employers get no deductions for withholding their employees' state income taxes.

California, Hawaii, New Jersey, New York, Rhode Island, and Washington State (starting in 2019) have state disability insurance that provides employees with coverage for injuries or illnesses that are not related to work. Employers in these states must withhold their employees' disability insurance contributions from their pay. Employers must also make their own contributions in Hawaii, New Jersey, New York, and Washington State (starting in 2019); these employer contributions are deductible.

In addition, subject to some important exceptions, employers in all states must provide their employees with workers' compensation insurance to cover work-related injuries. Workers' compensation is not a payroll tax. Employers must purchase a workers' compensation policy from a private insurer or state workers' compensation fund. Your worker's compensation insurance premiums are deductible as a business insurance expense. (See Chapter 13 for more on deducting business insurance.)

Bookkeeping Expenses Are Deductible

Figuring out how much to withhold, doing the necessary record keeping, and filling out the required forms can be complicated. Professionals often hire a bookkeeper or payroll tax service to do the work. Amounts you pay a bookkeeper or payroll tax service are deductible business operating expenses.

Be aware, however, that even if you hire a payroll service, you remain personally liable if your payroll taxes are not paid on time. The IRS recommends that employers: (1) keep their company address on file with the IRS, rather than the address of the payroll service provider, so that the company will be contacted by the IRS if there are any problems; (2) require the payroll service provider to post a fiduciary bond in case it defaults on its obligation to pay any penalties and interest due to IRS deficiency notices; and (3) ask the service provider to enroll in and use the Electronic Federal Tax Payment System (EFTPS) so the employer can confirm payments made on its behalf.

CAUTION
Employers in California must withhold for parental leave. Employers in California are also required to withhold (as part of their disability program) for parental leave. For more information on the program, go to www.edd.ca.gov.

Employee Fringe Benefits

There is no law that says you must provide your employees with any fringe benefits—not even health insurance (except in Hawaii and Massachusetts), sick pay, or vacation. Large employers (those with 50 or more full-time employees in 2016 and later) are required to provide health insurance to their full-time employees or pay a penalty to the IRS. However, the tax law encourages you to provide employee benefits by allowing you to deduct the costs as business expenses. (These expenses should be deducted as employee benefit expenses, not employee compensation.) Moreover, your employees do not have to treat the value of qualified fringe benefits as income on which they must pay tax. So you get a deduction, and your employees get tax-free goodies. Tax-free employee fringe benefits include:

- health insurance (see Chapter 11)
- accident insurance
- Health Savings Accounts (see Chapter 11)
- dependent care assistance
- educational assistance
- group term life insurance coverage—limits apply based on the policy value
- qualified employee benefit plans, including profit-sharing plans, stock bonus plans, and money purchase plans
- employee stock options
- lodging on your business premises
- moving expense reimbursements
- achievement awards

- commuting benefits
- employee discounts on the goods or services you sell
- supplemental unemployment benefits
- de minimis (low-cost) fringe benefits such as low-value birthday or holiday gifts, event tickets, traditional awards (such as a retirement gift), other special occasion gifts, and coffee and soft drinks, and
- cafeteria plans that allow employees to choose among two or more benefits consisting of cash and qualified benefits. (Starting in 2011, small employers—those with 100 or fewer employees—were able to offer their employees a simple cafeteria plan not subject to the nondiscrimination requirements of traditional cafeteria plans.)

Employee fringe benefits are covered in detail in Chapter 15.

Reimbursing Employees

There may be times when your employees must pay for a work-related expense. Most commonly, this occurs when an employee is driving, traveling, or entertaining while on the job. However, depending on the circumstances, an employee could end up paying for almost any work-related expense—for example, an employee might pay for office supplies or parking at a client's office.

All these employee payments have important tax consequences, whatever form they take. The rules discussed below apply whether the expenses are incurred by an employee who is not related to you or by an employee who is your spouse or child.

Reimbursement Under an Accountable Plan

The best way to reimburse or otherwise pay your employees for any work-related expenses is to use an accountable plan. Basically, this means the employee must submit all his or her documentation to the practice in a timely manner and return any excess payments. An accountable plan need not be in writing (although it's not a bad idea). All you need to do is set up procedures for your employees to follow that meet the requirements for accountable plans. (See Chapter 16 for more on accountable plans.)

When you pay employees for their expenses under an accountable plan, two great things happen:

- You don't have to pay payroll taxes on the payments.
- The employees won't have to include the payments in their taxable income.

Moreover, the amounts you pay will be deductible by you, just like your other business expenses, subject to the same rules.

> **EXAMPLE:** The ABC Medical Corporation decides that Manny, its senior nurse, should attend a nursing convention in Las Vegas. Manny pays his expenses himself. When he gets back, he fully documents his expenses as required by Acme's accountable plan. These amount to $2,000 for transportation and hotel and $1,000 in meal and entertainment expenses. Acme reimburses Manny $3,000. Acme may deduct as a business expense the entire $2,000 cost of Manny's flight and hotel and deduct 50% of the cost of the meals and entertainment. Manny need not count the $3,000 reimbursement as income (or pay taxes on it), and Acme need not include the amount on the W-2 form it files with the IRS reporting how much Manny was paid for the year. Moreover, Acme need not withhold income tax or pay any Social Security or Medicare taxes on the $3,000.

The reimbursements can be made through advances, direct reimbursements, charges to a company credit card, or direct billings to the employer.

The accountable plan rules are intended to prevent employees from seeking payment for personal expenses (or nonexistent phony expenses) under the guise that they are business expenses. Employees used to do this all the time to avoid paying income tax on the reimbursed amounts (employees must count employer reimbursements for their personal expenses as income, but not reimbursements for the employer's business expenses).

Unreimbursed Employee Expenses

Unless you've agreed to do so or your state's labor laws require it (see the warning below), you have no legal obligation to reimburse or pay employees for job-related expenses they incur. Employees are entitled to deduct from their own income any ordinary and necessary expenses arising from their employment that are not reimbursed by their employers. In this event, you (the employer) get no deduction, because you haven't paid for the expense.

> ⊘ **CAUTION**
> **Some states require reimbursement.** Check with your state's labor department to find out the rules for reimbursing employee expenses. You might find that you are legally required to repay employees, rather than letting your employees deduct the expenses on their own tax returns. In California, for example, employers must reimburse employees for all expenses or losses they incur as a direct consequence of carrying out their job duties. (Cal. Labor Code § 2802.)

Employees may deduct essentially the same expenses as business owners, subject to some special rules. For example, there are special deduction rules for employee home office expenses (see Chapter 7), and employees who use the actual expense method for car expenses may not deduct car loan interest.

However, it's much better for employees to be reimbursed by their employer under an accountable plan and let the employer take the deduction. Why? Because an employee can deduct unreimbursed employee expenses only if the employee itemizes his or her deductions and only to the extent that these deductions, along with the employee's other miscellaneous itemized deductions, exceed 2% of the employee's adjusted gross income. Adjusted gross income (AGI) is the employee's total income, minus deductions for IRA and pension contributions and a few other deductions (shown on Form 1040, Line 35).

Employing Your Family

Whoever said "never hire your relatives" must never have read the tax code. The tax law promotes family togetherness by making it highly advantageous for small business owners, including professionals, to hire their spouses or children. If you're single and have no children, you're out of luck.

Employing Your Children

Believe it or not, your children can be a great tax-savings device. If you hire your children as employees to do legitimate work in your practice, you may deduct their salaries from your business income as a business expense. Your children will have to pay tax on the salary only to the extent it exceeds the standard deduction amount for the year—$6,350 in 2017. Moreover, if your child is under 18, you won't have to withhold or pay any FICA (Social Security or Medicare) tax on the salary (subject to a couple of exceptions).

These rules allow you to shift part of your business income from your own tax bracket to your child's bracket, which should be much lower than yours (unless you earn little or no income). This can result in substantial tax savings.

A child need only pay a 10% tax on taxable income up to $9,325— taxable income means total income minus the standard deduction. Thus, a child could earn up to $15,675 and pay only a 10% income tax.

> **EXAMPLE:** In 2017, Carol hires Mark, her 16-year-old son, to perform computer inputting services for her medical practice, which she owns as a sole proprietor. He works ten hours per week and she pays him $20 per hour (the going rate for such work). Over the course of a year, she pays him a total of $9,000. She need not pay FICA tax for Mark because he's under 18. When she does her taxes for the year, she may deduct his $9,000 salary from her business income as a business expense. Mark pays tax only on the portion of his income that exceeds the $6,350 standard deduction—so he pays federal income tax only on $2,650 of his $9,000 salary. With such a small amount of income, he is in the lowest federal income tax bracket—10%. He pays $265 in federal income tax for the year.

No Payroll Taxes

As mentioned above, one of the advantages of hiring your child is that you need not pay FICA taxes for your child under the age of 18 who works in your trade or business, or your partnership if it's owned solely by you and your spouse.

Moreover, you need not pay federal unemployment (FUTA) taxes for services performed by your child who is under 21 years old.

However, these rules do not apply—and you must pay both FICA and FUTA—if you hire your child to work for:

- your corporation, or
- your partnership, unless all the partners are parents of the child.

You need not pay FICA or FUTA if you've formed a one-member limited liability company and hire your child to work for it. For tax purposes, a one-member LLC is a "disregarded entity"—that is, it's treated as if it didn't exist.

No Withholding

In addition, if your child has no unearned income (for example, interest or dividend income), you must withhold income taxes from your child's pay only if it exceeds the standard deduction for the year. The standard deduction was $6,350 in 2017 and is adjusted every year for inflation. Children who are paid less than this amount need not pay any income taxes on their earnings.

> EXAMPLE: Connie, a 17-year-old girl, is paid $4,000 a year to help out in her mother's chiropractic practice. She has no income from interest or any other unearned income. Her parents need not withhold income taxes from Connie's salary because she has no unearned income and her salary was less than the standard deduction amount for the year.

However, you must withhold income taxes if your child has more than $350 in unearned income for the year and his or her total income exceeds $1,050 (in 2017).

> EXAMPLE: If Connie (from the above example) is paid $4,000 in salary and has $500 in interest income, her parents must withhold income taxes from her salary because she has more than $350 in unearned income and her total income for the year was more than $1,050.

Employing Your Spouse

You don't get the benefits of income shifting when you employ your spouse in your business, because your income is combined when you file a joint tax return. You'll also have to pay FICA taxes on your spouse's wages, so you get no savings there either. However, you need not pay FUTA tax if you employ your spouse in your unincorporated business. This tax is usually less than $50 per year, so this is not much of a savings.

The real advantage of hiring your spouse is in the realm of employee benefits. You can provide your spouse with any or all of the employee benefits discussed in "Tax Deductions for Employee Pay and Benefits," above. You'll get a tax deduction for the cost of the benefit, and your spouse doesn't have to declare the benefit as income, provided the IRS requirements are satisfied. This is a particularly valuable tool for health coverage—you can give your spouse health insurance coverage and reimbursements for uninsured expenses as a tax-free employee benefit. (See Chapter 11 for a detailed discussion.)

Have Your Spouse Work at Home

Having your spouse spend all day with you at your office might sound like too much togetherness and could even cause problems with your other staff members. Fortunately, there is no law that says your spouse must work in your office. He or she can work at home. Professionals' spouses typically do accounting, collections, or marketing work for family practices. All these activities can easily be conducted from a home office.

Having your spouse work at home has tax benefits as well. If you set up a home office for your spouse that is used exclusively for business purposes, you'll get a home office deduction. Your spouse has no outside office, so the home office will easily pass the convenience of the employer test. (See Chapter 7.) Moreover, you can depreciate or deduct under Section 179 the cost of office furniture, computers, additional phone lines, copiers, fax machines, and other business equipment you buy for your spouse's use on the job.

Rules to Follow When Employing Your Family

The IRS is well aware of the tax benefits of hiring a child or spouse, so it's on the lookout for taxpayers who claim the benefit without really having their family members work in their businesses. If the IRS concludes that your children or spouse aren't really employees, you'll lose your tax deductions for their salary and benefits, and they'll have to pay tax on their benefits. To avoid this, you should follow these simple rules.

Rule 1: Your Child or Spouse Must Be a Real Employee

First of all, your child or spouse must be a bona fide employee. Their work must be ordinary and necessary for your business, and their pay must be for services actually performed. Their services don't have to be indispensable, only common, accepted, helpful, and appropriate for your business. Any real work for your business can qualify—for example, you could employ your child or spouse to clean your office, answer the phone, perform word processing, do photocopying, stuff envelopes, input data, or do filing. You get no business deductions when you pay your child for personal services, such as babysitting or mowing your lawn at home. On the other hand, money you pay for yard work performed on business property could be deductible as a business expense.

The IRS won't believe that an extremely young child is a legitimate employee. How young is too young? The IRS has accepted that a seven-year-old child may be an employee (*Eller v. Comm'r*, 77 T.C. 934 (1981)), but probably won't believe that children younger than seven are performing any useful work for your practice.

You should keep track of the work and hours your children or spouse perform by having them fill out time sheets or timecards. You can find these in stationery stores or make a timesheet yourself. It should list the date, the services performed, and the time spent performing the services. Although not legally required, it's also a good idea to have your spouse or child sign a written employment agreement specifying his or her job duties and hours. These duties should be related only to your practice.

Junior's Timesheet

Date	Time In	Time Out	Total Work Time	Services Performed
1/9	3:30 pm	5:30 pm	2 hours	copying, some filing
1/14	3:30 pm	5:00 pm	1 1/2 hours	printed out bills and prepared them for mailing
1/15	3:45 pm	5:15 pm	1 1/2 hours	copying and filing
1/24	10:00 am	3:00 pm	5 hours	answered phones
1/30	3:30 pm	5:30 pm	2 hours	copying and filing
1/1	10:00 am	2:00 pm	4 hours	cleaned office

Rule 2: Compensation Must Be Reasonable

When you hire your children, it is advantageous (taxwise) to pay them as much as possible. That way, you can shift as much of your income as possible to your children, who are probably in a much lower income tax bracket. Conversely, you want to pay your spouse as little as possible since you get no benefits from income shifting. This is because you and your spouse are in the same income tax bracket (assuming you file a joint return, as the vast majority of married people do). Moreover, your spouse will have to pay the employee's share of Social Security taxes on his or her salary—an amount that is not tax deductible. This tax is 7.65% up to the annual ceiling. (As your spouse's employer, you'll have to pay employment taxes on your spouse's salary as well, but these taxes are deductible business expenses.) The absolute minimum you can pay your spouse is the minimum wage in your area.

However, you can't just pay any amount you choose: Your spouse's and/or your child's total compensation must be reasonable. Total compensation means the sum of the salary and all the fringe benefits you provide your spouse, including health insurance and medical expense reimbursements, if any. This is determined by comparing the amount paid with the value of the services performed. You should have no problem as long as you pay no more than what you'd pay a stranger for the same work—don't try paying your child $100 per hour for office cleaning just to get a big tax deduction. Find out what workers performing similar services in your area are being paid. For example, if you plan to hire your teenager to do word processing, call an employment agency or temp agency in your area to see what these workers are being paid.

To prove how much you paid (and that you actually paid it), you should pay your child or spouse by check, not cash. Do this once or twice a month as you would for any other employee. The funds should be deposited in a bank account in your child's or spouse's name. Your child's bank account may be a trust account.

Rule 3: Comply With Legal Requirements for Employers

You must comply with most of the same legal requirements when you hire a child or spouse as you do when you hire a stranger. These rules are explained in detail in Publication 15, Circular E, *Employer's Tax Guide,* and Publication 929, *Tax Rules for Children and Dependents.* You can download them from the IRS website at www.irs.gov or get free copies by calling the IRS at 800-TAX-FORM.

Tax Deductions When You Hire Independent Contractors

As far as tax deductions are concerned, hiring independent contractors is very simple. Most of the time, the amounts you pay an IC to perform services for your practice will be deductible as business operating expenses. These expenses are deductible as long as they are ordinary, necessary, and reasonable in amount.

> EXAMPLE: Emily, an architect, hires Don, an attorney, to sue a client who failed to pay her. He collects $5,000, and she pays him $1,500 of this amount. The $1,500 is an ordinary and necessary business operating expense—Emily may deduct it from her business income for the year.

Of course, you get no business deduction if you hire an IC to perform personal services.

> **EXAMPLE:** Emily pays lawyer Don $2,000 to write her personal will. This is a personal expense. Emily cannot deduct the $2,000 from her business income.

If you hire an IC to perform services on your behalf in the start-up phase of your business, to manufacture inventory, or as part of a long-term asset purchase, the rules for deducting those types of expenses must be followed.

> **EXAMPLE:** Don hires Ralph, a business broker, to help him find a good dental practice to buy. After a long search, Ralph finds the right practice and Don buys it for $200,000. He pays Ralph a $12,000 broker's fee. This fee is a business start-up expense, of which Don may deduct $5,000 during the first year he's in practice and the remaining $7,000 over the first 180 months he's in business.

No Deductions for ICs' Taxes

When you hire an independent contractor, you don't have to withhold or pay any state or federal payroll taxes on the IC's behalf. Therefore, you get no deductions for the IC's taxes; the IC is responsible for paying them.

However, if you pay an unincorporated IC $600 or more by cash, check, or direct deposit during the year for business-related services, you must:

- file IRS Form 1099-MISC telling the IRS how much you paid the IC, and
- obtain the IC's taxpayer identification number.

You need not file a 1099-MISC if you pay an independent contractor electronically through a third-party payment organization—for example, through PayPal—or by credit card. The IRS may impose a $250 fine per violation if you intentionally fail to file a Form 1099 when required. But, far more serious, you'll be subject to severe penalties if the IRS later audits you and determines that you misclassified the worker.

If you're not sure whether you must file a Form 1099-MISC for a worker, go ahead and file one. You lose nothing by doing so and will save yourself the consequences of not filing if you were legally required to do so.

RESOURCE

For a detailed discussion of how to file a 1099 form and the consequences of not filing one, see *Working With Independent Contractors*, by Stephen Fishman (Nolo).

Paying Independent Contractors' Expenses

Independent contractors often incur expenses while performing services for their clients—for example, for travel, photocopying, phone calls, or materials. Many ICs want their clients to separately reimburse them for such expenses. The best practice is not to do this. It's better to pay ICs enough so they can cover their own expenses, rather than paying them less and having them bill you separately for expenses. This is because ICs who pay their own expenses are less likely to be viewed as your employees by the IRS or other government agencies.

However, it's customary in some businesses and professions for a client to reimburse an IC for expenses. For example, a lawyer who handles a business lawsuit will usually seek reimbursement for expenses such as photocopying, court reporters, and travel. If this is the case, you may pay these reimbursements.

When you reimburse an IC for a business-related expense, you, not the IC, get the deduction for the expense. Unless the IC fails to follow the adequate accounting rules discussed below, you should not include the amount of the reimbursement on the 1099 form you must file with the IRS reporting how much you paid the IC. The reimbursement is not considered income for the IC. Make sure to require ICs to document expenses with receipts that you save in case the IRS questions the payments.

The rules differ depending on whether the IC provides you with an "adequate accounting."

Adequate Accounting for Travel and Entertainment Expenses

To make an adequate accounting of travel and entertainment expenses, an IC must comply with all the record-keeping rules applicable to business owners and employees. The IRS is particularly suspicious of travel, meal, and entertainment expenses, so there are special documentation requirements for these. (See Chapter 18 for more on record keeping.) You are not required to save the IC's expense records except for records for entertainment expenses.

You may deduct the IC's travel, entertainment, and meal expenses as your own business expenses; but remember that meal and entertainment expenses are only 50% deductible. You do not include the amount of the reimbursement you pay the IC on the Form 1099 you file with the IRS reporting how much you paid the IC.

> EXAMPLE: Tim hires Mary, a self-employed marketing consultant, to help him increase his business's sales. In the course of her work, Mary incurs $1,000 in meal and entertainment expenses while meeting potential customers. She makes an adequate accounting of these expenses and Tim reimburses her the $1,000. Tim may deduct 50% of the $1,000 as a meal and entertainment expense for his business; Mary gets no deduction. When Tim fills out the 1099 form reporting to the IRS how much he paid Mary, he does not include the $1,000. Tim should save all the documentation Mary gave him showing her entertainment expenses.

No Adequate Accounting for Travel and Entertainment Expenses

If an IC doesn't properly document travel, meal, or entertainment expenses, you are probably not under any legal obligation to pay him or her. However, if you decide to pay some of these expenses, you may have to keep records of these items. You may reimburse the IC for the expenses and deduct the full amount as IC payments, provided they are ordinary, necessary, and reasonable in amount. The IC should provide you with some type of records to establish this. You are deducting these expenses as IC compensation, not as travel, meal, or entertainment expenses, so the 50% limit on deducting meal and entertainment costs does not apply. You must include the amount of the reimbursement as income paid to the IC on the IC's 1099 form.

Professionals Who Incorporate

I f you've incorporated your practice, or are thinking about it, this chapter is for you. When you form a professional corporation, you will ordinarily work as its employee, and be a shareholder as well. Your employee status presents some unique tax problems and opportunities.

If your practice is an LLC, an LLP, or a partnership, you can elect to be taxed as a corporation, so you also may be interested in learning about corporate tax treatment.

Automatic Employee Status

If you form a professional corporation to own and operate your practice and you continue to actively work in the practice, you automatically become an employee of your corporation. So even though you own the corporation (alone or with others in a group practice), you are also an employee of your corporation. In effect, you wear two hats: corporate shareholder and employee. Typically, you also serve as an officer of your corporation—president, vice president, secretary, or treasurer. In a one-shareholder corporation, one person holds all these officer positions and is an employee as well.

You're not an employee if your practice is organized in any other way—as a sole proprietorship, an LLC, a partnership, or an LLP. Even though you actively work in your unincorporated practice, you remain a self-employed business owner. It's only when you form a corporation that your status changes to that of an employee.

The tax rules that apply to you as an employee of a business that you own or co-own are the same as those that apply to any corporation with employees. The tax consequences of being an employee instead of a self-employed business owner are significant—with a mix of good and bad.

First, let's look at some of the disadvantages of being an employee:

- Your corporation must pay half of your employment taxes from its funds, withhold the other half from your pay, and send the entire amount to the IRS.
- Your corporation must send a W-2 form to the IRS each year showing how much you were paid.

- Your corporation must pay unemployment taxes on your behalf (see Chapter 14).
- Your corporation will probably have to provide you with workers' compensation coverage.
- Business expenses that are not reimbursed by your corporation must be deducted on your personal return as miscellaneous itemized deductions or characterized as shareholder loans (see Chapter 16).
- You'll qualify for the home office tax deduction only if your use of your home office is for the convenience of your employer (see Chapter 7).
- You can't deduct interest on a car loan for a car you use for business driving (see Chapter 5).

However, there are certain tax benefits that you get by incorporating and becoming an employee. If your corporation is taxed as a C corporation, you qualify for various tax-free employee fringe benefits. If your corporation is taxed as an S corporation, you don't get tax-free fringe benefits but you may be able to reduce your employment taxes by paying part of your compensation as a corporate distribution.

In the rest of this chapter, we focus on how incorporated professionals can fine-tune their compensation—with a mix of salary, employee benefits, dividends, and loans—to minimize the taxes they must pay and take advantage of their employee status. And we go over the differences in how to do this with a C corporation and an S corporation.

Paying Yourself

When you have an incorporated practice, one of your most important decisions is how much to pay yourself and what form the payments should take. Your decision will have important tax consequences. This is not the case when your practice is a sole proprietorship, an LLC or LLP, or a partnership. The owners of these entities pay personal income taxes on all their business profits each year, so it doesn't matter how they take the money out of their businesses.

Forget About Being a Nonemployee Shareholder

To avoid paying employment taxes, many incorporated professionals who actively work in their practices have tried to claim that they were not employees of their corporations and that the money they received from their corporations was dividends—not employee compensation. All have lost.

The courts have consistently held that corporation officer/shareholders who provide more than minor services to their corporation and receive remuneration are employees.

In one case, an accountant who was the president and owner of an S corporation claimed he was not an employee of his corporation, even though he did all of the accounting for the corporation and signed all of its tax returns. The accountant characterized the money he took out of his corporation as corporate dividends. The court found that the accountant provided substantial services that were essential to the corporation and that he was an employee (not an independent contractor), so the dividends were actually wages subject to employment taxes. (*Spicer Accounting, Inc. v. United States*, 1988 U.S. Dist. LEXIS 16891 (D. Idaho 1988); *aff'd* 918 F.2d 90 (9th Cir. 1990).)

Even if you avoid serving as a corporate officer, you will still be an employee of your corporation if you spend all your time working for it.

If, like most shareholders of professional corporations, you work as your corporation's employee, you can make payments to yourself in any of the following ways:

- employee compensation—salary, bonus, and fringe benefits such as health insurance and pension benefits
- corporate distributions, and/or
- loans from your corporation to you.

Of course, corporation shareholders can also liquidate (bring an end to) their corporation and distribute its assets to themselves. But this can only be done once, and can have substantial tax costs.

Most of your payments will likely be as employee salary, bonuses, benefits, and distributions. It is very important to get the mix between distributions and employee compensation right. Depending on whether your professional corporation is a C or an S corporation, too much of one or the other can result in extra taxes.

The Tax Treatment of Compensation Versus Distributions

Compensation that an incorporated business, including a professional practice, pays its employee is a deductible business expense provided the compensation is:

- ordinary and necessary
- paid for services actually performed, and
- reasonable in amount.

If your corporation is a C corporation, it deducts employee compensation on its own corporate tax return. You get no personal deduction for it. If your corporation is an S corporation, the deduction decreases the S corporation's profits that pass through the corporation to the shareholders' personal tax returns. (See Chapter 2.)

Corporate dividends are not tax deductible but they are taxable income to the shareholder who receives them. A dividend is not a payment for a shareholder-employee's services to the corporation as its employee. Rather, it represents a return on the capital the person has invested in the corporation as a shareholder.

On the other hand, employee wages are not only subject to income tax, but also to employment tax—this is a 12.4% Social Security tax up to an annual ceiling ($127,200 in 2017), and a Medicare tax on all employee earnings. Medicare taxes consist of a 2.9% tax up to an annual ceiling—$200,000 for single taxpayers and $250,000 for married couples filing jointly. All income above the ceiling is taxed at a 3.8% rate. Corporate distributions are not subject to any employment tax because they constitute payments to shareholder-employees as shareholders, not for their services as employees.

So, which is better to receive when you are a shareholder-employee of a professional corporation—employee compensation or shareholder distributions? It all depends on whether your corporation is a C corporation or an S corporation.

> ### LLCs, LLPs, and Partnerships Can Also Be Taxed Like C Corporations
>
> You don't necessarily have to have a corporation to obtain C corporation tax treatment for your practice. Although they are normally taxed as pass-through entities, LLCs, LLPs, and partnerships can obtain C corporation tax treatment by filing an election with the IRS. However, sole proprietors may not do this; they must form a C corporation to obtain such tax treatment. (See Chapter 2.)

C Corporations and the Advantages of Employee Compensation

If your professional corporation is a C corporation—that is, a taxpaying entity (see Chapter 2)—it is usually advantageous to take money out of the corporation in the form of employee compensation. This is because C corporations are subject to double taxation. The corporation must pay corporate income tax on its annual profit, and then the shareholders pay personal income tax on the same profits if they are distributed to them as dividends by the corporation.

Small C corporations, including most professional corporations, avoid double taxation by making sure their corporation has little or no profit at the end of the tax year. To accomplish this, the corporation's tax deductions must offset (zero out) all or most of its income, leaving it with no taxable profit. (See Chapter 2.) Employee compensation is usually the largest single tax deduction professional corporations have. Because they are not deductible, paying out dividends will not avoid double taxation—indeed it will promote it.

> EXAMPLE 1: DDS, Inc., is a professional corporation owned by Mark, a dentist, who is its sole shareholder and employee. DDS had a net income of $100,000 during the year ($400,000 revenue minus $100,000 operating expenses, and a $200,000 employee salary for Mark). DDS distributes its profits by giving Mark a $100,000 dividend. DDS, Inc., gets no tax deduction

for the distribution. Thus, it's left with the $100,000 profit at the end of the year on which it must pay corporate income tax. It pays this tax at a 35% flat rate because it is a personal services corporation. Mark must then pay a combined 18.8% capital gains and Medicare net investment income tax on the dividend distribution he receives. The distribution is not subject to employment taxes. DDS must pay $35,000 in corporate income tax on the $100,000 dividend (35% × $100,000 = $35,000). That leaves $65,000 to distribute to Mark, on which he must pay $12,220 in tax (18.8% x $65,000 = $12,220). The total tax paid on the $100,000 dividend is $47,220.

EXAMPLE 2: Assume that DDS does not pay any dividends to Mark. Instead, it pays the $100,000 profit to him as an employee bonus. Because employee salaries and bonuses are a deductible business expense, DDS now has no profits for the year on which it must pay corporate income tax ($100,000 profit − $100,000 bonus = $0 net profit). Mark must pay a 33% income tax and 3.8% employment tax (Medicare payroll tax) on his $100,000 bonus. The total tax on the $100,000 employee bonus is $36,800. Mark and his corporation save $10,420 in taxes by characterizing the $100,000 as a bonus instead of a dividend.

These examples illustrate that a C corporation's shareholder-employees have a strong incentive to pay themselves as much employee compensation as possible to avoid double taxation. Paying large salaries to C corporation employees has another advantage—it increases the amount you can contribute to tax-advantaged retirement accounts each year.

The IRS, however, is well aware of all this. Unfortunately, it likes double taxation and has a powerful weapon to help maintain it: If the IRS determines that a corporation has paid a shareholder-employee an unreasonably high salary for the services actually performed, the IRS can treat the excess part of the salary as a dividend. Such a pretend dividend is called a constructive dividend. The C corporation will lose its deduction for that amount and will have to pay income tax on it. For most professional corporations, this means a 35% income tax because they are personal service corporations. The shareholder-employee who receives the payment will have to pay capital gains tax on the amount. Currently, the top income tax on distributions is 23.8% (see Chapter 2).

However, in some cases, the IRS will not permit salary disallowed as unreasonable to be treated as a constructive dividend to the shareholder (although it is treated that way for the corporation). Instead, the payment remains as compensation in the hands of the employee-shareholder who must pay income tax on it at ordinary personal income tax rates, usually far above 23.8%. Employment tax must be paid on the amount as well. (*Stemo Sales Corp.*, 345 F.2d 552 (Ct. Cl. 1965).)

Thus, if you're the shareholder-employee of a C corporation, it is crucial for you to know how much the corporation can pay you as employee compensation without bringing down the IRS's wrath. You must be able to prove to the IRS that your pay is reasonable.

CAUTION

You can't use Section 179 if you zero out your corporation's profits. This could be a big drawback taxwise for your business. Section 179 allows businesses to deduct the cost of equipment and other tangible personal property bought for the business. However, the deduction is limited to the business's annual profits. No profit, no deduction. Thus, if you want to use the Section 179 deduction, you need to make sure that your C corporation has enough profit left at the end of the tax year. Alternatively, you may be able to use bonus depreciation, which is not subject to a business income limitation. (See Chapter 9 for a detailed discussion of Section 179 and bonus depreciation.)

What Is Reasonable Compensation?

There is no mathematical formula for determining whether compensation is reasonable. Rather, the IRS looks at all the facts and circumstances. The general rule is that reasonable pay is the amount that like enterprises would pay for the same, or similar, services. Among the factors the IRS and courts consider are:

- the duties performed by the employee
- the volume of business handled
- the type of work and amount of responsibility
- the complexity of the business
- the time and effort devoted to the business

- the timing and manner of paying bonuses to key people
- use of a formula to determine compensation
- the cost of living in the locality
- the ability and achievements of the individual employee performing the service
- the pay compared with the gross and net income of the business, as well as with distributions to shareholders
- the company's policy regarding pay for all employees, and
- the payment history for each employee.

These factors are judged based on the circumstances that exist when you contract for the services, not those that exist when reasonableness is questioned by the IRS. No single factor is determinative, and not all are considered in every case. Indeed, some courts consider only one factor: whether an independent financial investor (a person with no interest in the company, other than stock ownership) would be willing to pay the compensation involved.

One-Person Corporations

If you have a one-person professional corporation for which you perform all the professional services, it's often easy to figure out how much you should be paid. Usually, it's the corporation's entire profit (that is, an amount equal to its gross income minus its operating expenses, not counting your compensation). The reasoning behind this is simple: A professional corporation earns its income from providing a service; thus, if you're the only one providing that service for the corporation, your services must be worth all that the corporation earns, less operating expenses.

> **EXAMPLE:** Richard Ashare, a Michigan attorney, formed a professional corporation of which he was sole shareholder and professional employee. For several years, Ashare's firm devoted itself to a single class action lawsuit which it won, obtaining a $70 million judgment. The firm was awarded a $12.6 million fee. Ashare had his corporation pay him $12.24 million of the fee over five years as employee salary. The tax court held that the compensation was reasonable because Ashare's personal services had earned the fee. (*Ashare v. Comm'r*, T.C. Memo 1999-282.)

Corporations With Multiple Shareholder-Employees

What if a professional corporation is owned by two or more professionals who provide employee services? You should not have a problem with the IRS if each shareholder-employee's compensation is based on the amount of money he or she brings into the practice. Compensation may also be added for the value of work a shareholder-employee does that does not directly lead to collections, such as administrative and management duties, business development, and community relations. (*Richlands Medical Association v. Comm'r*, T.C. Memo 1990-660.)

However, the IRS will become suspicious if the shareholder-employees' compensation is based on the proportion of their stock ownership of the corporation, rather than the actual value of their work as employees. For example, if a three-person professional corporation where each person owns one-third of the stock always pays each shareholder-employee one-third of the profits, the IRS will likely raise the issue of unreasonable compensation in an audit.

Corporations With Nonshareholder Employees

Where professional corporations can really run into problems with unreasonable compensation is when they have nonshareholder employees who provide professional services for the corporation, as well as shareholder-employees. The shareholder-employees' compensation cannot include amounts derived from the nonshareholders' work. A shareholder-employee can be paid only for the reasonable value of the services he or she actually performs, not those performed by others.

> EXAMPLE: Pediatric Surgical Associates, a professional corporation taxed as a C corporation, had shareholder surgeons who received monthly salaries and cash bonuses based on the corporation's net profit, and nonshareholder surgeons who received only monthly salaries. The corporation deducted the entire amount paid to the shareholder surgeons as employee compensation. Both the IRS and tax court found that part of the salaries paid to the shareholder surgeons was unreasonable because it exceeded the value of their services to the corporation based on their collections. Rather, the excessive amounts represented the profits the corporation earned through

the services of the nonshareholder surgeons. These profits could not be distributed to the shareholder surgeons as employee compensation because they were not for work actually performed by them. (*Pediatric Surgical Associates, P.C. v. Comm'r,* T.C. Memo 2001-81.)

Strategies to Avoid Unreasonable Compensation Problems

It's up to you to prove that your salary is reasonable if you are audited by the IRS. The time to think about how you will do this is long before you hear from the IRS. Here are some things you can do to prove you're worth what your corporation pays you.

Keep records of your work. Keep detailed records showing why you are worth what you're being paid. These should show the number of hours you worked, your contributions to the practice that may not directly result in collections (such as management and administrative tasks), and any other factors which could affect how much you're paid.

Keep records of your training and accomplishments. Employees with specialized training and/or experience can justify higher salaries than those without it. Professionals ordinarily have substantial training and other accomplishments they can brag about to the IRS. Maintain a file of all education credits, seminars, degrees, certificates, notable accomplishments, honors, and achievements that relate to your practice. Also keep records of what you earned as a professional before you established your corporation. These can provide strong evidence of what your services are worth. In one case, a court held that an incorporated dentist was entitled to a salary equal to what he had earned as a sole proprietor. (*Bianchi v. Comm'r,* 66 T.C. 324 (1976).)

Document your employment relationship. Draw up a written employment agreement and corporate resolution detailing your abilities, qualifications, and responsibilities. These should show why you're worth what your corporation is paying you. If your pay is more than your professional services are worth, the agreement should detail all the administrative duties you must perform and how much pay they merit above and beyond compensation for your professional services.

Whenever you receive a raise or a salary, a corporate resolution should also be drafted that documents the reasons for the increase in pay—for example, the substantial income your efforts bring in to the corporation. (For examples of such a corporate resolution, see *The Corporate Records Handbook: Meetings, Minutes & Resolutions*, by Anthony Mancuso (Nolo).)

Avoid large year-end bonuses. Try to avoid paying yourself large discretionary bonuses at the end of the year after your corporation's annual profits have been calculated. Such bonuses look like an effort to avoid corporate income tax, not pay you for your employee services to the corporation. If possible, the amount of any bonuses should be established in your employment agreement and based on a quantifiable figure, such as your annual billings. Bonuses should never be a percentage of the corporation's net profit or based on your stock ownership.

Establish annual salary in advance. One way to establish your annual salary is for a specific amount to be provided in your employment agreement. This will have to be redone at the beginning of each year. Another approach is to use a formula to set shareholder-employee salaries. If this is done, the formula should not be based on the corporation's net profits—this makes it look like a distribution. Instead, base the formula on the monetary value of the shareholder-employee's actual services. For example, you could base it on a percentage of collections the shareholder-employee brings in, plus the value of other administrative or managerial services.

Pay some distributions. It's best for a professional corporation to pay its shareholder-employees at least some distributions, some years. These should be more than a token amount or they won't impress the IRS. However, professional corporation distributions are ordinarily smaller than those issued by most other business corporations because professional corporations typically have less capital invested. Talk to your tax pro about how much your corporation should distribute as a dividend.

Consider all your compensation. All your compensation should be considered when determining whether it will pass muster with the IRS as reasonable. This includes not just your salary and bonus, but employee benefits, retirement plan contributions, and fringe benefits like company cars.

S Corporations and the Advantages of Corporate Distributions

If you are the shareholder-employee of a professional corporation that is an S corporation, you want to pay yourself as little employee wages and as much in S corporation distributions as possible. This, of course, is the exact opposite of a C corporation. The reason distributions are good when you have an S corporation is that distributions are not subject to employment taxes. Employee wages, on the other hand, are subject to such taxes. The fact that distributions are not deductible is meaningless for an S corporation because it is a pass-through entity—it pays no taxes. (See Chapter 2.)

> **EXAMPLE:** Senator John Edwards ran as the Democratic Party vice presidential candidate in 2004. Prior to his political career, he was one of the most successful medical malpractice lawyers in the United States. In 1995, he converted his law firm to an S corporation of which he was the sole shareholder. He paid himself an employee salary of $600,000 in 1996 and $540,000 in 1997, on which he and his firm paid employment taxes. As the sole stockholder, Edwards received distributions from his S corporation of $5 million for each of those two years, or $10 million total. He only had to pay income tax, not employment taxes, on the $10 million in distributions. How much did this save him? Had the $10 million been paid out as employee compensation, he would have had to pay 2.9% Medicare tax on this amount. (He wouldn't owe Social Security tax because his annual salary was well above the Social Security tax ceiling.) The Medicare tax really adds up, though, when you earn $5 million per year. In this case, Edwards saved a total of $290,000 ($10,000,000 × $2.9% = $290,000). Even though Edwards was subjected to criticism in the press during the 2004 campaign for his S corporation, his tax strategy was perfectly legal. If Edwards did this today, he'd save even more in Medicare tax because the Medicare tax rate for higher-income taxpayers was increased to 3.8% effective 2013.

It's up to the people who run an S corporation—its officers and directors—to decide how much salary to pay the corporation's employees. When you are employed by an S corporation that you own (alone or with others), you'll be the one making this decision. In fact, 70% of all

S corporations are owned by just one person, so the owner has complete discretion to decide on his or her salary.

However, an S corporation must pay reasonable employee compensation (subject to employment taxes) to a shareholder-employee in return for the services the employee provides before a distribution (not subject to employment taxes) may be given to the shareholder-employee. Whether compensation paid by an S corporation is reasonable is determined according to the same standards as those used for C corporations. (See "C Corporations and the Advantages of Employee Compensation," above.)

If you don't pay yourself enough employee compensation, the IRS can reclassify all or part of the distribution as employee salary. This is particularly likely to occur if you pay yourself no employee compensation at all. For example, a CPA who incorporated his practice took a $24,000 annual salary from his S corporation and received $220,000 in dividends that were free of employment taxes. The IRS said that his salary was unreasonably low and that $175,000 of the dividends should be treated as wages subject to employment taxes. The court upheld the IRS's power to recharacterize the dividends as wages subject to employment tax. (*Watson v. United States*, (D.C. Iowa 05/27/2010) 105 AFTR 2d. 2010–908.)

How low can you go and still pay yourself a reasonable salary? There are no precise guidelines. IRS officials have stated that they make the determination on a case-by-case basis. After examining all the circumstances, they establish a range of reasonable salaries, from low to high. In one case, the IRS concluded that a reasonable salary for an Arkansas certified public accountant was $45,000 to $49,000. The accountant in that case had paid himself no salary and received $83,000 in corporate distributions. The IRS used salary information from a large financial services recruiting firm to determine what was reasonable. (*Barron v. Comm'r*, T.C. Summ. 2001-10.) Some IRS offices have software that provides salary information for a variety of occupations throughout the country.

Paying yourself the minimum wage likely won't be considered reasonable by the IRS. Some tax professionals believe that you'll have no problems as long as you pay yourself an amount at least equal to the Social Security tax ceiling—$127,200 in 2017. However, it is unclear if this is really true. A good approach is to find out what professionals performing similar services as employees are being paid in your area, and pay yourself on the low side of the salary range.

Also, keep in mind that there is a downside to paying yourself a small employee salary: You may end up reducing the amount you can contribute each year to a tax-advantaged retirement plan. This is because your annual tax-deductible contribution limit is based on your employee salary. The smaller your salary, the less you may contribute and the smaller your deduction will be. To maximize their retirement plan contributions, some S corporation shareholder-employees elect to pay themselves the highest-level salary that is used to determine the maximum annual contribution amount. This amount changes each year. In 2017, it was $270,000. The shareholders take the rest of their compensation, if any, as S corporation distributions. It seems highly unlikely that the IRS would claim that an S corporation shareholder-employee who is paid $270,000 is not receiving a reasonable salary.

Employee Fringe Benefits

The most significant tax advantage that C corporations have over pass-through entities (sole proprietorships, partnerships, LLCs, LLPs, and S corporations) is in the area of employee fringe benefits. The main reason some professionals continue to form C corporations (or obtain C corporation tax treatment for an LLC or LLP or a partnership) is to obtain these benefits.

An employee fringe benefit is a form of payment for the employee's services. However, instead of paying the employee money, the employer provides the employee with property or services—for example, health insurance, retirement benefits, and company cars.

Qualified Fringe Benefits

Ordinarily, employee fringe benefits are treated the same as employee salary or bonus: They are tax deductible by the C corporation employer as a business expense, but their cost or value must be added to the recipient employee's taxable wages. This means that both income and employment taxes must be paid on the benefit's costs.

However, certain types of fringe benefits are tax free—that is, the corporate employer may deduct them as a business operating expense, and the employees don't need to include the benefits' cost in their income. The tax law lists the benefits that can be tax free and establishes requirements that must be met to obtain this coveted status. Benefits that meet the requirements are said to be "qualified." Nonqualified benefits are taxable to the employee.

The rules are different for retirement benefits. They are not tax free to the employee, but tax on them is deferred until the employee collects the benefits, which can be many years in the future.

If your professional practice is taxed as a C corporation and you work as its employee (which incorporated professionals ordinarily do), you can have your company provide employee benefits to you in your capacity as an employee, which can result in tax savings.

> **EXAMPLE:** Marvin is a dentist who has formed a professional corporation taxed as a C corporation. He is the sole shareholder and the only employee. Marvin has his corporation pay the premiums for a generous disability insurance policy for him. He also establishes a medical reimbursement plan to have his corporation reimburse him for health-related expenses not covered by insurance. The total cost of these benefits is $10,000 per year. His corporation gets to deduct the cost of the insurance, and he doesn't have to include the cost in his employee income. He's in the 33% federal income tax bracket, so this saves him $3,300 in income tax that he would have had to pay had he taken $10,000 in employee salary and purchased the insurance with his personal funds. He and his corporation also avoid paying employment taxes on the amount.

Professionals whose practices are taxed as sole proprietorships, partnerships, LLCs, LLPs, or S corporations must include in their incomes, and pay tax on, the value of any fringe benefits they receive from their companies. For example, if Marvin in the above example had his practice organized as an LLC and taxed as a partnership, the LLC could have deducted the insurance premiums and medical reimbursements, but Marvin would have had to include them in his taxable income—thus, he would have $10,000 more in self-employment income to pay both income and self-employment tax on.

However, when it comes to the most important benefits—health insurance and retirement plans—things aren't nearly as bad for owners of pass-through entities as they used to be. Pass-through entity owners may deduct 100% of their health insurance expenses as a special personal income tax deduction (see Chapter 11). They can also establish their own retirement plans that are just as good as those for employees.

Pass-through entity owners, however, may not obtain tax-free medical reimbursement plans for themselves. This is a huge advantage for C corporations. But there is one way professionals who have pass-through entities can obtain tax-free treatment for medical reimbursement plans and all the other employee fringe benefits: The professional can hire his or her spouse as an employee and provide the spouse with the benefits. The spouse must be a legitimate employee, however. (See Chapter 11.)

Also, S corporation shareholder-employees who own less than 2% of the corporate stock receive the same treatment as C corporation shareholder-employees. However, few professionals own so little stock in their corporations (an S corporation shareholder can't stay under the 2% ownership ceiling by transferring stock to a spouse or other family member).

CAUTION

The IRS scrutinizes employee fringe benefits. Some companies try to avoid paying any taxes on profits by distributing them to employees in the form of money or reimbursements for bogus tax-free fringe benefits. In one case, an employer paid its employees $180 per month for nonexistent parking expenses. Because employee parking expenses are a tax-free employee fringe benefit (within certain limits), they didn't pay any income or employment tax on the payments. The IRS discovered the subterfuge and recharacterized the payments as taxable employee wages. (IRS Rev. Rul. 2004-98.) If you pay yourself for an employee benefit, make sure it's a legitimate benefit, and keep proper records.

Types of Fringe Benefits

The most important employee fringe benefits are:

- health insurance and other health benefits (see Chapter 11), and
- working condition fringe benefits (see Chapter 16).

Health benefits are so important that they have their own chapter. Working condition fringes are covered in the chapter on paying expenses.

Other fringe benefits are discussed below. Most have dollar limits. If the limit is exceeded, the employee must pay tax on the excess. In addition, to qualify for tax-free treatment, many of these fringe benefits must be offered to C corporation employees on a nondiscriminatory basis—that is, the corporation cannot provide the benefits just to highly compensated employees. These are employees who:

- own 5% or more of the corporation stock, or
- whose compensation exceeds a threshold amount.

If the nondiscrimination rules are violated, the cost or value of the benefit must be included in the highly compensated employee's income for tax purposes. What this means is that providing a tax-free fringe benefit could get very expensive if a C corporation has many nonshareholder employees. As a result, many small professional corporations do not provide employee fringe benefits that are subject to nondiscrimination rules. The benefits subject to these rules are noted below.

 RESOURCE
For more information on these fringe benefits, refer to IRS Publication 15-B, *Employer's Tax Guide to Fringe Benefits.* It can be found on the IRS website at www.irs.gov, or you can obtain a copy by calling 800-TAX-FORM.

Group Term Life Insurance

A corporation may provide up to $50,000 in group term life insurance to each employee tax free. If an employee is given more than $50,000 in coverage, the corporation still gets to deduct the full premium, but the employee must pay tax on the excess amount. However, this tax is paid at very favorable rates.

For a group term life insurance plan to qualify for tax-free treatment, it must cover at least ten full-time employees. If the corporation has fewer than ten employees, all insurable employees must be covered. In addition, the plan must not discriminate in favor of key employees. An employee life insurance plan does not discriminate if any of the following is true:

- The plan benefits at least 70% of all employees.
- At least 85% of all participating employees are not key employees.
- The plan benefits employees who qualify under a classification that is set up by the employer and found by the IRS not to discriminate in favor of key employees.

Disability Insurance

If a professional corporation pays disability insurance premiums for an employee (and the employee is the beneficiary), the premiums are excluded from the employee's income. However, the employee must pay income tax on any disability benefits received under the policy. There is an important exception, however: Disability payments for the loss of a bodily function or limb are tax free.

An employee can obtain disability benefits tax free by paying for the premiums. If an employee pays for disability insurance him- or herself, any disability benefits paid to the employee under the policy are not taxable to the employee. The IRS has ruled that an employee need only pay the disability premiums in the policy year the disability occurred to obtain tax-free treatment; the employer can pay the premiums for the preceding years. (IRS Private Letter Ruling 8027088.) The company can withhold the premiums from the employee's salary, or the employee can pay the premiums directly.

Educational Assistance

Employers may pay employees up to $5,250 tax free each year for educational expenses, such as tuition, fees, and books. However, there is a strict nondiscrimination requirement: No more than 5%

of the benefits may be paid to shareholder-employees who are highly compensated employees. This rule eliminates this benefit for most professional corporations.

No Additional Cost Services

You may provide your employees (or their spouses or dependent children) with a service that you regularly provide to your clients. However, this benefit is tax free only as long as it does not cause the company to incur any substantial additional costs. Additional costs usually include the cost of labor, materials, and supplies. If substantial additional costs are incurred, the cost of the *entire* service is taxable income to the employee, not just the added costs. Thus, for example, a medical corporation can't perform an operation on an employee and treat it as a tax-free benefit. The entire cost of the operation would have to be added to the employee's income.

This benefit is also subject to nondiscrimination rules. A highly compensated employee must include this cost in his or her income unless it's offered to all employees, or a group of employees defined under a reasonable classification you set up that does not favor highly compensated employees.

Employee Discounts

Employees may be given discounts of up to 20% for an employer's services or products. For example, a professional medical corporation can give employees a 20% discount for medical services. This benefit is subject to nondiscrimination rules.

Dependent Care Assistance

Up to $5,000 in dependent care assistance may be provided to an employee tax free. For example, the company could help pay for day care for an employee's child. This benefit is subject to nondiscrimination rules. Unlike all the other benefits covered in this chapter, this benefit may be provided to owners of pass-through entities.

Moving Expense Reimbursements

Employees may also be paid or reimbursed for moving expenses. However, this benefit is tax free to the employee only if the expense would be deductible if the employee paid for it. The move must meet both a distance test and time test. The distance test requires that the new job location be at least 50 miles farther from the employee's old home than the old job location. The time test is met if the employee works at least 39 weeks during the first 12 months after arriving in the general area of the new job location.

Meals

Any meal or meal money you provide to an employee is tax free if it has so little value (taking into account how frequently you provide such meals) that separately accounting for it makes no sense. This includes, for example:

- coffee, doughnuts, or soft drinks
- occasional meals or meal money provided to enable an employee to work overtime, and
- occasional parties or picnics for employees and their guests.

Meals you provide your employees on your business premises are also tax free if they are furnished for your convenience—that is, for a substantial business reason. Boosting employee morale is not a good reason.

Athletic Facilities

If a corporation has an on-premises gym or other athletic facility, it can allow its employees to use it tax free if substantially all use of the facility during the year is by corporation employees, their spouses, and their dependent children.

De Minimis (Minimal) Benefits

De minimis (minimal) employee benefits are also tax free. A de minimis benefit is property or service you provide to an employee that has so little value that accounting for it would be unreasonable. Cash, no matter how little, is never excludable as a de minimis benefit, except for occasional meal money or transportation fare.

Examples of de minimis benefits include:

- holiday gifts, other than cash, with a low fair market value
- group term life insurance payable on the death of an employee's spouse or dependent if the face amount is not more than $2,000
- occasional parties or picnics for employees and their guests, and
- occasional tickets for entertainment or sporting events.

Transportation Benefits

De minimis (minimal) transportation benefits may be provided to employees tax free. These cost so little that it makes no sense to keep track of them—for example, the occasional transportation fare given to an employee because the employee is working overtime. Employers may also pay up to $255 per month for employee parking or for mass transit passes for those employees who don't drive to work. These are the limits for 2017. They are adjusted for inflation each year. In addition, employees who regularly commute to work by bicycle may be paid up to $20 per month to reimburse them for expenses such as bike storage.

Cafeteria Plans

A cafeteria plan (also called a flexible spending account) allows employees to choose benefits from a range of choices such as health insurance, dental plans, short-term disability coverage, and life insurance. They are called cafeteria plans because the option is similar to choosing a meal in a cafeteria. Typically, these plans also allow employees to lower their income and employment taxes by making their own contributions and deducting them from their salaries. However, starting in 2013, such employee contributions must be limited to no more than $2,500 per year. If a cafeteria plan does not comply with this requirement, all benefits offered under the plan must be included in the employee's gross income.

Unfortunately, classic cafeteria plans are subject to nondiscrimination rules. Highly compensated employees must include benefits from such plans in their taxable income if they receive more than 25% of plan benefits. For this reason, professional corporations often don't use such plans. However, small employers (those with 100 or fewer employees) can offer their employees a simple cafeteria plan—a plan not subject to the nondiscrimination requirements of traditional cafeteria plans. Such plans enable employers to provide discriminatory benefits for highly compensated and key employees, while allowing other employees to benefit from the plan. This should make these plans especially attractive for professional corporations. These plans do have restrictions: Minimum contributions must be made for all qualified employees. The plan must also satisfy minimum eligibility and participation requirements.

Benefits That Are Not Tax Deductible

Some types of fringe benefits are not tax deductible at all—the corporate employer may not deduct them, and the recipient employee must include their cost or value in his or her income. Any benefit provided by a corporation to an employee is nondeductible if it also couldn't be deducted as a business expense if the employee personally bought it. This includes, for example:

- paying for an employee's membership in country clubs
- paying for meals and entertainment that are not de minimis and do not meet the requirements for deductibility set forth in Chapter 4
- paying for an employee's personal vacations or other nonbusiness travel
- permitting an employee to use corporate property for personal purposes free of charge—for example, using a company car for a personal vacation
- allowing an employee to rent corporate property at below market rates
- allowing an employee to purchase corporate property at below market rates, and
- giving an employee any other property or service used solely for personal purposes.

The cost or fair market value of all such nondeductible benefits must be added to the employee's taxable income.

> EXAMPLE: Phil, the shareholder-employee of an engineering firm, has his company purchase a cell phone that he takes home and gives to his daughter. The cost of the phone would not be deductible as a business expense by Phil if he bought it himself because the phone is used only for personal purposes. Therefore, the cost of the phone must be added to Phil's employee income by his professional corporation employer.

Shareholder Loans

Borrowing money from your corporation can appear to be a very attractive option because a loan is tax free: It is not taxable income to you, and the company need not pay employment taxes on the amount. In the past, small business owners avoided taxes by making cash advances to shareholders and treating them as loans, even though there was no intention that the money would ever be paid back. Today, there are strict IRS rules to prevent such abuses.

CAUTION
Loans are not a deductible expense. A loan is not a deductible expense for the lender. Thus, a C corporation that makes a loan to a shareholder from its corporate earnings must pay corporate income tax on the amount of the loan, even though the money is no longer in the corporation's bank account. Professional corporations normally pay income tax at the 35% personal service corporation rate. This result can be avoided only if the shareholder/borrower pays back the money before the corporation files its tax return, or if the corporation has losses that can be used to offset the loan. If a loan is made to a shareholder of an S corporation, no corporate income tax will be due because S corporations don't pay income tax. The money will pass through the corporation to the shareholder's personal returns, however, and the shareholder will have to pay personal income tax on it. Again, this can be avoided only through timely repayment or offsetting losses.

Only Bona Fide Loans Are Recognized by the IRS

A corporate loan to a shareholder-employee must be a bona fide (real) loan, or the IRS will recharacterize it as employee compensation or a corporate distribution. A bona fide loan is made with the intention that it be repaid by the borrower.

The loan should have all the characteristics of a loan made by a bank: There should be a signed promissory note with a stated interest rate requiring repayment on a specific date or in installments. Banks ordinarily don't make unsecured personal loans, so the loans should also be secured by the shareholder-employee's personal property, such as the employee's corporate stock, or a house or car. The loan should be listed on the company's balance sheet as a receivable, and the corporation's minutes should reflect approval of the loan. Most important, the terms of the loan must be followed—that is, the shareholder-employee must repay the loan on time.

If an IRS auditor concludes that a shareholder-employee loan is not bona fide, it will be recharacterized as something else for tax purposes. If the corporation is an S corporation, IRS auditors will usually try to reclassify a bogus loan as employee compensation, with the con-sequences described above—income and employment taxes will be due on the money, as well as penalty taxes for underpayment of taxes. If the corporation is a C corporation, the IRS auditor will likely reclassify the loan as a taxable constructive dividend.

Below-Market Loans

Even if a shareholder-employee loan is bona fide, there will still be tax problems if it is a below-market loan—a loan for no interest or interest below the applicable federal rate. The applicable federal rate is based on the rate the federal government pays on new borrowings and is adjusted monthly. The rate can be found on the IRS website (www.irs.gov). There are three different rates: short-term (for loans not over three years), midterm (for four- to nine-year loans), and long-term (for loans over nine years). In late 2017, the annual short-term rate was 1.29%, the midterm rate was 1.95%, and the long-term rate was 2.58%. If the corporation charges at least this much interest, the IRS will not complain.

However, if no interest is charged, or if the rate is below the applicable federal rate, interest will be imputed by the IRS. That is, the IRS will pretend that interest equal to the applicable federal rate was charged on the loan. The corporation will be treated as transferring the imputed interest to the shareholder-employee as additional compensation and the employee will have to pay tax on it. However, this interest might be deductible as a personal deduction by the shareholder if the loan proceeds are used for investment purposes.

There is one important exception to the below-market loan rules: A shareholder can borrow up to $10,000 from the corporation interest free, and the IRS will not impute any interest. However, this exception does not apply if one of the principal purposes of the loan is tax avoidance.

How You Pay Business Expenses

Does it make any difference how you pay for a business expense? In other words, is an expense's deductibility affected by whether you pay the expense out of your own pocket or from business funds? The short answer is, yes!

Consider this example: Clarence, an attorney and partner in a ten-lawyer law firm organized as an LLC, receives a $500 bill for his state bar association dues. He pays the bill with his personal funds and then has his firm reimburse him. Sounds simple. But how is this transaction treated for tax purposes? Is the $500 reimbursement income that Clarence must pay taxes on? Can Clarence's practice deduct the expense? Would it make any difference if Clarence's firm paid the bill directly?

This chapter discusses the different ways you can pay business expenses and how this affects their deductibility.

SKIP AHEAD

Sole proprietors can skip ahead to "Your Client Reimburses You." The material in "Your Practice Pays" and "Using Personal Funds to Pay for Business Expenses" does not apply to professionals who are sole proprietors or owners of one-person LLCs taxed as sole proprietorships. It makes no difference if you pay an expense from your personal funds or business funds because your practice and personal finances are one and the same.

Your Practice Pays

The best way to pay for business expenses you incur is to have your practice pay for them. This can be done in several ways:

- The practice can pay the expense directly—that is, the practice pays the bill with money from its own bank account.
- The practice can give you a cash allowance that you use to pay for the expense.
- The practice can give you a company credit card to pay for the expense.

Tax Treatment

Your practice will be entitled to deduct the cost of anything it pays for that you use for your work. Such expenses fall under a broad category of deductible business expenses called working condition fringe benefits—property and services a business provides to its workers so that they can perform their jobs. Anything can be a working condition fringe benefit as long as it is used, at least part of the time, by the worker for his or her job. This includes many of the more common business expenses, such as:

- local and long-distance travel for business
- business-related meals and entertainment
- professional association dues
- professional liability insurance
- professional publications
- business equipment, such as computers and telephones, and
- company cars.

The worker can be an employee of an incorporated practice or the owner of a practice taxed as a partnership (which includes most LLCs, LLPs, and partnerships), or even an independent contractor. For purposes of working condition fringe benefits, all such people are treated alike—we'll refer to them as workers.

A working condition fringe benefit is tax free to a worker to the extent that the worker would be able to deduct the cost of the property or services as a business or depreciation expense if he or she personally paid for it. If the worker uses the benefit 100% for work, it is 100% tax free. But the value of any personal use of a working condition fringe benefit must be included in the worker's compensation and the worker must pay tax on it.

> EXAMPLE: Lloyd, the shareholder-employee of a small incorporated engineering firm, has his company purchase a cell phone that he uses to keep in touch with his office and clients when he's in the field. If Lloyd uses the cell phone 100% for his work, it is tax free to him. But if he uses it only 50% of the time for work and 50% of the time for personal purposes, he would have to pay income tax on 50% of its value. Either way, Lloyd's corporation gets to deduct 100% of its payment for the cell phone.

The value of the personal use is determined according to its fair market value.

> **EXAMPLE:** It costs Lloyd, Inc., $100 a month to pay for the cell phone used by Lloyd, the employee. If Lloyd uses the cell phone 50% of the time for work and 50% of the time for nondeductible personal uses, he would have to add $50 per month to his taxable compensation.

Documentation Requirements

For a working condition fringe benefit to be tax free, all applicable documentation requirements must be satisfied. There must be documentation showing that the expense was business related, which the company should keep. At a minimum, this means that there must be a receipt (except for travel, meal, or entertainment expenses of less than $75) and proof of payment, such as a canceled check or credit card statement. Additional documentation is required for meal, entertainment, and travel expenses. If the property is listed property—for example, cars, computers, or cell phones—the amount of business and personal use must be documented. (See Chapter 18 for a detailed discussion of all these documentation requirements.)

In addition, if, instead of paying the bill directly, the practice gives you a cash allowance or a credit card or another cash equivalent, you must follow the accountable plan rules covered in "Accountable Plans," below.

Using Personal Funds to Pay for Business Expenses

It's better not to pay for a business expense from your personal funds; however, this may not always be possible. If you do pay for something yourself, you need to understand and follow the rules. Failure to follow the rules could result in the complete loss of the deduction—and even extra taxes for you. The rules differ depending on how your practice is legally organized.

LLCs, Partnerships, and LLPs

If you're involved in a group practice organized as a multi-member LLC, a partnership, or an LLP, your practice will ordinarily receive partnership tax treatment (although you can elect to be taxed as a corporation; see Chapter 2). Your practice and your personal finances are separate, and your LLC, LLP, or partnership must have a separate bank account. There are two ways to deal with business expenses you pay from your own pocket:

- obtain reimbursement from the practice, or
- deduct the expense on your personal return.

Obtaining Reimbursement

Unless your partnership, LLP, or LLC makes clear in writing, or by an established unwritten policy, that it will *not* reimburse you for the type of expense you've paid yourself while performing services for the partnership, you must obtain reimbursement from the LLC, LLP, or partnership. If the accountable plan rules discussed below in "Accountable Plans" are followed, the reimbursement will not be taxable income to you, and the practice may deduct the amount as an operating expense.

It is very important to understand that if a partner or an LLC member has the right to be reimbursed for an expense, he or she is *not entitled to any tax deduction for the expense.* The reasoning behind this rule is that if a partner or an LLC member has the right to be reimbursed for an expense, it is not a "necessary" expense for that LLC member or partner, and only necessary business expenses are deductible. Obviously, it is a necessary expense for the LLC, LLP, or partnership. (IRS Private Letter Ruling 931600.)

For a reimbursed expense to be deductible by your LLC, LLP, or partnership, and not be taxable income to you, the reimbursement must be made under an accountable plan. An accountable plan is a set of procedures intended to ensure that your practice doesn't reimburse you for personal expenses and then take a deduction for it.

In brief, you must:

- make an adequate accounting of the expense—that is, follow all the applicable record-keeping and other substantiation rules for the expense
- timely submit your expense report and receipts to your LLC, partnership, or LLP, and
- timely return any payments that exceed what you actually spent for business expenses.

These rules apply not only when you are reimbursed for an expense, but also to cash advances and allowances. They also apply when you use a company credit card. (See "Accountable Plans," below, for a detailed discussion of accountable plan rules.)

If the accountable plan rules are followed, your LLC, LLP, or partnership lists the reimbursed expense on its own tax return (IRS Form 1120) as an operating expense deduction. You don't list it on your personal return. It is combined with all the other deductions for the business, and then subtracted from its income to determine if the practice had a profit or loss for the year. The profits or losses then pass through the business entity to the owners' individual tax returns. The owners pay individual tax on their share of the profits. Thus, in effect, the LLC members or partners share all the tax deductions for expenses reimbursed by the practice.

> **EXAMPLE:** Louis is a surgeon who is a member of a group practice organized as an LLC and taxed as a partnership. He takes a trip to Paris to attend a medical convention that costs $5,000. He charges the whole amount on his personal credit card. When he gets back home, he quickly submits an expense report, along with all required receipts, to the LLC, which then reimburses him for the expense. Because he has followed the accountable plan rules, the $5,000 is not taxable income to Louis. The reimbursement is an LLC tax deduction that is listed on the LLC's tax return, not Louis's. It is deducted from all the income the LLC earned during the year to determine the LLC's annual profit. The $5,000 deduction reduces the LLC's annual profit from $305,000 to $300,000. Louis and his two partners each pay personal tax on their one-third share of these profits.

If reimbursement of a working condition fringe benefit is not made under an accountable plan, the money you receive is treated as compensation to you from your LLC, LLP, or partnership and is subject to both income and self-employment taxes. Your LLC, partnership, or LLP may be able to deduct the payment as a guaranteed payment to you. But you get no deduction for the expense on your personal tax return—as explained above, as a partner or an LLC owner you may not take a personal deduction for an expense that the partnership or LLC will reimburse you for.

> **EXAMPLE:** Assume that Louis from the above example fails to follow the accountable plan rules for his $5,000 reimbursement. His LLC doesn't get to deduct the $5,000 and must report it as taxable compensation to Louis, who will have to pay income and self-employment tax on it. Louis may not deduct the $5,000 as a business expense on his own tax return.

Deducting the Expense on Your Personal Tax Return

Another approach is for a partner or an LLC member to deduct as a business expense on his or her own personal tax return the expenses incurred while providing services to the practice. This way, you get the total deduction instead of having to share it with the other LLC members or partners. The deduction not only reduces your taxable income for income tax purposes, but reduces self-employment income as well, so you pay less Social Security and Medicare tax.

However, a personal deduction is allowed only if either of the following is true:

- A written partnership agreement or LLC operating agreement provides that expenses will not be reimbursed by the partnership or LLC.
- The business has an established routine practice of not reimbursing expenses.

Absent such a written statement or practice, no personal deduction may be taken. Instead, you must seek reimbursement from the partnership, LLP, or LLC.

> **EXAMPLE:** Dr. Magruder, a pathologist, was a member of a South Carolina group medical practice organized as a partnership. He regularly invited medical technologists employed by various hospitals he dealt with to join him for lunch and paid the cost out of his own pocket. Dr. Magruder did not seek to have the lunch expenses reimbursed by his partnership; instead, he tried to deduct them as business expenses on his personal tax return. The IRS and tax court disallowed the expenses because Magruder failed to show that his partnership had a written policy, or unwritten practice, denying reimbursement for such expenses. (*Magruder v. Comm'r*, T.C. Memo 1989-169.)

The moral is clear: Unless your LLC, LLP, or partnership has a written policy, or well-established unwritten policy, of *not* reimbursing an expense, you should always seek reimbursement. Otherwise, the expense may not be deductible at all.

If you want to take a personal deduction for an expense but your partnership, LLP, or LLC agreement doesn't require that you pay it personally, you'll have to amend the agreement to make clear that partners or LLC members will not be reimbursed for specified expenses. A partnership agreement can be amended as late as the due date for the partnership return for the tax year (excluding extensions) and still be effective for the entire partnership year. For example, a partnership agreement could be amended as late as April 15, 2014 and the change would be effective for all of 2013. (IRC § 761(c).)

In addition, you must comply with all applicable record-keeping and documentation requirements for the expense—for example, you should use a mileage log to document car expenses. (See Chapter 5.) Keep these records and receipts with your personal tax records. You don't need to provide them to the LLC, LLP, or partnership because it isn't taking the deduction.

To deduct business expenses on your personal return, list them on Schedule E (Form 1040), Part II. Check the "yes" box on Line 27 to indicate that you're claiming unreimbursed partnership expenses. List the unreimbursed partnership expenses themselves on a separate line in

Column (h) of Line 28. Write "UPE" or "Unreimbursed Partnership Expenses" in Column (a) of Line 28.

If you deduct a business expense on your personal tax return, you may not also obtain reimbursement from your LLC, LLP, or partnership— no "double dipping" is allowed.

Corporations

If your practice is incorporated (whether it's taxed as a C or an S corporation), you'll ordinarily be its employee for tax purposes. You have three options for dealing with expenses you incur while performing services for your corporation:

- Seek reimbursement from the corporation.
- Deduct the expense on your personal tax return.
- Make a shareholder loan to the corporation.

These rules apply to all employees, including family members who work as your employees.

Obtaining Reimbursement

From a tax standpoint, the best option is to have your corporation reimburse you for your expenses. You must comply with all the documentation rules for the expense and your reimbursement should be made under an accountable plan. As described below in "Accountable Plans," an accountable plan is a set of procedures that ensures that employees don't get reimbursed for personal expenses.

If you comply with the requirements for an accountable plan, your corporation gets to deduct the expense and you don't have to count the reimbursement as income. The reimbursement should not be included in the W-2 form the corporation files with the IRS showing how much you were paid for the year.

If you fail to follow the rules, any reimbursements must be treated as employee income subject to tax. Thus, the corporation must include them on your W-2. You'll then have to deduct the expense on your personal tax return as described below.

Deducting the Expense on Your Personal Tax Return

Another option is simply to pay the expense yourself, forgo reimbursement from your corporation, and deduct it on your personal tax return. However, a corporate employee is entitled to a personal deduction for an unreimbursed employee expense only if he or she does not have the right to be reimbursed for the expense by the corporation. If an employee has a right to reimbursement, but fails to claim it, a personal deduction for the employee's expenses is not allowed because the employee's expenditures are not "necessary." (*Heidi v. Comm'r*, 274 F.2d 25 (7th Cir. 1959).)

> EXAMPLE: Burten Schaeffer, a medical doctor employed by a Cleveland hospital, traveled to Chicago to attend a presentation on antibiotics and to look into purchasing laboratory equipment for the hospital's pathology laboratory. Dr. Schaeffer never sought reimbursement for his expenses from the hospital. Instead, he deducted the cost of the trip on his personal tax return. The IRS and tax court disallowed the deduction because Schaeffer failed to show that the hospital would not have reimbursed him for the expense had he asked for it. (*Schaeffer v. Comm'r*, T.C. Memo 1994-227.)

How do you prove to the IRS that you don't have the right to be reimbursed for an expense from your corporation? The best way is for the corporation's directors to adopt a corporate resolution that the corporation's employees will not be reimbursed for the type of expense involved. Alternatively, a written policy may be drafted. Another method is to ask the corporation for reimbursement and be refused in writing.

If you fail to show that you would not have been reimbursed for an employee expense you paid yourself, your payment will be treated by the IRS either as a contribution to your corporation's capital or as a loan from you to the corporation (see below). If it's characterized as a loan, it may be deductible by the corporation. (*Deputy v. Du Pont*, 308 U.S. 488 (1940).)

If you are able to deduct the unreimbursed expense on your personal return, it must be listed on IRS Schedule A, Form 1040, as a miscellaneous itemized deduction. You must also file IRS Form 2106, *Employee Business Expenses*, reporting the amount of the expense.

However, it's much better for you to be reimbursed by your employer (your corporation) under an accountable plan and let the corporation take the deduction. Why? Because employees can deduct unreimbursed employee expenses only as miscellaneous itemized deductions. Thus, they are deductible only if they itemize their deductions and only to the extent that these deductions, along with any other miscellaneous itemized deductions, exceed 2% of the employee's adjusted gross income. Adjusted gross income (AGI) is an employee's total income, minus deductions for IRA and pension contributions and a few other deductions (shown on Form 1040, Line 37).

Shareholder Loan to the Corporation

Instead of obtaining reimbursement or personally deducting an expense you pay yourself, you may be able to treat the payment as a loan from you, a shareholder, to your corporation. However, the payment must be handled like a real loan—that is, it should be properly documented as a loan on your corporation's books and the corporation must pay it back. If more than a nominal amount is involved, the loan should be documented with a signed promissory note and corporation resolution approving the loan and repayment. If you fail to treat your payment as a true loan, the IRS may recharacterize it as a contribution by you to your corporation's capital and any loan repayments you receive as taxable dividends.

It's best to charge your corporation interest for any payments you treat as loans. However, your corporation may borrow up to $10,000 from you interest free, so long as it is not done to avoid taxes. (IRC § 7872(c) (3).) The $10,000 limit is an aggregate figure—that is, your corporation cannot owe you more than a total of $10,000 at any one time. If you lend more than $10,000 to your corporation, you must charge interest at market rates or the IRS may impute interest—that is, it will pretend that interest equal to the applicable federal rate was charged on the loan. (See Chapter 15.) Repayment of the loan is not taxable income to you, the lender; but any interest you receive from your corporation, or that the IRS imputes, is taxable income.

Your Client Reimburses You

Many professionals—for example, attorneys and accountants—typically have all or some of the expenses they incur while working for a client reimbursed by the client. This is particularly common for local and long-distance travel expenses. These types of expenses are working condition fringe benefits.

Obviously, if you incur a deductible expense while performing services for the client, and the client does not reimburse you, you may deduct the expense on your own return. (If your practice is a partnership, an LLP or LLC, or a corporation, "you" means the business entity, not you personally.) Your client gets no deduction for the expense, because it didn't pay it.

But, if your client reimburses you for an expense, your client gets the deduction, not you. However, you need not include the reimbursement in your income if you provide an adequate accounting of the expenses to your client—you should follow the accountable plan rules discussed in the next section. If the reimbursement is for entertainment expenses, the client must keep your records documenting each element of the expense. The reimbursement should not be included in any 1099-MISC form the client files with the IRS reporting how much you were paid for the year.

> **EXAMPLE:** Jason, an attorney based in Chicago, is hired by Acme Corp. to handle a trial in Albuquerque, New Mexico. He incurs $5,000 in travel expenses, which he fully documents. Acme reimburses Jason for the $5,000 expense. Jason need not include this amount in his income for the year. Acme may deduct it as a business expense.

If you do not adequately account to your client for these expenses, the client still gets to deduct the expense, but *you must pay tax on the reimbursement.* Moreover, the client must include the amount of the reimbursement in any 1099-MISC it files with the IRS reporting how much it paid you for your services.

EXAMPLE: Assume that Jason doesn't keep proper records of his travel expenses, but is still reimbursed $5,000 by Acme. Acme must include the $5,000 payment in the 1099-MISC form it files with the IRS reporting how much it paid Jason. Jason will have to pay tax on the $5,000.

For simplicity in bookkeeping, some professionals routinely deduct all expenses they incur, even those that were reimbursed by clients. But, they also include the amount of all the reimbursements they receive from their clients in their income and pay tax on them. This is fine with the IRS. What you cannot do is deduct an expense and not report as income a reimbursement you received for it.

Deducting all your expenses yourself does not lessen the IRS's record-keeping requirements. If you lack proper documentation for an expense, your deduction will be disallowed by the IRS in the event of an audit.

Clients Often Improperly Include Reimbursements in 1099s

Clients should not include expense reimbursements in the 1099-MISC forms they file with the IRS (reporting how much they paid you) if you provided an adequate accounting for the expense. However, some clients do it anyway. If this happens, you should report the entire amount on the 1099-MISC as income and deduct the amount of the reimbursement as a business expense. That way, everything will even out.

EXAMPLE: Annie, a sole proprietor accountant, is reimbursed $5,000 by ABC, Inc., for expenses she incurred performing accounting work. Annie provided an adequate accounting to ABC, but ABC included the $5,000 in the 1099-MISC it filed with the IRS. Thus, the 1099 shows Annie receiving $10,000 in income from ABC, instead of $5,000. Annie should include the whole $10,000 in her income on her tax return and deduct the $5,000 in expenses on her Schedule C.

Accountable Plans

The accountable plan rules are a set of procedures intended to prevent workers from seeking reimbursement for personal expenses under the guise that they were business expenses. You need to understand and follow the accountable plan rules if any of the following apply:

- Your practice gives you cash or a credit card (or other cash equivalent) to pay a business-related expense.
- Your practice reimburses you for an expense you pay for yourself.
- A client reimburses you for expenses.

If you follow the rules, any reimbursement or allowance you receive will not be taxable income to you. But, if you fail to follow the rules, you'll have to pay tax on the amount.

What Is an Accountable Plan?

An accountable plan is an arrangement in which a company agrees to reimburse or advance worker expenses only if the worker:

- pays or incurs expenses that qualify as deductible business expenses while performing services for the company
- adequately accounts to the company for the expenses within a reasonable period of time, and
- returns to the company within a reasonable time any amounts received in excess of the actual business expenses incurred.

An accountable plan need not be in writing (although it's not a bad idea). What you need to do is set up procedures for you and other company workers to follow that meet the following three requirements.

The expense must be for business. The expense must have a business connection—that is, the worker must have paid it while performing services for the company. The expense must have been deductible as a business expense had the worker paid for it with his or her own money.

The worker must make an adequate accounting. The worker must provide the company with an "adequate accounting" for the expense within a reasonable time after it was paid or incurred. This means the worker must document and follow all the applicable record-keeping and other substantiation rules for the expense. For example, the worker must keep receipts for all expenditures (except for travel, meal, and entertainment expenses below $75, or travel and meal expenses paid on a per diem basis).

Excess payments must be timely returned. Workers who are advanced or reimbursed more than they actually spent for business expenses must return the excess payments to the company within a reasonable time.

Payments a company makes under an accountable plan should be deducted on the company's tax return in the proper category. For example, reimbursements for business travel should be deducted as travel expenses.

Time Limit to Make Adequate Accounting

A worker can't wait forever to meet the accountable plan requirements. An adequate accounting must be provided to the company within a reasonable time. If this is not done, the entire amount the company paid the worker must be added to the worker's income. Likewise, any excess payments must be returned within a reasonable time. Any amounts not so returned are treated as taxable compensation for the worker.

There are three ways to meet the reasonable time requirement:
- **Fixed date method.** Under this method, the expense must be substantiated by the worker within 60 days after it is paid or incurred. If the worker received more money from the company than he or she actually spent on business expenses, the excess amount must be returned to the company within 120 days after the expenses were paid or incurred. If the company gives the worker an advance to cover expenses, it may be paid no more than 30 days before the expense is incurred.
- **Periodic statement method.** Under this method, the company provides the worker with a periodic statement (at least quarterly) listing any excess amounts that the worker must return to the company. The worker must substantiate all expenses and return any excess payments within 120 days after receiving the statement. This gives the worker as much as 210 days to meet the requirements.

- **Other reasonable method.** You may use any other time periods that are reasonable under the circumstances—for example, a worker on an extended business trip might be given a longer period to substantiate expenses and return any excess allowance than a worker on a single overnight trip.

EXAMPLE: Tom is the sole shareholder and employee of his engineering consulting firm, which is a C corporation. He has his corporation give him a $5,000 cash advance to cover his expenses for a business trip—in other words, he takes $5,000 out of the corporation's bank account and puts it in his pocket. While on the trip, he spends $4,000 on his travel and meal expenses, which he fully documents. He files his expense diary and receipts with his corporation tax records within 60 days after he paid his expenses. He returns the excess $1,000 payment to his corporate bank account within 120 days after he paid his expenses. Tom has complied with the accountable plan rules. If he had failed to return the extra $1,000 within 120 days, it would have had to be added to Tom's W-2 as part of his annual wages.

Payments Not Made Under an Accountable Plan

Any payments to workers for business-related expenses that do not comply with the accountable plan rule are deemed to be made under an "unaccountable plan." The result is that the payments are considered to be taxable compensation to the worker.

If your practice is a corporation and you work as its employee, this means that all of the following apply:

- You must report the payments as income on your tax return and pay tax on them.
- You may deduct the expenses—but only as an itemized deduction (unreimbursed employee expenses) on your Schedule A—and you must have the documentation to back up the deduction if you're audited.

- Your corporation may deduct the payments as employee wages paid to you.
- The corporation must withhold your income taxes and share of Social Security and Medicare taxes from the payments.
- The corporation must pay its share of your Social Security and Medicare taxes on the payments.

If your practice is a multi-member LLC, a partnership, or an LLP, you will not be its employee; thus the payments will not be characterized as employee wages and there will be no withholding. Instead, they will be taxable distributions to you from your business entity. You must report the payments as income on your personal tax return and pay both income and self-employment taxes on them. Your LLC, partnership, or LLP may be able to deduct the payments as a guaranteed payment to you. You may deduct them as business expenses on your personal return; but, again, you must have the documentation to back them up if you're audited by the IRS.

IRS Audits

RS audits are no fun. Unfortunately, high-income professionals are more likely to be audited, particularly if they make use of tax shelters.

RESOURCE

Need more information on dealing with the IRS? For a detailed discussion of audits and other IRS procedures, see *Stand Up to the IRS*, by Frederick W. Daily and Erica Good Pless (Nolo).

Anatomy of an Audit

You can claim any deductions you want to take on your tax return; after all, your tax preparer (or you) fills it out, not the government. However, all the deductions you claim are subject to review by the IRS. This review is called a tax audit.

How Small Business Owners Get in Trouble With the IRS

When auditing small business owners, including professionals, the IRS is most concerned about whether you have:

- **Underreported your income.** Unlike employees who have their taxes withheld, business owners who are not employees have no withholding—and many opportunities to underreport how much they earned.
- **Claimed tax deductions to which you were not entitled.** For example, you claimed that nondeductible personal expenses, such as a personal vacation, were deductible business expenses.
- **Properly documented the amount of your deductions.** If you don't have the proper records to back up the amount of a deduction, the IRS may reduce it, either entirely or in part. Lack of documentation is by far the most common reason taxpayers lose deductions when they get audited.

Records Available to Auditors

An IRS auditor is entitled to examine the business records you used to prepare your tax returns, including your books, check registers, canceled checks, and receipts. The auditor can also ask to see records supporting your business tax deductions, such as a mileage record if you took a deduction for business use of your car. The auditor can also get copies of your bank records, either from you or your bank, and check them to see whether your deposits match the income you reported on your tax return. If you deposited a lot more money than you reported earning, the auditor will assume that you didn't report all of your income, unless you can show that the deposits you didn't include in your tax return weren't income. For example, you might be able to show that they were loans, inheritances, or transfers from other accounts. This is why you need to keep good financial records.

IRS Audit Technique Guides

Would you like to know what the IRS examiner is supposed to look for when you are audited? You may be able to find out. The IRS has created a series of audit technique guides to train its examiners in how to audit many types of businesses, including some types of professional practices. Many of these guides are available on the IRS website at www.irs.gov/Businesses/Small-Businesses-&-Self-Employed/Audit-Techniques-Guides-ATGs.

The audit technique guides of interest to professionals are those for:
- architects
- attorneys
- business consultants
- partnerships, and
- veterinary medicine (also useful for medical doctors and dentists).

Tax Shelters, Scams, and Schemes

Abusive tax shelters, scams, and schemes have been much in the news lately, and are a growing preoccupation of the IRS and Congress. High-income professionals are prime targets for promoters of questionable tax shelters and schemes, and many have gotten into tax trouble for participating in them.

The basic rule for avoiding abusive tax shelters and tax scams is simple: If it sounds too good to be true, it probably is. Before you invest or participate in any shelter that promotes substantial tax benefits in return for a minimal investment, obtain expert advice from a tax professional not involved in selling the shelter. Do not rely on legal opinions provided by the shelter's promoter.

For more information on tax shelters, visit the IRS website at www.irs.gov.

Tax Shelters

A tax shelter is any investment designed to reduce or avoid income taxes. There is nothing wrong with sheltering your income from taxes—people do it all the time. You'll have no trouble with the IRS so long as your shelter is legitimate. A legitimate tax shelter not only reduces taxes, it also has a real business purpose. Often, a tax shelter comes with an opinion letter by an attorney stating that it is legal (although this won't help you if the IRS decides it is not).

An investment in low-income property that provides rental income is a good example of a legitimate tax shelter. Such an investment can save you taxes through depreciation and other tax deductions, but tax savings are not the only reason for the investment—you also own a property from which you receive rental income. The investment involves a risk of loss that is proportionate to the expected tax benefits—for example, you might have trouble renting the property and end up losing the money you've invested.

What the IRS doesn't like are "abusive tax shelters." Tax professor Michael Graetz devised the best definition of an abusive tax shelter: "A deal done by very smart people that, absent tax considerations, would be very stupid."

An abusive tax shelter is an investment or transaction entered into solely to obtain tax deductions or other tax benefits. There is no legitimate business purpose. Signs that a tax shelter is abusive include:

- The shelter's promoters promise investors a larger tax write-off than the amount invested; often much greater than two-to-one after five years—that is, after five years, you'll save more than twice as much in taxes as you invested in the shelter.
- The shelter involves the purchase of assets at grossly inflated prices so that investors can claim larger deductions for depreciation, interest, and other items.
- The shelter is heavily promoted or marketed to the public by salespeople who earn substantial commissions.
- Investors must sign confidentiality agreements promising not to tell anyone about the shelter.
- The shelter includes a money-back guarantee—a promise in writing that the promoter's fees will be fully or partially refunded if the investor doesn't receive all the projected tax benefits from the shelter.
- The investment is very complex, but actually involves little risk, despite outward appearances.

An example of a very simple abusive tax shelter involves investment in a motion picture. The investors purchase a film for a grossly inflated price. They make a cash down payment for what the film is really worth, and enter into a loan agreement for the remaining balance due. The loan has to be repaid only if the investors earn money from the film. The investors obtain substantial tax deductions by depreciating the film at its inflated price, and from investment tax credits. It's highly unlikely that the investors will ever earn a profit from this transaction, but their tax deductions will far exceed the cash they invested.

Many more examples of abusive tax shelters can be found at the following website, which tracks all kinds of tax scams: www.quatloos.com.

The IRS has begun to wage war on abusive tax shelters and has established the Office of Tax Shelter Analysis (OTSA) to coordinate its efforts. A major focus is disclosure of "potentially abusive" tax shelters to the IRS so it can prevent them from being widely used. Expanded disclosure rules require tax shelter promoters to provide statements to the OTSA describing potentially abusive tax shelters and to maintain lists of the clients who buy them. The OTSA is creating databases from these disclosure statements and other sources to enable it to cross-check information reported on tax returns filed by investors in abusive tax shelters.

In addition, the IRS has identified many tax shelters as abusive and listed them in IRS notices and on its website (www.irs.gov).

The organizers and promoters of potentially abusive or listed tax shelters must register them with the IRS. Each shelter is given an identification number. Anyone who invests in a registered tax shelter must include the identification number on his or her tax return. This will often lead to an audit, with the taxpayer required to pay more tax, plus penalties and interest.

Tax Scams and Schemes

Tax scams and schemes involve outright fraud or other forms of illegal tax evasion. This is in contrast to tax shelters which involve investments that could arguably be legitimate. Scam artists and scheme promoters often prey on busy professionals who don't have a lot of time to focus on their finances. As a result, the IRS says that it has seen an increase in tax fraud in the professional community, especially by health care professionals.

Common tax scams and schemes marketed to professionals include the following:

Abusive trust schemes. Abusive trust schemes involve a series of domestic and/or foreign trusts layered upon one another. The scheme gives the appearance that the taxpayer has given up control of his or her business to a trust and progressively reduces the income distributed to the trust beneficiaries by charging administrative or other expenses at each level. The reality is that nothing ever changed. The taxpayer still exercises full control over his or her business and assets. A network of promoters, who may charge $5,000 to $70,000 for their trust packages, market these schemes.

International business corporations. The taxpayer establishes a corporation in a foreign tax haven. This corporation has the exact same name as the taxpayer's incorporated business in the United States. As checks from clients, customers, or patients are received, the taxpayer sends them to the foreign country to be deposited in the foreign corporation's bank account. This way, the taxpayer avoids reporting income to the IRS.

False billing schemes. A taxpayer sets up a corporation in a tax haven country with someone else as the owner, usually the scheme's promoter. A bank account is opened for the corporation, with the taxpayer listed as a signatory. The promoter then issues invoices to the taxpayer's business for goods allegedly purchased by the taxpayer. The taxpayer sends payments to the corporation which get deposited into the joint account held by the corporation and the taxpayer. The taxpayer takes a business deduction for the payments to the corporation, thereby reducing his or her taxable income and safely placing the unreported income into the foreign bank account.

Investors in abusive tax schemes are liable for taxes, interest, and civil penalties. Violations of the Internal Revenue Code with the intent to evade income taxes may also result in a civil fraud penalty or criminal prosecution. Civil fraud can include a penalty of up to 75% of the underpayment of tax attributable to fraud, in addition to the taxes owed. Criminal convictions of promoters and investors may result in fines up to $250,000 and up to five years in prison.

Your Duty to Report Foreign Bank Accounts

If you have money or assets in an account at a foreign financial institution, you may have to file an annual *Foreign Bank Account Report* (FBAR, Form TD F 90-22.1) with the IRS. An FBAR must be filed with the IRS by June 30 of each year (April 15 for 2017 and later) whenever a taxpayer has an interest in, or signature authority over, a foreign financial account with a value over $10,000 any time during the prior calendar year. The FBAR must be filed electronically with the Department of Treasury Financial Crimes Enforcement Network using the BSA efile system at http://bsaefiling.fincen. treas.gov/main.html. For more details, see IRS's Report of Foreign Bank and Financial Accounts (FBAR) webpage at www.irs.gov/businesses/small-businesses-self-employed/report-of-foreign-bank-and-financial-accounts-fbar.

Record Keeping and Accounting

When you incur business expenses, you get tax deductions and save money on your taxes. But those deductions are only as good as the records you keep to back them up. Failure to keep proper records is by far the most common reason taxpayers lose deductions when they are audited by the IRS.

This is what Dr. Maureen Polsby, a sole proprietor neurologist, found out when she got audited. Dr. Polsby frequently drove from her home office to the Social Security Administration office in Baltimore to review disability claims. She claimed a $7,011 car expense deduction. Unfortunately, she failed to keep adequate records such as a diary or mileage logbook to document her business trips. As a result, the IRS and tax court completely disallowed her deduction. (*Polsby v. Comm'r*, T.C. Memo 1998-459.)

Any expense you forget to deduct (or lose after an IRS audit because you can't back it up) costs you dearly. For example, if you're in the 28% federal income tax bracket, you'll have to pay $28 more in federal tax for every $100 deduction you fail to take, not to mention additional state income taxes and self-employment or employment taxes.

Luckily, it's not difficult to keep records of your business expenses. In this chapter, we'll show you how to document your expenditures so you won't end up losing your hard-earned business deductions.

Recording Your Expenses

Recording your expenses is what we normally think of as "keeping the books." Every business should have a record of what it spends and what it earns. Without this information, it will be impossible for you to know how much profit your practice earns (if any); and it will be much more difficult to prepare your taxes.

Most professionals use accountants or bookkeepers to perform these recording functions. However, if your practice is small, you may choose to do it yourself and save the money.

RESOURCE

For an excellent overall guide on how to do small business book-keeping yourself, refer to *Small Time Operator,* **by Bernard B. Kamoroff (Taylor Trade Publishing).** A good (and fun to read) introduction to basic accounting principles is *The Accounting Game: Basic Accounting Fresh from the Lemonade Stand,* by Darrell Mullis and Judith Orloff (Sourcebooks).

Your Accounting System

Your practice should have an accounting system that allows you to keep track of all the financial information you need to do your taxes and make good business decisions. Keeping track of your expenses is just one part of this system. An accounting system for a service business ordinarily includes a series of journals and ledgers (or their computerized functional equivalents).

Today most professionals use computerized accounting systems that perform the same recording functions that used to be done on paper. Many different types of accounting software are available.

There are a number of generic programs that are designed to be used by any type of business. The simplest financial programs are those like *Quicken* that work off of a computerized checkbook. More sophisticated accounting software includes *QuickBooks* and *QuickBooks Pro* by Intuit. This software can accomplish more complex bookkeeping tasks, such as double-entry bookkeeping, tracking inventory, payroll, billings, handling accounts receivable, and maintaining fixed asset records.

However, you'll probably be better off using a program specially designed for your type of practice. Such a program will probably cost more than generic software, but it won't require as much customizing for your particular needs. There are specialized accounting programs available for every profession. Consult your accountant or bookkeeper about which program to use.

> ### Hiring an Accountant
>
> You should hire an accountant experienced with your type of practice to set up your accounting system. After that, a much less expensive book-keeper or staff member can perform routine recording functions and balancing accounts. But the accountant should be available to handle any problems that come up.

Documenting Your Deductions

The IRS lives by the maxim that "figures lie and liars figure." It knows very well that you can claim anything in your books and on your tax returns, because you create or complete them yourself. For this reason, the IRS requires that you have documents to support the deductions you list in your books and claim on your tax return. In the absence of a supporting document, an IRS auditor may conclude that an item you claim as a business expense is really a personal expense, or that you never bought the item at all. Either way, your deduction will be disallowed.

You can hire an accountant or a bookkeeper to record your deductions in your books, but you must document your deductions yourself. You need to learn the IRS's documentation rules and live by them each day. The most common business deductions—travel, meals, and entertainment—require especially good documentation.

What Supporting Documents Do You Need?

The supporting documents you need to prove that a business deduction is legitimate depend on the type of deduction involved. However, at a minimum, every deduction should be supported by documentation showing what, how much, and who. That is, your supporting documents should show:

- what you purchased for your practice
- how much you paid for it, and
- who (or what company) you bought it from.

Additional record-keeping requirements must be met for local transportation, travel, entertainment, meal, and gift deductions, as well as for certain long-term assets that you buy for your business. ("Entertainment, Meal, Travel, and Gift Expenses," below, covers these rules.)

You can meet the what, how much, and who requirements by keeping the following types of documentation:

- canceled checks
- sales receipts
- account statements
- credit card sales slips
- invoices, or
- petty cash slips for small cash payments.

Documentation for Expenses Reimbursed by Clients

You need exactly the same documentation for an expense that is reimbursed by a client as you do for an expense you pay yourself. Unless you provide your client with an adequate accounting for the expense and follow the accountable plan rules discussed in Chapter 16, any reimbursement you receive must be included in your taxable income. An adequate accounting includes providing the client with proper documentation of the expense. The client is supposed to keep your documentation for any entertainment expenses it reimburses you for.

Canceled Check + Receipt = Proof of Deduction

Manny, a sole proprietor architect, buys a $500 digital camera for his practice from the local electronics store. He writes a check for the amount and is given a receipt. How does he prove to the IRS that he has a $500 business expense?

Could Manny simply save his canceled check when it's returned from his bank? Many people carefully save all their canceled checks (some keep them for decades), apparently believing that a canceled check is all the proof they need to show that a purchase was a legitimate business expense. This is not the case. All a canceled check proves is that you spent money for something. It doesn't show what you bought. Of course, you can write a note on your check stating what you purchased, but why should the IRS believe what you write on your checks yourself?

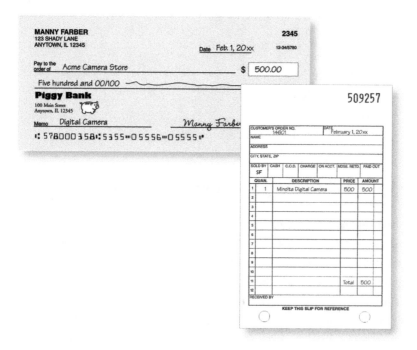

Does Manny's sales receipt prove he bought his camera for his business? Again, no. A sales receipt only proves that somebody purchased the item listed in the receipt. It does not show who purchased it. Again, you could write a note on the receipt stating that you bought the item. But you could easily lie. Indeed, for all the IRS knows, you could hang around stores and pick up receipts people throw away to give yourself tax deductions. There are also websites that, for a fee, will create legitimate-looking fake receipts.

However, when you put a canceled check together with a sales receipt (or an invoice, a cash register tape, or a similar document), you have concrete proof that you purchased the item listed in the receipt. The check proves that you bought something, and the receipt proves what that something is.

This doesn't necessarily prove that you bought the item for your practice, but it's a good start. Often, the face of a receipt, the sales slip, or the payee's name on your canceled check will strongly indicate that the item you purchased was for your business. But if it's not clear, note what the purchase was for on the document. Such a note is not proof of how you used the item, but it will be helpful. For some types of items that you use for both business and personal purposes—cameras are one example—you might be required to keep careful records of your use. (See "Listed Property," below.)

Make Digital Copies of Your Receipts

According to an old Chinese proverb, the palest ink is more reliable than the most retentive memory. However, when it comes to receipts, ink is no longer so reliable. Receipts printed on thermal paper (as most are) fade over time. By the time the IRS audits your return, you may find that all or most of the paper receipts you've carefully retained in your files are unreadable.

Because of the fading problem, you should photocopy your receipts if you intend to rely on hard copies. Obviously, this is time-consuming and annoying. But there is an easier alternative: Make digital copies of your receipts and throw away the hard copies.

Making a digital copy of a receipt used to require a scanner, which could be cumbersome and inconvenient. This is no longer necessary. If you have an iPhone or other smartphone with a camera, you can use that to take digital photographs of receipts. Because you are likely to have your phone with you anyway, this is easy and convenient. After a business dinner, simply make a digital copy of your receipt and then throw it away. You don't have to worry about losing it or storing it.

There are many inexpensive smartphone applications you can use to copy and keep track of receipts. Two of the most popular are Shoeboxed.com and Expensify.com. Using these and other similar apps, you can add notes and then upload the digital photos to an online account for permanent storage. These apps can even automatically categorize your expenses, and you can export your data to *QuickBooks, Quicken, Excel, FreshBooks*, and other accounting software.

Credit Cards

Using a credit card is a great way to pay business expenses. The credit card slip will prove that you bought the item listed on the slip. You'll also have a monthly statement to back up your credit card slips. If you're a sole proprietor, you should use a separate credit card for your practice. If your practice is organized as a corporation, an LLC or LLP, or a partnership, it's best that the card be in the practice's name. That way, you avoid paying for business expenses with your personal funds and then having to go to the trouble of being reimbursed by your practice.

Account Statements

Sometimes, you'll need to use an account statement to prove an expense. Some banks no longer return canceled checks, or you may pay for something with an ATM card or another electronic funds transfer method. Moreover, you may not always have a credit card slip when you pay by credit card—for example, when you buy an item over the Internet. In these events, the IRS will accept an account statement as proof that you purchased the item. The chart below shows what type of information you need on an account statement.

Proving Payments With Bank Statements	
If payment is by:	**The statement must show:**
Check	Check number Amount Payee's name Date the check amount was posted to the account by the bank
Electronic funds transfer	Amount transferred Payee's name Date the amount transferred was posted to the account by the bank
Credit card	Amount charged Payee's name Transaction date

Automobile Mileage and Expense Records

If you use a car or another vehicle for business purposes other than just commuting to and from work, you're entitled to take a deduction for gas and other auto expenses. You can either deduct the actual cost of your gas and other expenses or take the standard rate deduction based on the number of business miles you drive. (See Chapter 5 for more on car expenses.)

Either way, you must keep a record of:
- your mileage
- the dates of your business trips
- the places you drove for business, and
- the business purpose for your trips.

The last three items are relatively easy to keep track of. You can record the information in your appointment book, calendar, or day planner. Or, you can record it in a mileage log.

Calculating your mileage takes more work. The IRS wants to know the total number of miles you drove during the year for business, commuting, and personal driving other than commuting. Commuting is travel from home to your office or other principal place of business. If you work from a home office, you'll have no commuting mileage. (See Chapter 5 for more on commuting and automobile expenses.) Personal miles other than commuting include all the driving you do other than from home to your office—for example, to the grocery store, on a personal vacation, or to visit friends or relatives.

To keep track of your business driving, you can use either a paper mileage logbook that you keep in your car or an electronic application. Logbooks are available in any stationery store and there are dozens of apps that you can use to record your mileage with an iPhone or similar device.

Whichever you choose, there are several ways to track your mileage; some are easy, and some are a bit more complicated.

52-Week Mileage Log

The hardest way to track your mileage—and the way the IRS would like you to do it—is to keep track of every mile you drive every day,

52 weeks a year, using a mileage logbook or business diary. This means you'll list every trip you take, whether for business, commuting, or personal reasons. If you enjoy record keeping, go ahead and use this method. But there are easier ways.

Claiming a Car Is Used Solely for Business

If you use a car 100% for business, you don't need to keep track of your personal or commuting miles. However, you can successfully claim to use a car 100% for business only if you:
- work out of a tax-deductible home office
- have at least two cars, and
- use one car just for business trips.

If you don't work from a home office, your trips from home to your outside office are nonbusiness commuting, so the car you take from home to your office is not used 100% for business, even if you drive it only for business after you get to your office and then drive straight home.

Tracking Business Mileage

An easier way to keep track of your mileage is to record your mileage only when you use your car for business. If you record your mileage with an electronic app, check the manual to see how to implement this system. If you use a paper mileage logbook, here's what to do:
- Note your odometer reading in the logbook at the beginning and end of every year that you use the car for business. (If you don't know your January 1 odometer reading for this year, you might be able to estimate it by looking at auto repair receipts that note your mileage.)
- Record your mileage and note the business purpose for the trip every time you use your car for business.
- Add up your business mileage when you get to the end of each page in the logbook. (This way, you'll only have to add the page totals at the end of the year instead of all the individual entries.)

- If you commute to your office or another workplace, figure out how many miles you drive each way and note in your appointment book how many times you drive to the office each week.

Below is a portion of a page from a mileage logbook.

Mileage Log

Date	Business Purpose	Odometer Reading Begin	End	Business Miles
5/1	Visit Art Andrews—potential client	10,111	10,196	85
5/4	Delivered documents to Bill James in Stockton	10,422	10,476	54
5/5	Picked up office supplies	10,479	10,489	10
5/8	Meeting—Acme Corp.—Sacramento	10,617	10,734	117
5/10	Lunch with Stu Smith—client	10,804	10,841	37
5/13	Meeting—Acme Corp.—Sacramento	10,987	11,104	117
5/15	Breakfast—Mary Moss—client	11,201	11,222	21
5/15	Lunch—Sam Simpson—potential client	11,222	11,247	25
5/15	Attend sales seminar—Hilton Hotel	11,247	11,301	54
5/17	Bank	11,399	11,408	9
5/18	Meeting—ABC Company	11,408	11,436	28
5/20	Sales presentation—Smith Bros. & Co.	11,544	11,589	45
Total				602

At the end of the year, your logbook will show the total business miles you drove during the year. You calculate the total miles you drove during the year by subtracting your January 1 odometer reading from your December 31 reading.

If you use the actual expense method, you must also calculate your percentage of business use of the car. You do this by dividing your business miles by your total miles.

EXAMPLE: Yolanda, a fundraising consultant, uses her car extensively for business. At the beginning of the year, her odometer reading was 34,201 miles. On December 31, it was 58,907 miles. Her total mileage for the year was therefore 24,706. She recorded 62 business trips in her mileage logbook for a total of 9,280 miles. Her business use percentage of her car is 37% (9,280 ÷ by 24,706 = 0.366). Yolanda commuted to her office every day, 50 weeks a year. She determined that her office was ten miles from her home. So Yolanda had 5,000 miles of commuting mileage for the year.

Sampling Method

There is an even easier way to track your mileage: Use a sampling method. Under this method, you keep track of your business mileage for a sample portion of the year and use your figures for that period to extrapolate your business mileage for the whole year.

This method assumes that you drive about the same amount for business throughout the year. To back up this assumption, you must scrupulously keep an appointment book showing your business appointments all year long. If you don't want to keep an appointment book, don't use the sampling method.

Your sample period must be at least 90 days—for example, the first three months of the year. Alternatively, you may sample one week each month—for example, the first week of every month. You don't have to use the first three months of the year or the first week of every month; you could use any other three-month period or the second, third, or fourth week of every month. Use whatever works best—you want your sample period to be as representative as possible of the business travel you do throughout the year.

You must keep track of the total miles you drove during the year by taking odometer readings on January 1 and December 31 and deduct any atypical mileage before applying your sample results.

> EXAMPLE: Tom, a doctor, uses the sample method to compute his mileage, keeping track of his business miles for the first three months of

the year. He drove 6,000 miles during that time and had 1,000 business miles. His business use percentage of his car was 17%. From his January 1 and December 31 odometer readings, Tom knows he drove a total of 27,000 miles during the year. However, Tom drove to the Grand Canyon for vacation, so he deducts this 1,000-mile trip from his total. This leaves him with 26,000 total miles for the year. To calculate his total business miles, he multiplies the yearlong total by the business use percentage of his car: 17% × 26,000 = 4,420. Tom claims 4,420 business miles on his tax return.

Keeping Track of Actual Expenses

If you take the deduction for your actual auto expenses instead of the standard rate (or are thinking about switching to this method), you must keep receipts for all of your auto-related expenses, including gasoline, oil, tires, repairs, and insurance.

Use a Credit Card for Gas

If you use the actual expense method for car expenses, use a business credit card when you buy gas. The monthly statements you receive will serve as your gas receipts. If you pay cash for gas, you must either get a receipt or make a note of the amount in your mileage logbook.

Parking and Tolls

Costs for business-related parking (other than at your office) and for tolls are separately deductible whether you use the standard rate or the actual expense method. Get and keep receipts for these expenses.

Entertainment, Meal, Travel, and Gift Expenses

Deductions for business-related entertainment, meals, and travel are a hot-button item for the IRS because they have been greatly abused by many taxpayers. You need to have more records for these expenses than for almost any others, and they will be closely scrutinized if you're audited.

Whenever you incur an expense for business-related entertainment, meals, gifts, or travel, you must document the following five facts:

- **The date.** The date the expense was incurred will usually be listed on a receipt or credit card slip; appointment books, dayplanners, and similar documents have the dates preprinted on each page, so entries on the appropriate page automatically date the expense.
- **The amount.** How much you spent, including tax and tip for meals.
- **The place.** The nature and place of the entertainment or meal will usually be shown by a receipt, or you can record it in an appointment book.
- **The business purpose.** Show that the expense was incurred for your practice—for example, to obtain future business, encourage existing client relationships, and so on. What you need to show depends on whether the business conversation occurred before, during, or after entertainment or a meal. (See Chapter 4 for more on deducting meal expenses.)
- **The business relationship.** If entertainment or meals are involved, show the business relationship of people at the event—for example, list their names and occupations and any other information needed to establish their business relation to you.

The IRS does not require that you keep receipts, canceled checks, credit card slips, or any other supporting documents for entertainment, meal, gift, or travel expenses that cost less than $75. However, you must still document the five facts listed above. This exception does not apply to lodging—that is, hotel or similar costs—when you travel for business. You do need receipts for these expenses, even if they are less than $75.

CAUTION

The $75 rule applies only to travel, meals, gifts, and entertainment. The rule that you don't need receipts for expenses less than $75 applies only to travel, gift, meal, and entertainment expenses. It does not apply to other types of business expenses. For example, if you go to the office supply store and buy $50 worth of supplies for your business and then spend $70 for lunch with a client, you need a receipt for the office supplies, but not the business lunch. If you find this rule hard to remember, simply keep all of your receipts.

All this record keeping is not as hard as it sounds. You can record the five facts you have to document in a variety of ways. The information doesn't have to be all in one place. Information that is shown on a receipt or canceled check or another item need not be duplicated in a log, an appointment book, a calendar, or an account book. Thus, for example, you can record the five facts with:

- a receipt, credit card slip, or similar document alone
- a receipt combined with an appointment book entry, or
- an appointment book entry alone (for expenses less than $75).

No matter how you document your expense, you are supposed to do it in a timely manner. You don't need to record the details of every expense on the day you incur it. It is sufficient to record them on a weekly basis. However, if you're prone to forget details, it's best to get everything you need in writing within a day or two.

Receipt or Credit Card Slip Alone

An easy way to document an entertainment, gift, travel, or meal expense is to use your receipt, credit card slip, invoice, or bill. A receipt or credit card slip will ordinarily contain the name and location of the place where the expense was incurred, the date, and the amount charged. Thus, three of the five facts you must document are taken care of. You just need to describe the business purpose and business relationship if entertainment or meals are involved. You can write this directly on your receipt or credit card slip.

EXAMPLE: Mary, a consulting engineer, has lunch with Harold, president of Acme Technologies, Inc., to discuss doing some programming work for Acme. Her restaurant bill shows the date, name, and location of the restaurant, the number of people served, and the amount of the expense. Mary just has to document the business purpose for the lunch and identify who it was with. She writes on the receipt: "Lunch with Harold Lipshitz, President, Acme Technologies, Inc. Discussed signing contract for programming services." All five facts Mary must prove to document her meal expense are on the receipt.

This is all Mary needs. She need not duplicate the information elsewhere—for example, in her appointment book or dayplanner.

```
            GREENS RESTAURANT
            FORT MASON, BLDG A
               SF, CA 94123
              (415)771-6222
    Server: LES              05/26/2013
    Table 28/1                 1:35 PM
    Guests: 2                    30005

    Bowl of soup                   6.50
    Sampler                       12.00
    Filo                          19.75
    Ravioli                       21.00

    Sub Total                     59.25
    Tax                            5.04

    Total                         64.29

    Balance Due            64.29
```

$10.00 tip

*Lunch with Harold Lipshitz,
President, Acme Technologies, Inc.
Discussed signing contract for
programming services.*

Receipt Plus Appointment Book

You can also document the five facts you need to record for an expense by combining the information on a receipt with entries in your appointment book, dayplanner, calendar, diary, or similar record.

EXAMPLE: Assume that Mary, from the above example, saves her receipt from the restaurant where she had her business lunch. She writes nothing on the receipt. She still needs to document the five facts. Her receipt contains the date, name, and location of the restaurant, and the amount of the lunch. She records whom the lunch was with and the business purpose by writing a note in her appointment book: "Lunch—Harold Lipshitz, President, Acme Technologies. Greens Restaurant. Discussed signing contract for programming services."

```
                    Appointment Book
 ┌────────────────────────────────────────────────────────┐
 │ 19  Thursday          232/134                            │
 │  7                                                       │
 │  8                                                       │
 │  9                                                       │
 │ 10                                                       │
 │ 11                                                       │
 │ 12  Lunch—Harold Lipshitz, President, Acme Technologies. Greens Restaurant. │
 │  1  Discussed signing contract for programming services.  $74.29 │
 │  2                                                       │
 │  3                                                       │
 │  4                                                       │
 │  5                                                       │
 │  6                                                       │
 │ 20  Friday            233/133                            │
 │  7                                                       │
 │  8                                                       │
 └────────────────────────────────────────────────────────┘
```

Appointment Book Alone

If your expense is for less than $75, you don't need to keep a receipt (unless the expense is for lodging). You may record the five facts in your appointment book, dayplanner, daily diary, or calendar, or on any other sheet of paper.

> EXAMPLE: Assume that Mary, from the above example, doesn't keep her receipt from her lunch. Because lunch cost less than $75, she does not need it. Instead, she documents the five facts she needs to record in her appointment book. She writes: "Lunch—Harold Lipshitz, President, Acme Technologies. Greens Restaurant. Discussed signing contract for programming services. $74.29." This short entry records the place of the lunch, who it was with, the business purpose, and the amount. She doesn't need to add the date because this is already shown by her appointment book.

Proof Required for Travel, Entertainment, and Gift Deductions

Records must show:	Amount	Time	Place or Description	Business Purpose and Relationship
Travel	Cost of each separate expense for travel, lodging, meals. Incidental expenses may be totaled in categories such as taxis, daily meals, and so on.	Dates you left and returned for each trip, and the number of days spent on business	Name of city, town, or other destination	Business purpose for the expense, or the benefit gained or expected to be gained
Entertainment (including meals)	Cost of each separate expense. Incidental expenses such as taxis, telephones, etc. may be totaled on a daily basis.	Date of entertainment	Name and address or location of place of entertainment Type of entertainment, if not otherwise apparent For entertainment directly before or after business discussion: date, place, nature, and duration	Nature of business discussion or activity Identities of people who took part in discussion and entertainment Occupations or other information (such as names or titles) about the recipients that shows their business relationship to you Proof you or your employee were present at business meal
Gifts	Cost of gift	Date of gift	Description of gift	Same as for entertainment

Receipts to Keep	
Type of Expense	**Receipts to Save**
Travel	Airplane, train, or bus ticket stubs; travel agency receipts; rental car; and so on
Meals	Meal check, credit card slip
Lodging	Statement or bill from hotel or another lodging provider; your own written records for cleaning, laundry, telephone charges, tips, and other charges not shown separately on hotel statement
Entertainment	Bill from entertainment provider; ticket stubs for sporting event, theater, or other event; credit card slips

Listed Property

Listed property refers to certain types of long-term business assets that can easily be used for personal as well as business purposes. Listed property includes:

- cars, boats, airplanes, motorcycles, and other vehicles
- computers, and
- any other property generally used for entertainment, recreation, or amusement—for example, VCRs, cameras, and camcorders.

Because all listed property is long-term business property, it cannot be deducted like a business expense. Instead, you must depreciate it over several years or deduct it in one year under Section 179 or use bonus depreciation. (See Chapter 9 for more on deducting long-term assets.)

Special Record-Keeping Requirements

With listed property, the IRS fears that taxpayers might claim business deductions but really use the property for personal reasons instead. For this reason, you're required to document how you use listed property. Keep an appointment book, or a logbook, business diary, or calendar showing the dates, times, and reasons for which the property is used—

both business and personal. You also can purchase logbooks for this purpose at stationery or office supply stores.

> **EXAMPLE:** Bill, an accountant, purchases a computer he uses 50% for business and 50% to play games. He must keep a log showing his business use of the computer. Following is a sample from one week in his log.

Usage Log for Personal Computer			
Date	Time of Business Use	Reason for Business Use	Time of Personal Use
5/1	4.5 hours	Prepared client tax returns	1.5 hours
5/2			3 hours
5/3	2 hours	Prepared client tax returns	
5/4			2 hours

Exception to Record-Keeping Rule for Computers

You usually have to document your use of listed property even if you use it 100% for business. However, there is an exception to this rule for computers: If you use a computer or computer peripheral (such as a printer) only for business and keep it at your business location, you need not comply with the record-keeping requirement. This includes computers that you keep at your home office if the office qualifies for the home office deduction. (See Chapter 7.)

> **EXAMPLE:** John, a psychiatrist, works full time in his home office, which he uses exclusively for his practice. The office is clearly his principal place of business and qualifies for the home office deduction. He buys a $2,000 computer for his office and uses it exclusively for his psychiatric practice. He does not have to keep records showing how he uses the computer.

This exception applies only to computers and computer peripheral equipment. It doesn't apply to other items such as calculators, copiers, fax machines, or typewriters.

TIP
Rules for cell phones. Since 2010, cell phones and similar personal communication devices have not been considered listed property. Thus, the strict record-keeping requirements for listed property do not apply to these devices. In addition, you don't have to include the fair market value of a cell phone provided to an employee for business purposes in the employee's gross income for tax purposes, as long as the phone is provided to the employee for noncompensatory purposes (meaning business purposes not related to providing additional compensation).

How Long to Keep Your Records

You need to have copies of your tax returns and supporting documents available in case you are audited by the IRS or another taxing agency. You might also need them for other purposes—for example, to get a loan, mortgage, or insurance.

You should keep your records for as long as the IRS has to audit you after you file your returns for the year. These statutes of limitations range from three years to forever—they are listed in the table below.

To be on the safe side, you should keep your tax returns indefinitely. They usually don't take up much space, so this is not a big hardship. Your supporting documents probably take up more space. You should keep these for at least six years after you file your return. Keeping your records this long ensures that you'll have them available if the IRS decides to audit you.

Keep your long-term asset records for three years after the depreciable life of the asset ends. For example, keep records for five-year property (such as computers) for eight years.

IRS Statutes of Limitations	
If:	**The limitations period is:**
You failed to pay all the tax due	3 years
You underreported your gross income for the year by more than 25%	6 years
You filed a fraudulent return	No limit
You did not file a return	No limit

What If You Don't Have Proper Tax Records?

Because you're human, you may not have kept all the records required to back up your tax deductions. Don't despair, all is not lost—you may be able to fall back on the *Cohan* rule. This rule (named after the Broadway entertainer George M. Cohan, involved in a tax case in the 1930s) is the taxpayer's best friend. The *Cohan* rule recognizes that all businesspeople must spend at least some money to stay in business and so must have had at least some deductible expenses, even if they don't have adequate records to back them up.

If you're audited and lack adequate records for a claimed deduction, the IRS can use the *Cohan* rule to make an estimate of how much you must have spent and allow you to deduct that amount. However, you must provide at least some credible evidence on which to base this estimate, such as receipts, canceled checks, notes in your appointment book, or other records. Moreover, the IRS will only allow you to deduct the least amount you must have spent, based on the records you provide. In addition, the *Cohan* rule cannot be used for travel, meal, entertainment, or gift expenses, or for listed property.

If an auditor claims you lack sufficient records to back up a deduction, you should always bring up the *Cohan* rule and argue that you should still get the deduction based on the records you do have. At best, you'll probably get only part of your claimed deductions. If the IRS auditor disallows your deductions entirely or doesn't give you as much as you think you deserve, you can appeal in court and bring up the *Cohan* rule again there. You might have more success with a judge. However, you can't compel an IRS auditor or a court to apply the *Cohan* rule in your favor. Whether to apply the rule and how large a deduction to give you is within their discretion.

Reconstructing Tax Records

If you can show that you possessed adequate records at one time, but now lack them due to circumstances beyond your control, you may reconstruct your records for an IRS audit. Circumstances beyond your control would include acts of nature, such as floods, fires, earthquakes, or theft. (Treas. Reg. 1.275.5(c)(5).) Loss of tax records while moving does not constitute circumstances beyond your control. Reconstructing records means you create brand-new records just for your audit or obtain other evidence to corroborate your deductions—for example, statements from people or companies from whom you purchased items for your practice.

Accounting Methods

An accounting method is a set of rules used to determine when and how your income and expenses are reported. Accounting methods might sound like a rather dry subject, but your choice about how to account for your business expenses and income will have a huge impact on your tax deductions. You don't have to become as expert as a CPA on this topic, but you should understand the basics.

You choose an accounting method when you file your first tax return for your practice. If you later want to change your accounting method, you must get IRS approval. If you operate two or more separate businesses, you can use a different accounting method for each—for example, a dentist who also operates a separate lab business may use separate accounting methods for each business. (A business is separate for tax purposes only if you keep a separate set of books and records for it.)

There are two basic methods of accounting: cash basis and accrual basis. Most professionals use the cash basis method.

Cash Method

The cash method is by far the simpler method. It is used by individuals who are not in business and by most small businesses that provide services and do not maintain inventory or offer credit. However, if you sell merchandise and keep an inventory, you might have to use the accrual method.

The cash method is based on this commonsense idea: You haven't earned income for tax purposes until you actually receive the money, and you haven't incurred an expense until you actually pay the money. Using the cash basis method, then, is like maintaining a checkbook. You record income only when the money is received and expenses only when they are actually paid. If you borrow money to pay business expenses, you incur an expense under the cash method only when you make payments on the loan.

Under the cash method, payments are "constructively received" when an amount is credited to your account or otherwise made available to you without restrictions. Constructive receipt is as good as actual receipt. If you authorize someone to be your agent and receive income for you, you are considered to have received it when your agent receives it.

You cannot hold checks or other payments from one tax year to another to avoid paying tax on the income. You must report the income in the year the payment is received or made available to you without restriction.

When Is an Expense Paid?

Although it's called the cash method, a business expense is paid when you pay for it by check, credit card, or electronic funds transfer, as well as by cash. If you pay by check, the amount is paid during the year in which the check is drawn and postal mailed or emailed—for example, a check dated December 31, 2017 is considered paid during 2016 only if it has a December 31, 2017 postmark or it's electronically paid by that date.

The general rule is that you can't prepay expenses when you use the cash method—you can't hurry up the payment of expenses by paying them in advance. An expense you pay in advance can be deducted only in the year to which it applies.

However, an important exception to the general rule, called the 12-month rule, went into effect in 2004. Under this rule you may deduct a prepaid expense in the current year if the expense is for a right or benefit that extends no longer than the earlier of:

- 12 months, or
- until the end of the tax year after the tax year in which you made the payment.

There is one small catch: If you previously followed the old rule under which expenses prepaid beyond the calendar year were not currently deductible, you must get IRS approval to use the 12-month rule. Approval is granted automatically by the IRS upon filing of IRS Form 3115, *Application for Change in Accounting Method*. You should attach one copy of the form to the return for the year of change and then send another copy to the IRS national office (not the service center where you file your return). The address is on the instructions for the form. Get a tax pro to help you with this form because it may require some adjustment of the deductions you've taken for prepaid expenses in previous years under the old rule.

Accrual Method

In accrual basis accounting, you report income or expenses as they are earned or incurred, rather than when they are actually collected or paid. The accrual method is not favored by professionals because (1) it can be complicated to use, and (2) it can require them to pay tax on income they haven't actually received.

When Income Is Received

With the accrual method, transactions are counted as income when services are provided, an order is made, or an item is delivered, regardless of when the money for them (receivables) is actually received or paid. As a result, you can end up owing taxes on income you haven't received. This is particularly bad news for professionals because they often have to wait a while (sometimes a long while) before they are paid for their services by their clients.

Obviously, if you have many clients who owe you money, you could end up having to pay substantial taxes on income you haven't received. If it turns out that a client never pays you, you may deduct the amount you're owed as a bad debt. But this will just wipe out the income you've already paid tax on in a prior year.

When Expenses Are Incurred

Under the accrual method, you generally deduct a business expense when the following are true:

- You are legally obligated to pay the expense.
- The amount you owe can be determined with reasonable accuracy.
- You have received or used the property or services involved.

Thus, when you use the accrual method, you can take a deduction for an expense you incur even if you don't actually pay for it until the following year. You can't do this under the cash basis method. There are obvious advantages to getting a tax deduction this year without actually having to shell out any money until a future year. However, for most professionals these advantages do not outweigh the disadvantage of having to pay tax on income that hasn't been received.

Businesses That Must Use the Accrual Method

The IRS likes the accrual method. Any business, however small, may use it if it wants to. But, as explained above, few professionals want to.

Unfortunately, some types of businesses are required to use the accrual method—for example, partnerships with average annual gross receipts exceeding $5 million that have C corporations as partners. Ordinarily, C corporations with average annual gross receipts exceeding $5 million must also use the accrual method. However, personal service corporations may use the cash method even if they earn this much. Most corporations formed by professionals qualify as personal service corporations (see Chapter 2).

Obtaining IRS Permission to Change Your Accounting Method

You choose your accounting method by checking a box on your tax form when you file your tax return for the first year you are in business. Once you choose a method, you can't change it without getting permission from the IRS. Permission is granted automatically for many types of changes, including using the 12-month rule to deduct prepaid expenses (see "Cash Method," above). You must file IRS Form 3115, *Application for Change in Accounting Method*, with your tax return for the year you want to make the change (if the change is automatically granted).

Automatic approval can also be obtained to change to the cash method if you've been using the accrual method and come within one of the exceptions discussed above. However, this type of change can have serious consequences, so consult a tax professional before doing so.

Businesses that sell, produce, or purchase merchandise and maintain an inventory are ordinarily required to use the accrual method. Thus, in the past, the IRS required some professionals, such as optometrists and veterinarians who sold merchandise, to use the accrual method. However, an important rule change took effect in 2001 that permits most professionals to use the cash method, even if they carry an inventory.

The rule change created two big exceptions to the requirement that businesses with inventories use the accrual method:

- **Exception #1—businesses that earn less than $1 million:** Even if you deal in merchandise, you may use the cash basis method if your average annual gross receipts were $1 million or less for the three tax years ending with the prior tax year.
- **Exception #2—some businesses that earn less than $10 million:** Even if your practice earns more than $1 million per year, you may use the cash basis method if your average annual gross receipts were $10 million or less for the three tax years ending with the prior tax year, and your principal business is providing services. (Rev. Proc. 2001-10, Rev. Proc. 2001-21.)

So, as long as your practice earns less than $10 million per year, you can use the cash method even if you sell clients merchandise as well as provide them with services. However, you may deduct only the cost of inventory that you sell during the year.

Tax Years

You are required to pay taxes for a 12-month period, also known as the tax year. Sole proprietors, partnerships, limited liability companies, S corporations, and personal service corporations are required to use the calendar year as their tax years—that is, January 1 through December 31.

However, there are exceptions that permit some small businesses to use a tax year that does not end in December (also known as a fiscal year). You need to get the IRS's permission to use a fiscal year. The IRS doesn't like businesses to use a fiscal year, but it might grant you permission if you can show a good business reason for it.

To get permission to use a fiscal year, you must file IRS Form 8716, *Election to Have a Tax Year Other Than a Required Tax Year.*

Index

⚖ NOLO *Online Legal Forms*

Nolo offers a large library of legal solutions and forms, created by Nolo's in-house legal staff. These reliable documents can be prepared in minutes.

Create a Document

- **Incorporation.** Incorporate your business in any state.
- **LLC Formations.** Gain asset protection and pass-through tax status in any state.
- **Wills.** Nolo has helped people make over 2 million wills. Is it time to make or revise yours?
- **Living Trust (avoid probate).** Plan now to save your family the cost, delays, and hassle of probate.
- **Trademark.** Protect the name of your business or product.
- **Provisional Patent.** Preserve your rights under patent law and claim "patent pending" status.

Download a Legal Form

Nolo.com has hundreds of top quality legal forms available for download—bills of sale, promissory notes, nondisclosure agreements, LLC operating agreements, corporate minutes, commercial lease and sublease, motor vehicle bill of sale, consignment agreements and many more.

Review Your Documents

Many lawyers in Nolo's consumer-friendly lawyer directory will review Nolo documents for a very reasonable fee. Check their detailed profiles at **Nolo.com/lawyers**.

On Nolo.com you'll also find:

Books & Software

Nolo publishes hundreds of great books and software programs for consumers and
business owners. Order a copy, or download an ebook version instantly, at Nolo.com.

Online Legal Documents

You can quickly and easily make a will or living trust, form an LLC or corporation, apply
for a trademark or provisional patent, or make hundreds of other forms—online.

Free Legal Information

Thousands of articles answer common questions about everyday legal issues
including wills, bankruptcy, small business formation, divorce, patents,
employment, and much more.

Plain-English Legal Dictionary

Stumped by jargon? Look it up in America's most up-to-date source for
definitions of legal terms, free at nolo.com.

Lawyer Directory

Nolo's consumer-friendly lawyer directory provides in-depth profiles of lawyers all
over America. You'll find all the information you need to choose the right lawyer.

DEPO13